D1548662

The Invisible Chain

Also by Jean-Pierre Durand

LIVING LABOUR: Life on the Line at Peugeot France (*with N. Hatzfeld*)

AFTER FORDISM (*with Robert Boyer*)

TEAMWORK IN THE AUTOMOBILE INDUSTRY: Radical Change or Passing Fashion? (*co-edited with Paul Stewart and Juan José Castillo*)

The Invisible Chain

Constraints and Opportunities in the New World of Employment

Jean-Pierre Durand

Professor of Sociology, and Director of the Centre Pierre Naville
University of Paris-Evry, France

First published 2007 by
PALGRAVE MACMILLAN
Houndmills, Basingstoke, Hampshire RG21 6XS and
175 Fifth Avenue, New York, N.Y. 10010
Companies and representatives throughout the world

PALGRAVE MACMILLAN is the global academic imprint of the Palgrave Macmillan division of St. Martin's Press, LLC and of Palgrave Macmillan Ltd. Macmillan® is a registered trademark in the United States, United Kingdom and other countries. Palgrave is a registered trademark in the European Union and other countries.

ISBN-13: 978-0-230-01363-6
ISBN-10: 0-230-01363-5

This book is printed on paper suitable for recycling and made from fully managed and sustained forest sources. Logging, pulping and manufacturing processes are expected to conform to the environmental regulations of the country of origin.

A catalogue record for this book is available from the British Library.

Library of Congress Cataloging-in-Publication Data
Durand, Jean-Pierre, 1948-
[Chaîne invisible. English]
The invisible chain : constraints and opportunities in the new world
    of employment / Jean-Pierre Durand.
    p. cm.
Includes bibliographical references.
ISBN-10: 0-230-01363-5
ISBN-13: 978-0-230-01363-6 (cloth)
1. Industrial sociology–Europe. 2. Industrial sociology–OECD countries.
    3. Work–Sociological aspects. I. Title.
HD6957.E8D8713 2007
306.3–dc22
                                                          2007060023

10   9   8   7   6   5   4   3   2   1
16   15   14   13   12   11   10   09   08   07

Printed and bound in Great Britain by
Antony Rowe Ltd, Chippenham and Eastbourne

Contents

List of Tables

List of Figures

Acknowledgements

I would like to thank my colleagues at the Centre Pierre Naville with whom I have been able to build the environment of trust and intellectual independence that is so necessary in any scientific endeavour. I owe a special debt of gratitude to Daniel Bachet, who was kind enough to read through the sections dealing with alternative managerial structures and the present state of globalization. His suggestions have done much to enrich and enhance the text. Thierry Pillon has also helped immensely through his astute and pertinent comments. I would also like to thank GERPISA (Groupe d'Etudes et de Recherche Permanent sur l'Industrie et les Salariés de l'Automobile) for encouraging and helping with the international comparisons that have given this work its global (and interdisciplinary) perspective. The English translation is by Nikhil Virani, with the help of Paul Stewart. I would like to thank them both.

Finally, the patience and serenity of Joyce Sebag have sustained me throughout the long and arduous journey of research and discovery. Without her, this book would not have seen the light of day.

JEAN-PIERRE DURAND

Introduction

To say that labour has changed is actually saying two things at once: on the one hand, the working conditions, the manner of working and the work itself have gradually been transformed; and on the other, the way in which society perceives labour – and employment – has changed significantly since the 1970s. Labour no longer holds the central position as it did for so long.

The first change was towards less physical labour. All over the world, in the industrialized nations and those that form part of the OECD (Organization for Economic Cooperation and Development), work has become physically less demanding and at the same time often more interesting. Workshops have become cleaner and are now sometimes even comfortable. But while office work and work within the service industries continues to grow, it is at the expense of the amount of labour devoted to agriculture and to industries, in broad terms. The decline in the number of labourers and farmers has been accompanied by a proportional increase in the number of mid-level professionals, employees and executives. This transformation in the employment structure naturally affected working conditions in general – if working habits change, so does the work itself. This in no way inhibits us from investigating autonomy in work, the nature of management, and the satisfaction and growth possibilities afforded by work. One might be an executive or a labourer, blessed with a comfortable working environment and yet be an unhappy employee, weighed down by stress that fell as much on the low-level employee as on the team leader who understands and respects the strong social links existing within any collective work. On the other hand, the idea of limitless growth of qualifications and/or of the availability of work in the service sector needs to be reconsidered, and perhaps moderated.

According to the Institut National de Statistiques et d'Etudes Economiques (INSEE), the steady decline in the number of manual workers in France, which began in the 1970s, tailed off at the turn of the twenty-first century and at the time of working the number of people in this category constitutes a growing percentage of the active population. According to Castells, if the trend in job creation seen in the service sector is replicated in the IT industries, the employment opportunities for semi-skilled workers will continue to rise rapidly and very soon constitute a sixth of the active population in the OECD countries.[1] With regard to the developing world (not dealt with in this book) the situation is evidently different. Developing countries must manage their own industrialization while 'benefiting' from the relocation of the secondary and tertiary activities that are no longer profitable in the developed countries. It is clear that strong unions, working conditions, and in particular salaries, in developing countries are in most cases much worse than those in Europe during the twentieth century or even the nineteenth. Though the degree of industrialization and the growth of the service sector in China, Indonesia, India, Africa and Latin America differ greatly from those of the industrialized countries, by standardizing the production methods of goods and services worldwide, globalization has homogenized many of the questions and issues. We could thus learn much from an analysis of the developments in Europe and the USA, and throw considerable light on the question and concerns surrounding these issues.

The second major transformation that has affected working conditions in the OECD countries, is the dwindling role of labour as a means of defining the self. While the need to assert oneself was growing ever more strident, the nature of work no longer provided the same support and satisfaction as before. As the typical, secure, full-time job in a large enterprise, became a thing of the past during the period 1950s to 1970s, the concomitant decline of personal status in the workplace caused a fundamental change in people's outlook towards work. A secure, well-paid job became such a rare commodity that the new entrants to the labour market did not even bother to look for one. Increasing unemployment and uncertainty, especially for the young, for women who wanted to return to work after raising their children, and for older workers (be they labourers, executives or specialists), completely shattered the notion of work as the principal source of social investment. At the same time, the rising educational level, the reduction in the number of working hours[2] and the growing amount of leisure time available meant that people began looking beyond their work for something more fulfilling. Some found societies and special-purpose institutions that provided openings for self-expression and diverse opportunities for personal growth,[3] further eroding the role of employment as a social investment that conferred status, prestige and satisfaction. Both men and women began to gain access to a wide range of activities that would give them at least as much social recognition as their work, with the added satisfaction of these being chosen rather than imposed activities, and the feeling that they were doing it for themselves, of their own free will.

The mutations of labour

The change in work patterns has the double aspect of its place in society and its internal transformation. This book deals primarily with the changes in work looked at from within. The argument is that the worldwide crisis of capital accumulation at the end of 1970s forced business leaders as well as government ministers and economists to invent a different productive model. As a result of a simultaneous decrease in productivity gains as well as demand, invested capital could no longer give the same returns as was seen during the economic boom of the golden age. The 1990s saw a new *combinatoire productive*[4] emerge. Though essentially different from Fordism (which had been the dominating force in the post-war period) it nevertheless retained some of its characteristics, especially those of Taylorism. The present labour system, in the industrial as well as the service sectors, borrows from the past while developing and transforming its essential points.

The crisis of capital accumulation in the 1970s changed inter-company relations radically by simultaneously intensifying competition and ushering in an era of massive restructuring of the production apparatus, be it for goods or services (mergers, buy-outs, the growth of smaller enterprises under the umbrella of large groups, and so on). But the point is, more than in any reorganization of capital or the production system (see Chapter 1), the main development lay in the spread of the just-in-time method. This system insisted that all goods be delivered, whether within an enterprise or between companies, in the quantity and quality required and at the precise time stipulated by the client. This principle of just-in-time led to the elimination of stocks and 'outstandings', as demand could vary constantly. We thus arrive at the concept of *tight flow*, which incorporates just-in-time deliveries and the absence of stocks. In turn, to remain unbroken (a break in flow would mean a dissatisfied client), tight flow required a reorganization of labour and the prioritizing of its *collective* nature under new types of corporate structures including *group work* (see Chapter 2). At the same time, human resources had to be guaranteed by newer schemes that were systematized and found shape through the implementation of the *competency model* on the one hand (see Chapters 3 and 4), and the reorganization of the fragmented labour market on the other (see Chapter 5).

All these transformations took place against a backdrop of the widespread use of information and communication technologies (ICT) both at home and at work. At the same time, as this new force was radically changing and reorganizing the conceptualization, production and distribution of goods and services, it also transformed the requirements of the people themselves – the demands of the consumer. The service sector, both industry and customer-orientated, has continued to grow rapidly. And if its production has imitated and owes something to industrial methods, at the start of the twenty-first century its organizational methods have not only influenced but also permeated the entire production apparatus (see Chapter 6). This complete transformation of labour gives rise to a number of questions: What are the changes regarding the autonomy, constraints and corporate control of labour? and In the face of the problems cropping up here and there, how are we to explain the general buoyant mood in world production? It must be because there are compensations in the work itself – not necessarily salary-based – that makes even the employees who have been assigned the most daunting tasks, to give of their best (see Chapter 7).

Finally, the end of the family business, of the nation-state and difficulties of trade unionism with the new situation characterized by financialization and globalization of the economy turned everything upside down. What new functions are we to ascribe to trade unionism in this great upheaval? What can trade unionism do in the face of the crisis in pension funding, including the growth in the privatization of the pensions sector? What kind of global regulations should be put in place in order to try to limit, if not eliminate, the increasing inequalities that may give rise to further social violence?

The paradox of constrained involvement[5]

All these questions are at the very heart of human activity, because work, by regulating the relations between people and their environment, also influences social interaction between them. But now the period of certainties is at an end. While yesterday we had alternative – even radical – solutions to pit against the large owners, today these counter-proposals seem to have changed their character. Have they now become more acceptable? What are the chances of their being implemented?

There are two major pitfalls we have conscientiously avoided in our presentation: the first is a pessimistic view of the evolution of labour by seeing fear as the main motivating factor driving people to work. From this perspective, work is mainly about suffering. This neglects the joys and satisfactions that in fact explain why workers even accept the often sorry conditions under which they labour. The second pitfall would be to interpret all these reorganizations of work as so many different ways to achieve the sole purpose of individual growth, to increase autonomy, creativity and the *work ethic*. It is true that today, employment does encourage versatility, while the work itself has greatly diversified. But operational work, particularly under time constraints (directly linked to the tight flow), is becoming increasingly stringent and demanding, quashing any ideas of self-expression.

We would rather take the middle path, and think that a more realistic view lies somewhere between these two poles. Though the majority of the people who hold jobs (whether stable and secure or short-term) work harder than they did in the past – either because the work itself is harder, or because of longer working hours[6] – they still claim that, in general, they are more satisfied by work than they were before. Most opinion polls taken in the Anglo-Saxon countries, as well as surveys regarding the social climate in France, agree on this paradoxical finding. This somewhat surprising situation can be explained partly by the growing competition between companies, who are always alert to new markets and better returns on their investments, which results in an increase in the pressure and constraints on work. Apart from the gains brought by the ICTs, the reorganization of work made it more efficient, while demanding a greater involvement on the part of employees. We have thus coined the phrase *constrained involvement* to embody this paradox: the employees apply themselves more or less wholeheartedly to work because they cannot afford to do otherwise. The effort required to keep the flow tight (no breakdowns, no stoppage of the flow and so on), in addition to a salary structure based on the performance of the employees, has forced them to involve themselves more deeply than before. At the same time, this involvement has bought them some satisfaction in the course of their jobs: relatively greater autonomy for each worker, creativity being encouraged within limits, the evolution of corporate games in which individuals exert themselves in order to change the rules of the game and so on. These are all reasons to render the coercion acceptable.

Each chapter takes up and analyses one of the elements of this new, post-Fordian *combinatoire productive*, to see how it fits in with all the other elements and to show how, together, they form the efficient system that has been at the heart of the vast majority of companies since the 1990s. Each element has undergone such a gradual transformation, often through trial and error, with justifications and explanations coming *ex post facto*. Even those who were the most affected by the changes, including the employees and their unions, hardly realized or analysed these changes, which nevertheless carried profound implications. And thus we have a general acceptance of these radical transformations of work with no murmur of protest (we are not talking here of the job losses caused by rising efficiency, the result of the happy combination of work, organization and the ICTs). The paradoxical principle of *constrained involvement* gives a new gloss to the alienation of salaried labour. According to Karl Marx, the salaried worker (labourer) is alienated because the result of his work does not belong to him (because of the very production methods that separate the outcome from the worker), 'at work, the labourer does not belong to himself but to another'.[7] Even more than the economic perspective of this alienation, the worker's principle characteristic resides in a negation: the lack of freedom to dispose of the result of his/her work is a lack of personal freedom – however this might be denied by any individual. The negation of this alienation is intrinsic to the alienation itself. Within the paradigm of the forced application, which has been accepted against some symbolic compensations (as opposed to the Fordian system, in which the compensations were clearly monetary), alienation has now been redoubled by the salary structure and concessions given in the form of greater autonomy, job satisfaction and so on. The conditions of a new kind of voluntary servitude are once again in place.

1
Reforming Corporate Structures: Integrating Reticular Reasoning and Tight Flows

The main difference between the modern era and the period immediately following the Second World War is that not all of the goods and services being produced today will necessarily find purchasers. In the past, shortages forced people to wait a long time before they could finally receive, say, the car of their choice or the household appliance they wanted. Since the 1970s, these needs have been largely satisfied in industrialized countries with solvent populations. This has had the effect of intensifying competition among suppliers offering an ever-greater variety of cheaper and better-quality goods and services – which is why the credo *price, quality and variety* has become so important in companies' daily lives. In reality, suppliers have been the main drivers behind this variety and quality agenda, much more than consumers have been. Suppliers try to use quality, and especially variety, to gain market share from their competitors. Customers did not ask the world's three leading detergent manufacturers to come up with more than forty brands featuring almost identical levels of performance. Neither did the hypermarkets, which complain that an enormous amount of shelf space is being used up by products that are extremely similar in nature. Attributing responsibility for greater variety (and to a certain extent, higher quality) to suppliers instead of consumers has a philosophical and political significance that is akin to expressing praise for individuals or for individualism. Individual customers are not the ones who have 'naturally' become more demanding. This has occurred because the economic system has produced an ever-greater variety of higher-quality goods and services. Individual customers are more influenced by corporate behaviour than the reverse. This conception of the customer–supplier or individual–company relationship explains why consumers, who part of the time are also wage-earning employees, have been forced to accept work situations formatted by the effects of competition–circumstances they would ideally have liked to avoid.

A firm's *competitiveness* is its ability to associate the three components of the price, quality and variety credo.[1] The idea here is not to reduce competitiveness to a question of costs, but instead to view it as the end result of a whole range of phenomena that include quality and variety (and delays). A firm's overall competitiveness is predicated on its increasing *productive efficiency* – that is, on ensuring that a modicum of coherence exists between its technological and human resources. This has been a key success factor for top-performing firms (including extended companies, replete with their sub-contractors) whose overall organization has meshed well with their work organization and people management. In recent years, such drives have occurred against the backdrop of an intensive (and wilful) use of information and communications technologies (ICT).

Coherence is the key word in the currently emerging productive organization. Reducing tensions among an organization's components can increase the efficiency of work and of ICT simultaneously. The great reforms of the early twenty-first century are based primarily on the integration of research and industrialization, the objective being to make scientific or technological innovations available to consumers as quickly as possible. A secondary reform has been to bring suppliers operating at different levels in a business constellation closer to its first-tier contractor, thereby developing a veritable extended enterprise or *network firm*. The third and final restructuring process, which is internal in nature, organizes the transversality (or *functional integration*) that has tended to replace hierarchical verticality. This means that processes geared towards the integration either of activities with one another, or else of legally independent companies, have come to be associated with intensive network development efforts. We can condense this into a construct we call *reticular integration*, analysing it against the backdrop of an increasingly widespread reliance on ICT. These three main restructuring trends constitute the basis of what we call the new *combinatoire productive*, an expression referring to the advent, in a post-Fordian era, of new solutions to corporate competitiveness issues (especially profitability).

Integrating research and industrialization

Given the severe competition that characterizes capitalism's current phase, companies have been seeking new products or services to add to their portfolios that will allow them to capture new customers. This can involve entirely new products (think about the Sony Walkman), more attractive substitute products (for example, automatic bank tellers) or an integration of new technologies into a mature good (one case in point being cars with embedded IT systems). Another driver can be technologies that considerably improve manufacturing processes, to the point of revolutionizing them – examples include metal cutting or welding tools such as plasma torches or lasers, electron beams and so on. Products' new performances (resins for luggage, different types of glues, new stealth plane materials, ceramic cutting tools and so on) transform markets by creating new needs. In manufacturing, design or distribution processes, technologies like these have contributed to improvements in product quality and corporate responsiveness. Most importantly, they are seen as leading factors in cost cutting, one that translates specifically into the replacement of human workers, who come to be seen in cost terms and not as sources of value. Information systems are still viewed as factors that help to increase the apparent productivity of labour – that is, human productivity. At a secondary level, IT (and more generally ICT) is viewed as a possible source of responsiveness and quality, because it is the harbinger of precise data, traceability, reproducible processes and so on.

In all of these areas (product innovation, improvements in existing goods, process and distribution transformations), every company tries to be the first, or at least one of the first, to apply a scientific discovery to an industrial application, hoping to derive as much competitive advantage as possible before the discovery's subsequent diffusion nullifies this effect. Now, many economists remain focused on the idea that a firm's market entry costs will be even higher when the market in question is a mature one. Everyone remembers, for example, the phenomenal sums spent by Samsung's chief executive officer (CEO) when the company was trying to enter the global automobile market in the 1990s. Because the CEO loved beautiful cars and saw them as an avenue for promoting his entire *chaebol*, he launched Samsung Motors, which needed US$5 billion to build a factory in Pusan and launch a new vehicle design. The firm had plans to spend the same amount again on the product's global diffusion. In the end, Samsung Motors had to be auctioned off.

Firms not only have to be the first to benefit from a particular technological advantage, they must also negotiate successfully two very intertwined challenges: apprehending new scientific research discoveries as soon as possible; and applying, implementing and digesting such discoveries quickly, transforming them into the goods or services customers want before the competition takes advantage of the situation. The first challenge is a question of *informational watch*, which combines technological and economic watch. Senior executives use technological (and scientific) watch to scan research laboratory findings. Conferences, reviews and symposia spotlight discoveries and innovations that can be used by any company willing to purchase the necessary patents and licences. This watch has no resemblance to industrial espionage, and originates in every company's need to maintain high performance.

To complement this informational watch, firms also need economic watch structures[2] to track changes in private or corporate customers' expressed needs, and in rivals' practices. The aim here is to predict the disappearance of certain needs and the emergence of substitute products. Strategic watch focuses just as closely on rivals' investments (and on the best way of making or diffusing something) as it does on products and services *per se.*

Informational watch (and for our purposes, technological watch) must be accompanied by the ability to transform a scientific discovery or patent as soon as possible into a product corresponding to an existent demand, or to one the company must help to bring out. To be competitive when offering new goods or services, firms must shorten the time lag between research, development and industrialization. The globalization of our economies has turned existing situations upside down, highlighting the urgency of disseminating throughout a whole company a culture based on the integration of research with industrialization, alongside other forms of integration.

Functional integration in companies

Products and services pass through several functions: *marketing*, focused on customer desires; *design centres*, which design the product; *method departments*, which reflect on its industrialization (large-scale production to reduce costs while maintaining good quality); a *workshop* to manufacture it (including the entity responsible for data input operations, bank offices and so on); *sales*, which diffuse the good or service; and finally, *after-sales service*, dealing with any customer dissatisfaction. The product life chain pits different corporate services and structures against one another, entities that frequently do not even speak the same language, have different cultures, and consider themselves to be in a state of conflict with their neighbours. One could also view this product or service life chain as a type of information flow (conveying product ideas, plans, manufacturing ranges, quality procedures, improvement proposals, packaging innovations, shorter distribution channels and so on) that runs right through a company, despite the diversity of its business units and logics. Functional integration involves the removal of barriers between departments marked by cultural differences (organizational integration). It also means using ICT to unify languages and cultures, and rationalizing the information flow relating to the life of the product travelling through the company (data-driven integration). Note that organizational integration and ICT-based integration are themselves profoundly interrelated, and are being separated here only for analytical purposes.

Organizational integration: the example of simultaneous engineering

Before the early 1990s, products often encountered major barriers as they ran through their various phases. The time between a product's development and its commercialization could be very long indeed, and product design errors would be noticed only at a very late stage, often after manufacturing had begun. Tracing problems back upstream to find a solution could be very time-consuming. The requisite iterations delayed the product's market launch, handicapping any firm guilty of such tardiness if the product's innovative nature was in fact its main sale argument. This was also a very costly way of doing things, taking into account the many different types of modifications required. In the end, the final product would scarcely satisfy anyone, since it would always look like a compromise between a series of heterogeneous modifications, and be expensive to manufacture and assemble.

This explains why companies felt it was necessary to incorporate users' comments (compiled by their after-sales service) as quickly as possible into the next product generation's design. Even more crucial was the need to put an end to this system of successive product life stages. The solution found here involved bundling several stages into a single major phase encompassing the firm's design centre, methods department and particular manufacturing workshop. This was the birth of *simultaneous engineering*, sometimes called *concurrent engineering*, a better translation of the attempt to achieve convergence on the objectives among the various actors participating in a given project. Nowadays, almost all activity branches practice simultaneous engineering, mixing product or service design work with productive process design efforts (and increasingly, with the diffusion–commercialisation function). Finalized and formalized in the automobile industry[3], simultaneous engineering has also invaded other sectors such as aeronautics, motorcycles, household appliances, retail electronics, furniture and so on. It has penetrated the building industry, now marked by an ever-closer combination of programming, design and production. In the fast food business, all new product services are designed and thoroughly tested by teams comprised of people representing every department in the business, and monitoring the project's feasibility from industrial preparations all the way to sales facilities, even going as far as to ascertain possibilities for packaging disposal.

Another way of characterizing this integration approach consists of focusing on the notion of shared *projects* capable of occupying hundreds or thousands of technicians and engineers. Here the talk is of project orientation or *management by projects*, which differs from project management as a methodology for conducting an already established project in terms of the way it tracks costs, delays and even quality. Management by projects directs and gears everyone's activities towards collective objectives such as compliance with a product's specifications, product launch and sales of a good or service.

More concretely, some major organizational questions have been raised by simultaneous engineering's implementation. If a company brings all its engineers and technicians on to a single site, as did Renault with its Guyancourt *Technocentre*, it still needs to resolve the complexity of a collective work organization assembling two or three million people to work on the same (vehicle) project. What is clear is that these people cannot all work together on an ongoing basis, hence the need to devise sub-projects, whose particular specifications have to be prepared without any damage being done to the coherence of the whole. Every change in a sub-assembly has to be transmitted, as soon as it is validated, to colleagues in other functions so they can integrate it into their past or future outcomes. The project manager is responsible for overall coherence, and performs this function by operating within time and cost constraints, and by making sure that the quality objective always remains at the heart of the process. S/he acts like a veritable orchestra conductor, given that complex products such as motor vehicles or planes integrate a multiplicity of centrifugal logics, bringing together a whole range of businesses such as body manufacturers, mechanics, electricians, plastics specialists and so on – all of whom are driven by varying logics, depending on whether they come from a design centre, method department or workshop background. Each of these actors has acquired competencies and is specialized in a sub-system or a sub-fraction that will constitute his/her yardsticks and which s/he will find difficult to abandon. Furthermore, each new project must incorporate a maximum of research and development (R&D) results (new materials, embedded IT) something that calls in turn for the acquisition of new competencies. Lastly, many technicians or engineers do not work full-time on a single project, but must share their working time between two or three projects. As enriching as this is for the individuals or projects involved, the proliferation of interlocutors absorbs an ever-greater proportion of mental resources. The final shape of this already complex structure also has to integrate the activities and constraints of any sub-contractors and suppliers who may be working on-site – parties responsible these days for more than 70 per cent of a vehicle's total value.

The *simultaneous* nature of work shared by several hundred engineers and technicians employed on the same project resolves one major problem – any manufacturing hindrances, machining problems (which can translate into surplus costs) or potential production quality problems will be noticed at an early stage and can be sorted out during the actual product design phase – that is, during the good or service's virtual creation phase. Solving a problem before its manufacturing starts costs ten, a hundred or a thousand times less than making some unavoidable modification after production has begun. It remains that the establishment of a simultaneous design period for both product and process can trigger a multitude of modification requests. Furthermore, simultaneity means that during the first part of this period (and maybe even for longer), the project remains highly uncertain, in terms of the product's shape, and in particular regarding its assembly and sub-assembly sizes. Although transformation costs rise as the project progresses, irreversible decisions tend to be taken as late as possible, because the people involved always have a belated perception of any mistakes that have been made. This runs counter to simultaneous engineering's development-time reduction objective. The initial problem managers face is to decide at which moment they are going to establish the benchmarks based on certain irreversible decisions that must be made. It is only once the product's shapes or sizes are 'set in stone' that the project can progress with any certainty. Between these outcome-defining moments, engineers and technicians must continue their work, since it is this is that constitutes the very essence of simultaneous engineering.

Here we encounter the second problem with this method, which is how to weigh the value or the efficacy of the information emanating from upstream, until such time as the next project manager validation takes place. The further the information is from the next validation meeting, the less certain it is, hence the greater the likelihood that it might change. For the downstream side, information in this state has little value, because it is subject to change. Yet the earlier such information is delivered (and therefore the less its value for a employee downstream), the greater is its long-term value to the company, since it can encourage the employee to work using this information for a longer period of time, thereby enhancing its value. Senior executives and project managers will be happy to have everyone working as early as possible on the basis of uncertain data, but on the other hand, downstream technicians and engineers will be discouraged to see their work being undermined continually by updated information coming down from the upstream side, and would prefer invariable data that might serve as a fixed yardstick for their own efforts. If there is no way of resolving the contradiction between these two points of view, the organization will have to find a compromise that relates to work organization details, or weights the value of each piece of information depending on the project or sub-project's state of progress. After all, reducing tensions remains a pre-condition for all efficient design work.

Data-driven integration

Simultaneous engineering cannot be separated from data-driven integration, which involves sharing the same piece of information, and disseminating it intensively across a company's different functions. Information systems, along with internal or external telecommunications, constitute the core of this mechanism. CAD/CAM (computer aided design/computer-aided manufacturing) provide the first step for this data-driven integration of the major corporate functions, and nowadays ERP (enterprise resource planning) programmes accelerate it even further. One example of this is the automation of information processing, which frees up time for people to turn their attention to product design or to further development of these automated procedures.

It remains that data-driven integration is not necessarily accompanied by a removal of barriers between corporate departments and functions. It is not because people possess a 'communicating machine' that they will use it: by retaining information or only relinquishing it belatedly, a person may be able to accumulate greater resources (power, control over his/her own timetable) than if s/he delivered it immediately. At the same time, attitudes such as these hinder communications and render IT investments useless. In other words, it may be true that organizational integration or a data-driven removal of barriers/integration go hand-in-hand and are mutually supportive, constituting an intensification of the informational flows derived from the need for interfunctional co-operation, something that is sustained in turn by the density of information exchanges – yet this does not mean that determinism exists in one direction or the other. The removal of barriers does not always lead to a greater reliance on ICT, nor does heavy investment in these areas necessarily cause a removal of the barriers separating the main corporate functions, or the integration of these. Concomitant organizational integration and data-driven integration, leading to greater competitiveness, must be borne by corporate planning if it is to succeed. In many firms, even today, internal organizational barriers impede the utilization of all of IT's potentialities.

Within these new forms of integration born out of simultaneous engineering and management by projects, IT-driven integration shows how relevant the *network* logic has become. Diachronous sequentiality and synchronous point-to-point connections have been replaced by simultaneity and multipoint operations (the network), to the exclusion of any considerations of time, distance and business, even culture. On a more global level, integration achieved through simultaneous engineering has tended to generalize to all functions via the intranet, and more specifically via groupware[4] (see Chapters 4 and 6). Networks are replacing linearity in both companies and extended firms.

Integration in extended firms

In the Fordian productive system, first-tier contractors used to produce the lion's share of all value-added, relegating sub-contractors to the interstices of their activity, the nooks and crannies marked by lesser value-added work. Nowadays, first-tier contractors have a tendency to act as mere designer–assemblers, integrating as many technological advances as possible into the final product or service they design, before assembling and diffusing it and giving it a prestigious brand that conveys some highly valued image. In the past, automobile industry sub-contractors only accounted for 25 per cent to 30 per cent of their final product's value-added – today the amount is 70 per cent to 75 per cent! This turnaround can be attributed to the Western world's adoption of the Japanese model,[5] where most sub-contractors maintain a close financial relationship with their first-tier contractor, depending on it technologically and commercially, and frequently organizing staff exchanges.

Based on interpretations of studies by Coase or Williamson comparing company-internal transaction costs with market-based transaction costs,[6] researchers began to depict market advantages as something systematic in nature, contrasted with internal sourcing (vertical integration). Many went on to affirm that not only does the market not suffer from the kinds of bureaucratic distortion that plague large firms, but that it is not in firms' interests to produce an item if their internal needs are too small to justify the minimum equipment required to achieve scale effects. This well-known perception has become the catalyst behind the drive of many firms to refocus on their core business. Alongside this trend, many analysts hold that the *extended firm* limits negative transaction cost effects (uncertainty, access to information) found in the traditional market by allowing actors to establish contracts (if possible, long-term ones) that alleviate potentially damaging commercial uncertainty. In other words, extended firms are 'institutional arrangements' that minimize transaction (and production) costs.

In reality, corporate management will always find it easier to get better prices, higher quality and shorter time lags from the market than it will from internal actors who, if they are not being forced to compete with the outside world, will labour under the impression that they are operating in a monopoly situation, or else that they are faced with a captive market – both comfort zones that diminish their motivation to improve performance. Furthermore, large firms generally carry heavy production management structures, comprising sourcing, inventory and delivery operations, as well as cumbersome change management systems. A small structure specializing in just a few technologies and products can dispense with all these indirect costs and be more responsive to all kinds of modification requests and fluctuations in volume.

This productive apparatus flexibility is grounded in a workforce structure and management configuration that can be very different from the type found in larger companies. The adaptation of volume to demand has involved a systematic recourse to temporary staff, which can account for up to 80 per cent of all personnel in certain workshops. Labour costs are much lower in companies such as these because of the absence or quasi-absence of the social advantages that are so characteristic of larger companies: various bonuses, seniority payments, donations to worker charities and so on. The absence or weakness of unions and associated staff representation institutions mollifies factory workers, and even white-collar ones (particularly in terms of their wage demands). The final advantage of a small structure in comparison with the large firm is its conditional acceptance of overtime work whenever there is a need to absorb variations in demand.

The transfer of the production of most value-added activity from a first-tier contractor to its sub-contractors and suppliers has been accompanied by a structural recasting of the mutual relations interconnecting these parties. In the past, first-tier contractors would purchase a product – that is, a sub-assembly – in the marketplace. To guarantee the quality of the final good upon which its own good name would be based, the first-tier contractor had to control the quality of each element individually, something that took a great deal of time and wasted a plethora of materials as a result of rejects. Today, first-tier contractors are able to buy a complete function (such as a windscreen cleansing system) rather than merely an element (such as a windscreen wiper). Contracts no longer cover manufacturing alone, but the entire design, manufacturing and quality control process for the whole of a function. Because of the aforementioned simultaneous engineering considerations, sub-contractors today do not receive their definitive specifications in anything approaching a timely fashion. As a result, from the very outset they are associated with the overall project, however much this may fluctuate over time. After all, as a project unfolds, many of its constituent phases experience change (continuing our current automobile example, this can be the room left under the car's bonnet for windscreen wiper motors or fluids; the location of the indicator, beam and windscreen wiper controls on the dashboard; the windscreen's shape and so on). Sub-contractors will send their engineers to meetings with the first-tier contractor, who can allocate workstations to them on its own premises to encourage and intensify exchanges.

In turn, sub-contractors have grown to become medium- and even large-sized companies, and are no longer able to manufacture all the sub-assembly elements they are supposed to deliver. As a result, they now surround themselves with second-tier sub-contractors who subsequently choose third- or fourth-tier ones and so on. In this system of satellite of satellites orbiting around a first-tier contractor, the further a company is from the centre, the smaller it becomes. Such peripheral firms participate less and less in the elements' design; feature lesser general competencies; and make greater use of a workforce that is poorly qualified, low paid and lacking in any long-term job security. Some of these lower-tier sub-contractors are located in countries found on the periphery of the more developed regions: Mexico for the USA; North Africa, Turkey and Eastern Europe for Western Europe; China, Malaysia and Thailand for Japan and Korea.

The primary strategic relationships are between the first-tier contractors and their first- and second-tier sub-contractors. The former no longer want to be responsible for controlling the components that suppliers deliver, since this is much too expensive a process. They demand total quality, much as they do in their own plants, and incorporate first-tier sub-contractors into their total quality drives by organizing mixed teams that design manufacturing processes from which non-quality is banished (ISO 9002). They also certify other workshops using complex procedures that guarantee extremely high quality rates (Supplier Quality Insurance and ISO 9003).

In other words, in extended or reticular firms comprised of hundreds of satellites,[7] integration processes can involve simultaneous engineering, management by projects (organizational integration) as well as data-driven integration (using IT and telecoms). Actors in reticular firms work remotely and in real time, using shared data to design products and processes. Production management is very rigorous in such instances, since first-tier contractors require just-in-time deliveries of a given quantity at a given time. The delivery schedule (several times a day/daily/weekly/monthly) will depend on several factors: the sub-assemblies' physical volume, their strategic role in the finished product, their scope/variety, costs and so on. Synchronous deliveries occurring several times a day have become increasingly arduous because (still using our motor vehicle example) the order in which delivery trucks unload car seats has to correspond to the order in which cars arrive on the final assembly line. Any error will disturb the overall flow: the extra seats will have to be stored somewhere; and any car that cannot be finished will have to be 'derailed' (taken off the assembly line). Here the first-tier contractor would issue its orders in a three-phase sequence, starting with an indicative order (one month previous), a provisional one (one week) and a final order (the day before delivery, or the day itself).

The triple integration that characterizes the reticular firm is based on inter-company relationships that can no longer be governed solely by the marketplace, since this is too random and versatile in nature. It is in the long run that such relationships can be consolidated. The first-tier contractor organizes a competition among several suppliers submitting proposals. A short-list is drawn up before a final choice is made, following detailed proposals that include commitments relating to quality, delays and, most importantly, cost reductions (which can be as high as 25 per cent within two or three years). This helps to create relationships of trust among all the actors participating in the extended enterprise. In turn, this explains why first-tier contractors are so willing to promote partnerships now, compared to the purely market-based relationships that prevailed in the 1970s and 1980s. The constitution of corporate or consortium clubs orbiting around a first-tier contractor (yet another imitation of the Japanese model, except for the fact that, in Japan, cross-shareholding was the factor driving these *Kyoryokukni*, or corporate clubs) highlights a willingness to support smaller firms to enable them to perform as well as larger ones, something that works to the advantage of the reticular firm as a whole.

Such network firms are not without tensions or even contradictions, and each actor must check to see whether this self-interested support does not in fact translate into an attempt by the constellation's largest firm to exercise an increasingly stringent (and discrete) control over its smaller counterparts. Preoccupied as they are by value creation concerns, the people managing the world's most powerful firms have been trying constantly to control their allies, whose reaction has been to resist this trend, sometimes by camouflaging potential profit sources (where possible, by not delivering real-time accounting data). Sub-contractors used to fall victim to such pressures. Nowadays, however, first- and second-tier suppliers are usually fairly healthy financially. For example, motor vehicle makers such as Peugeot have shown no hesitation in acquiring their seats supplier company (in Peugeot's case, Bertrand Faure). In addition, having been delegated so many activities and responsibilities and so much initiative, suppliers have been able to achieve technological independence. This has had the effect of enhancing their mastery of technological innovation, to such an extent that they now constitute the main catalysts between networks' research/industrialization integration drives. In many different areas, suppliers have conquered a strategic position that allows them to pit automakers against one another, given the latter actors' interest in bringing out product innovations as quickly as possible. Since the 1980s, first-tier suppliers have been the initiators behind most of the automobile industry's non-driving system-related innovations. The strategic risk remains so high in this area, however, that some automakers have preferred to protect themselves by taking economic control of these competitors – especially since the latter have performed so well financially. All in all, the network form, having achieved its objectives, has come full circle. It has bolstered actors that used to be so subjugated that they were unable to take the initiatives they needed to become fully efficient. At the same time, the catalysts for these transformations have reinforced their economic control over their counterparts, just as the latter were finally achieving success.

The different meanings of a network

To a certain extent, everything has become a network in sociological or economic literature, with all social or commercial relationships now being interpreted in network terms.[8] Buzzwords like communication, connections, complexity and, especially, innovation have tended to make people forget that networks generally apply a hierarchical modus operandi (after all, one talks about the head of a network), and that they are marked by relationships of domination and subordination. Networks provide a basis for communications in our informational society, but there is nothing to indicate that their connections are equal in value, as the first variant of the network concept would have us believe. In other words, the operationality of the network construct should neither mask its various aspects nor the contradictory nature that remains the lot of most network realities.

In information transmission, networks possess certain advantages over point-to-point communication since they are capable of ensuring simultaneous transmission to several correspondents. In the past, any executory agents who wanted to communicate with someone operating at a similar level would transmit the information to his/her superior who, after validating it, would send it to another manager for transmission to the final executory agents. The proliferation of these types of communication would weigh so heavily on the productive system as to paralyse it. One key principle in bureaucracy is that information must always be validated by someone in charge. When the reticular organization removed this rule (with the end effect that everyone started to live in relative uncertainty), it transformed the conditions underlying the design and production of goods and services. The new rule no longer revolves around a priori validation, but is based instead on everyone acting within a normative framework or rule-based system whose outcome is to be validated a posteriori. However, it would be a mistake to try to generalize these conclusions about the network organization – after all, this is an organization that is only of interest to certain groups of employees. Others continue to operate under a more flexible or humanistic version of Taylorism, whether they are still doing their former jobs or have begun new activities (particularly in the service sector). Whenever a reticular organization starts to dominate the organizational forms described in this chapter, or other (indirect production) process supervision activities, it generally increases the productive system's responsiveness to demands originating in the outside world. Because networks increase the speed of multipoint communications, they reduce reaction times and can in fact accelerate the implementation of solutions to problems such as quality, or even cost overruns.

At the same time, networks lead to forced co-operation between the agents who are affected by them. Constraints no longer stem from a single (hierarchical) contact but become multipoint, hence inevitable. This explains why they often seem so unacceptable, forcing everyone involved to provide data of a certain quality by a certain deadline, so that the performance of the whole structure does not suffer. The network reality is also based on new technological resources (intranet, groupware, CAD and manufacturing software, for example), and its matrix organization serves to reinforce its management by projects logic. The end effect is that agents' direct correspondents have all increased by a factor of ten or twenty since the 1980s. In parallel to this, knowledge and skills have continued to broaden and grow. Companies are recruiting a rising number of graduates who are learning to share information in networks, specifically because their ability to be functional depends on this kind of sharing behaviour.

The pre-condition for the existence of a network is an actor's willingness to provide information or a service because s/he expects to receive a counter-gift at a later time, whenever an immediate need arises. This may be quite different from the gift/counter-gift paradigm anthropologists use, but the fact remains that networks do maintain themselves via similar forms of exchange, apart from the fact that, in this instance, gifts seem to be more of an investment made in the hope of a future return. Anthropologists have never resolved their debates about the unselfish nature of gift offering in early societies, but there is little doubt as to the self-interested nature of such actions in the networks found at the heart of our market-based societies, even when such giving is not rewarded with hard cash.

Hence the emergence of new competencies: on the one hand, employees must develop exchangeable resources so they can participate in one or several networks; but on the other, they must know where to find immediately, and for the lowest possible 'price', any strategic information that can be useful in overcoming hurdles or in advancing their own section(s) within the collective project. This becomes a new form of intelligence, in every sense of the term, and it is a variable that senior managers value highly. There is no remuneration *per se* for these new resources that are produced as part of employees' attempts to join a network, since activities of this ilk have almost nothing to do with the titular tasks or objectives that have been assigned to the employees. Nevertheless, such output should be viewed as a creation of value, since the new resources being produced (a pre-condition for membership in the network) will subsequently be integrated into the work object, thereby helping to enhance the value of capital. This goes to the very heart of the explanation given for the long-awaited miracle of e-business or the 'new economy', models that are supposed to integrate into the market-based system (and therefore into the capital accumulation process) resources and values that are produced 'free of charge', meaning outside of any market-based logic. More and more employees have been organizing ongoing individual watch systems that will enable them to solve whatever problems they face when fulfilling their function. This is the ransom of the generalized uncertainty that is so characteristic of the deregulated system, and exacerbated competition whose effects are nowadays felt by people all the way down to their workstations. Everyone is trying to improve or maintain his/her position by reducing any and all ancillary uncertainties. People are turning to networks in the hope that these can be used as support systems.[9]

Having to build up a network and then maintain it (involving two activities that, while being convergent, are different in nature) amplifies the constantly rising stress that typifies today's world of work, pressuring actors into a never-ending search for and production of resources. At the same time, the ability to produce such resources is distributed unequally, both among individuals and also in terms of the situations they occupy. In other words, people fight so bitterly to accumulate resources because this is indispensable for anyone who wants to join a network. Note that this process involves interiorizing a company's culture and aims, not so much by focusing on these two elements *per se* but more generally (or insidiously) by assessing which conditions govern membership in the networks that condition life in the company. The stressful yet playful efforts required to build up the resources that sustain such networks can translate into behavioural self-control (that is, fully-fledged compliance with locally established standards) that may involve, for example, hiding from oneself the contradictory nature of a firm's wage–labour nexus. Indeed, people's interest in building up and maintaining networks, and everyone's mobilization around such efforts, encourage any and all interested parties to have a positive perception of their own activities, making them forget that they are working for a wage that only corresponds to part of the value they create, depending on how the value-added is split between employees and the employer.

People do not need to maintain and catalyse all of their networks constantly, since this would be too costly and stressful a proposition. Quite the reverse, in fact: management through projects involves activating just one part of one's network(s), while leaving the rest dormant before using it at a later date:

> a *project* is an opportunity and a pretext for a connection. It assembles broadly disparate people on a temporary basis, assuming for a relatively short period of time the appearance of *one end of a highly activated network*, enabling the forging of more durable connections that will subsequently be put to sleep, although they do remain available. Projects enable production and accumulation in a world that, if it were purely connectionist in nature, would witness flows alone, meaning that nothing would have a chance to stabilise, accumulate or take shape. Everything would bob along on a continuous current of withered flotsam that, given its capacity for communicating everything to everyone, would constantly disseminate and dissolve whatever it is that had been gestated internally. A project is a very specific pile of active connections that are conducive to a gestation of forms, giving birth to objects and subjects by stabilising connections and making them irreversible. In other words, what we have is a temporary *pocket of accumulation* that, insofar as it creates value, responds to the network's need for further extension by encouraging connections.[10]

Analysts such as L. Boltanski and E. Chiapello may have underestimated the cost and energy required to maintain a network (even in a dormant stage), but in fact everyone labours under the impression that a project is acceptable because, at any given moment, it only mobilizes part of the network(s) to which the person involved belong(s). By focusing people's work on no more than the fraction of the network requiring activation, the project, as a modus operandi for the collective group and as a means for ensuring mobilization, does not completely exhaust people's potentialities.

In sum, the mobilizing power of a network (and of a project, as a special moment thereof) does not only stem from its metaphorical dimension, which is an ideal tool for focusing energies and knowledge on a particular objective. A network merits being thought of as a set of dual practices, based on a consumption of resources generated elsewhere, or by someone else following an exchange of self-interested gifts and counter-gifts, as well as an unequal production of resources by people seeking to participate in the various networks that drive communications and exchanges in companies and extended firms. This unequal production of resources produces, or reproduces, unequal status in networks. When combined with the above-mentioned resource production efforts, the potential value of these stressful yet playful inequalities is to help mask the true nature of existing production and domination-based relationships.

Since the project, and in particular, the network, condenses and mobilizes employees' subjectivity, it *captivates* them until they forget their subordination to the employer. Because of its eminently social nature, the network injects an emotional charge into a work activity, and into the extended enterprise in which this takes place. At the same time, the mobilization must be channelled in such a way as to serve the company's aims, and even more importantly people's expectations of returns on the company's capital. The social control of labour, which manifests in varying forms depending on the nature of the activity involved (employee skills in the present case), materializes nowadays in new mechanisms that are fully explained by reticular integration, as analysed above.

The emergence of a new *combinatoire productive*

In terms of the actual working process – that is the work organization, employee motivation, pay and so on – major changes have been taking place before our eyes without the main parties to such changes having taken any particular notice of them. Either the transformations have occurred on a step-by-step basis without any announcements being made about the overall project, or they have advanced tentatively through trial and error. One thing is certain, however – a lot of ground has been covered since the 1980s – the time when everybody was talking about rampant Japanization! In our current circumstances, efficiency derives from the coherence of the principles that are being implemented, both at the micro-social work-process level, and at the broader level of changes being made to the productive apparatus.

In general, the organisation of the production of goods and services has been covered by *just-in-time* principles (involving the delivery of goods and services in the right quantity and with the right quality at the right time) and the *tight flow* construct, whose foundations will be explained in the next chapter. Keeping productive flows lean requires a specific work organization – that is, *group work*, which is dominated by the collective dimension of work (see Chapter 2). Moreover, personnel management has been rooted increasingly in an individualized wage–labour nexus that finds its best expression in a competency logic as a workforce mobilization model (see Chapter 3). The three components are perfectly coherent. Moreover, they turn the work process that characterized the entire Fordian period completely upside down, in so far as each actor now relies on ICT in his/her own way. For example, it is hard to imagine just-in-time delivery or tight flows occurring in the absence of computer-assisted production management (CAPM). How could collective teamwork survive the break-up of a given team if computerized memory and telematic technologies did not exist? It would be impossible to implement a competency approach without an IT-based accumulation of data compiled from individual assessment interviews and staff biographies. In short, ICT is the factor driving this model's efficiency. This does not mean, however, that it should receive as much unadulterated praise as is currently the case. ICT does participate directly in productivity gains, but the results it achieves are partial at best and cannot explain all the gains achieved in recent years.

ICT has been an indirect source of productivity gains because it has opened the door to a new phase in work rationalization. One proof of this is CAPM, a system where information technology has opened the door to a very tight management of materials and people. Similarly, the constant rise in automated data exchanges has translated into an increasingly precise control of goods and service production activities, and to further productivity gains. Once integrated management applications such as ERP (enterprise resource planning) have hit their cruising speed, new productivity gains will stem more from work rationalization and from exchanges between people (or else between people and machine systems) than they will from the automated processing of information.

At present, most productivity and competitiveness gains stem from a reorganization of production and work, and from everything associated with this, the new workforce mobilization regime. These are all reorganizations that can be combined within the new *combinatoire productive* concept that began to take shape in the later decades of the twentieth century. The purpose of this construct is to highlight the goal of ensuring coherence between our three work process components (tight flows, group work and competency logic) and firms' reticular integration elements (their network link-up provisions and integration of available internal and external resources). At the same time, those elements and components that tend to be coherent with one another, clearly cannot escape the social contradictions that are so intrinsic to capitalism.

A company's level of productive efficiency is closely linked to the degree of coherence that exists between these elements of the *combinatoire productive*. Managers' more or less main objectives are to create a modicum of coherence between the four main paradigms we analyse in this book (reticular integration, tight flows, group work and competency logic). These paradigms, if embedded into the economic, social and political environment,[11] constitute something we can for the present refer to as the post-Fordist productive model. Yet there is no *single* path towards a firm's organization of production or work. There may be general principles (which we call paradigms), but their mutual coherence depends on the historical specificities of each company or country, and their implementation must be adapted to local, national and historical conditions to ensure a phasing of the company's two core markets – the market for goods or services and technologies – and the labour market. To ensure coherence between the components that make up the *productive combinatoire* presented above, consideration must be given to:

- the state of the labour market: skills/competencies, unionization, employment law (collective bargaining, role of the state), pay levels and systems, and so on; and
- the market for goods or services and technologies: consumers' degree of solvency, the competitive situation, the population's cultural level, technical and scientific environment, technological potential, technical norms (the state's regulatory role) and so on.

In other words, implementing productive paradigms means accounting for their host region's economic and social history in a way that constructs entrepreneurial realities that will be different every time, in so far as the coherence that has become so indispensable for the success of such undertakings demands a recognition of local social realities. Since managers also situate their own decisions within the history of the particular company for which they are working, we are able to trace corporate (or in certain cases, institutional) trajectories and develop industrial models[12] to highlight each of the original solutions for creating coherence between whatever productive models are being validated at a given moment in time, in a well-defined social context inherited from the past.

Using this meso-social analysis of a company and its production organ-ization, we can try to understand the main transformations that have taken place in the work process itself. From a very detailed analysis of working activities, we have seen to what extent the reforms engaged through the advent of new social-productive tools have led to an ever-greater involvement for employees. Note that this has sometimes occurred despite them – if not against them.

2
The Tight Flow Rules: Work under Time Constraints

Tight flow, the universal form of the just-in-time method, was conceived by T. Ohno in the mid-1950s and subsequently systematized by Toyota. At the same time as it was being spread throughout the industrial world by the global implementation of Toyotism, managers and directors in the service sector also began to take note of its advantages. The results are now quite evident: in the fast food business by the conspicuous absence of hamburgers languishing on grills between the kitchen and the counter; in retail business, stocks are always on the move, aboard trucks plying between the suppliers and the hypermarkets; in air transport, the concept of 'shuttles' or even *hubs* (connecting centres between flights), have transformed passengers and their luggage into a vast, continuous flux. There are no more (or hardly any) stocks: workers, material and information circulate non-stop in a vast, quasi-Brownian movement. Mass production, with its stocks (one of the definitions of Fordism) has given way to a new production method characterized by its fluidity, constant movement and the elimination of stocks and buffers between the manufacturing and service centres. The tight flow can thus be seen as the systematization and, in particular, the generalization of just-in-time. As we shall see in the course of this chapter, by using the term 'tight flow' instead of 'just-in-time' (coined and applied to the logistics of the motor vehicle industry), we gain much in terms of abstraction and generalization in order to bring to light a whole new production paradigm and its massive spillovers on to society at large.

The usage of this principle of the flow goes back to the end of the nineteenth century. In the so-called property industries (for example, chemicals, cement, energy, iron and steel, agri-food) the flow was linked to production itself, as it involved the transformation of the physico-chemical properties of the material, which changed its characteristics by going through successive phases in the same place. The manufacturing industries took more time to adopt this principle of the flow, as may be seen in the case of the slaughterhouses (end of the nineteenth century) and the motor vehicle industry (beginning of the twentieth). What is fundamentally new today is the concept of *tight* flow, that is to say, the elimination of the intermediate stock in the course of production (the buffers) of goods or services, and the disappearance of commercial stock between factory and outlet. In other words, while the attempt to create a production flow is not new, it has now been pushed up another notch in the manufacturing industry in the form of tight flow. Resulting in large part from the development of ICT, which allowed the implementation of complex flow structures, the sequential stages in production have been replaced by a continuous movement – as in the case of the 'proprietorship industries', also known as 'process industries'.

As we shall see throughout this book, the principle of tight flow grows by generalization. In addition to its concrete applications, which are easy to spot, it formed the bedrock of client–supplier relationships in the second half of the 1990s. The client, downstream to the supplier, expected the latter to provide him/her with goods or services at a fixed price (generally decreasing over time), in the quantity and the quality required at the instant *t*, with all the information having been duly set down and agreed upon. Every actor (an individual, a workshop, a service, a factory or a company), a client to a supplier, became in turn, the supplier to a client downstream – all the way down to the final consumer. This supplier–client chain, which functioned without any intermediary stock constituted a tight flow. With the coming together of the fluidity of the sequential industries (and a number of service industries) with that of the process industries, the organizers could bring together the concepts to such an extent as to introduce *management by process* in all the production activities, be they the manufacture of goods or in the service sector. From the point of view of quality control, the International Standards Organization (ISO) proposed that all production be repartitioned into an ensemble of *processes*, that is to say, into more or less autonomous sections that would each receive an input to which it would add value before passing it on to the next section. The exigencies of cost, quality, deadlines (or of diversity) tended to place the responsibility squarely on each section, which was tightly bound to its supplier behind it and its client ahead, as well as to the other support cells, resource units and, of course, the commissioning parties. The flow was thus as tight as the above exigencies made it by greatly reducing, if not completely eliminating, the buffers to reduce costs and increase the reactivity of each process, and ultimately, of the production system as a whole.

In France, this transition towards tight flow came about quietly and gradually, without any great fuss, as though it was a most natural outcome, a change that went hand in hand with the emerging technologies, increasing competition or simply progress in general. In Germany, IG Metall initiated a lively internal debate on the acceptance of 'lean production' as an outcome of the just-in-time concept. In the UK, a number of books questioned the 'Japanization' of industries and of the economy. In the USA, some unionists (especially in the car industry) and universities also questioned this change in the production paradigm.

In France, the trade unions, which were mainly preoccupied with retaining jobs, saw these changes as inevitable, not only accepting them without analysing them too deeply, but more importantly, without imposing obstacles to their introduction. Yet the modifications brought about by the principle of tight flow affected not only the manner of working – for example, by increasing each individual's responsibility – they transformed the obligations and constraints that came with the work, and thereby the contents (in some activities) and the significance given by the employee to his/her work or function. A short tour of the history behind just-in-time and the reasons that led to the generalizations behind the concept of tight flow will help greatly in appreciating its importance and understanding the significance of the changes it ushered in.

The genesis of just-in-time

Born during the inter-war period in the USA and subsequently generalized in Western Europe in the early 1950s, mass production was rarely concerned with questions of cost or quality: practically everything that was produced was sold. Standardized products satisfied the market demand. The manufacturing process consisted of long lines of parts arranged in series, which were fitted together and stored in enormous stockpiles (often approaching a month's buffer – that is, thousands of components languishing in warehouses) before being assembled into the finished product: motor vehicles, electrical household appliances, furniture and so on.

After the Second World War, Japan too adopted these Fordian methods of production, partly as a result of the pressure exerted by the American occupation and partly because it knew no other way. But these methods did not suit Japanese industry in that era – the markets were too small (a poor country, just emerging from the shambles of a devastating war), and there were too many suppliers. In other words, mass production with its stocks did not allow industrialists to make significant profits. The more daring among them were on the lookout for a miracle solution that would generate profits from short production runs – in effect, the opposite of the Fordian tradition.

T. Ohno, chief engineer and later director of the Toyota factories, came up with the following diagnosis: 'We kept reminding ourselves, however, that careless imitation of the American system could be dangerous. Making many models in small numbers cheaply – wasn't this something we could develop? And we kept thinking that a Japanese production system like this might even surpass the conventional mass production system.'[1] During the 1950s, he decided to implement in his workshops the principles behind the American supermarkets. Ohno had come to know of them from the published professional literature and from his own visit to the USA in 1956. For Ohno, 'a supermarket was, in fact, a place where the consumer could get the goods that he needed, at the time that he needed them and in the quantity needed ... As for the employees of the store, it was clear that it was up to them to ready and display their merchandise such that the consumers could come for their purchases at a time of their choosing.'[2]

The results of this concept on industrial production methods were far-reaching. In the first place, it eliminated the stockpiling of goods between factory and client. As in the supermarkets, in the new system at Toyota it was the consumer who put his/her requirements to the fore, and *downstream management* was born. Second, and by the same logic, every workstation or production section could ask its immediate neighbour upstream to deliver the required goods in (productive/due) time and in the volume considered necessary: just-in-time was born. As a workstation upstream would now produce and deliver only the quantity required and at precisely the time stipulated by the station downstream, there was no need to stock anything, and buffers were all but eliminated between production sections.

The engineers at Toyota, followed closely by the economists, were quick to point out the advantages of just-in-time and downstream management. An end to stockpiling meant a significant saving of space, which in Japan, because of its geography and the structure of its landholdings, was extremely expensive. The just-in-time system also reduced the capital locked in stock. Both these advantages could be savoured only once: at the moment that stock was eliminated (or at least greatly reduced). But the just-in-time method also offered other, more permanent, benefits: the absence of stock meant that a defective part was noticed immediately, instead of, as in the old system, after having been stockpiled with a number of units later found to be defective during assembly. Similarly, the just-in-time system immediately identified the bottlenecks and malfunctions in a production line: it required the immediate resolution of all problems.

Finally, downstream management brought the consumer closer to the production system by eliminating the stockpiling of finished goods. Now producers were directly in touch with their clients and could respond very quickly to their needs and changing tastes, and to the innovations launched by competitors.

The concepts of both just-in-time and downstream management appeared and were implemented by Toyota in the 1950s through the need to generate profits from short production runs. And it was this same requirement, shared by the whole of Japan, that ensured the success of 'the Toyota system' throughout the archipelago in the following decades. When the accumulation crisis hit the West in the 1970s, ever-increasing competition brought in and exacerbated a slew of problems, and industry leaders began to look frantically for solutions. It was not only that the race for volume (as was the case in the motor vehicle industry) caused them headaches, but the products themselves (motorcycles, video and hi-fi equipment and so on) were often more expensive and of lower quality than those coming from Japan. Moreover, the competition was not only with respect to price and quality, but also variety: everyone was trying to capture an ever-growing number of market niches by radically diversifying their products. We thus pass from the concept of *static flexibility* (which produced a delayed variety achieved by means of differing assembly methods from various components) to the *dynamic flexibility* that could satisfy a much more varied demand (and growing uncertainty) by making extensive use of management information systems (MIS) and better group training.[3]

In other words, European and American industrialists came up against the intrinsic limitations of the Fordian principles – they were now required to produce high-quality short-run job lots at low cost. In the meantime, their Japanese counterparts had already solved this conundrum, albeit under rather different historical circumstances, and had extracted considerable profits by inundating selected sectors of the world market with their products. Thus, the Japanese solution of just-in-time and downstream management came to be considered the indispensable 'model' for squaring the Fordian circle. The number of study missions to Japan increased exponentially, a large number of consultants and directors of Western corporations (in the USA and Europe) took to the principles of just-in-time and downstream management, and the *flexible mass production* system was born. All that had been learnt step by step, through trial and error over more than a decade at Toyota was theorized, systematized in its presentation and reconstructed *ex post facto* to become universally accepted (Womack *et al.* 1990). It contained, via the organizational coherence between the activities of production and interchange that it proposed, a logic that was at least as compelling as that of those who, at the beginning of the twentieth century, had invented the assembly line (around Ford) on the one hand and scientific management (after Taylor) on the other.[4]

The hidden core of tight flow

Downstream management, and in particular just-in-time production, required a considerable conceptual leap on the part of all involved. The elimination of buffers brought in an element of stress and constant insecurity at every workstation, and weighed heavily on workers because, if they failed to deliver, the whole production chain would come to a standstill, affecting the entire run. Doubts were raised and the conceptual leap required proved difficult to accomplish as it involved a major change in the outlook of every worker – they had first to be convinced of the necessity of these revolutionary changes. For his part, Ohno likened the maintenance of stock to the gut-reflexes of impoverished agriculturists and said:

> we must instead become a community of hunters, and taking courage in both hands, get for ourselves all that we need, at the moment that we need it and in the quantity that is needed. Actually, it is not a question of courage – in a modern, industrial society, it is simply a question of common sense. At the same time, it will require, what I will call a 'mental revolution' within the industrial community, a radical change in attitude and point of view. To maintain any sizeable stock in an environment of slow economic growth is wastage by over-production.[5]

For his part, Coriat concurred with Ohno's proposals and advocated 'thinking in reverse' about the Western way of working. In fact, in order to highlight the importance of this revolution in mind-set, he even named one of his books after it.[6]

By eliminating buffers and stock, just-in-time tightened the flow. Just as Taylor fought against the 'systematic idling' of workers, just-in-time aimed at getting rid of idling material – components, stock and products were to be constantly on the move. Tight flow increased productivity by, as the economists keep reiterating, reducing the amount of locked-up capital in the form of stock on the one hand and holding and handling charges on the other. This did not include the large savings in rework costs caused by the repeated handling of goods and material in stocking and destocking processes. But, it must be repeated, these savings were realized only once: only at the time when the corporation decided on the elimination of stock, or at least on a drastic stock reduction.

Our proposition is that tight flow had other, significantly more important and durable, benefits which were thus of much greater strategic value. This time, however, they do not deal with the material moved around in a tight flow, but rather the people themselves, who were placed all along the line and charged with keeping it tight. In effect, *tight* flow (compared to the traditional system with stock) was in essence, fragile. For us, the strength of tight flow as a production paradigm lay in this very fragility, in a vulnerability that required the complete attention of everyone working under it. Its fragility was not a defect that would have an adverse effect on its users, who might perhaps have underestimated its problems: on the contrary, it was a powerful managerial tool that highlighted the bottlenecks that needed to be addressed urgently while at the same time whipping the whole workforce on to a war footing in order to retain the 'tightness' of the flow. We could use the term *constrained involvement* to characterize the intrinsic nature of tight flow – from the moment a worker accepted the principle, the flow completely took over, in spite of himself, all his physical and intellectual faculties.

To the fragility of the system was then added an element of complexity. An analysis of the traditional manufacturing methods of complete products (for example, motor vehicles, electrical household appliances, furniture and electronics.) will reveal that as all of these are now produced with added functions and more sophisticated designs, their manufacture too had to keep up and become more complex. Thus this 'complexifying' of products and the associated processes increased the fragility that had been introduced by tight flow, and it was the responsibility of the workers to ensure the tautness of the flow – that is, to prevent any break in continuity. Their function was no longer limited just to production, without bothering, as in the past, about other details of the work. They now also had to consider and control the environment around their workstation, to ensure the continuity of the flow. The objective was no longer just the output in itself, assessed by the number of good pieces, for example, but rather the *tightness of the flow*, its continuity. This meant that further responsibilities were added to the workstation and resulted in new working methods with new organizational tools. In effect, preventing any break in the flow meant:

- the elimination of downtime by *preventive maintenance*;
- making sure that all the parts or services delivered were of *good quality*;
- being prepared to *change the tools quickly* to manufacture the parts required downstream; and
- the *continuous improvement* of the production plant.

Along with the implementation of just-in-time, Ohno was also busy with his engineers, designing the tools that were indispensable to the success of his venture. These tools were then modified substantially by his Japanese, American and European successors, and converted into ready-to-use methods that were then circulated widely via managerial literature. They included total productive maintenance (TPM); total quality management (TQM, which gave rise to a variety of 'quality processes'); the single minute exchange die (SMED); and *kaizen* (continuous improvement).

Just as in the case of the older tools that had been conceived of by the inheritors of Ford and Taylor, these tools, which were implemented from the 1980s, also need to be seen both as a means of reorganizing production and consequently work, as well as props for newer methods of managing the labour force (see also the next chapter). In fact, in a certain sense, this line of enquiry is bound to prove more fruitful for investigating the sources of the actual productivity gains instead of looking only at the reorganization of the production system.

Preventive maintenance and the 5Ss

The concept of TPM involved a complete reversal of the maintenance and repair culture. In the past, qualified workers and technicians were evaluated according to their speed and efficiency. This resulted in the creation of an implicit hierarchy, based on the skill with which any breakdowns or complex problems were tackled and resolved. For all practical purposes, these technicians were the masters of the game, as they controlled the whole flow by the way they handled any downtime. This conferred on them a special status in the workshop, a respect and solidarity that resulted in an accelerated rate of unionization. But with the coming of the concept of preventive maintenance and its prevalence in the modern workshop, the repair technicians were relegated to a subsidiary role and consigned to work in the shadows. The absence of a breakdown is always less spectacular than a speedy repair under adverse conditions (reworking of parts, tinkering and sometimes even the taking of physical risks to expedite a repair). Today, preventive maintenance, done unobtrusively in the time-gaps between production runs (for example, at night, weekends, specific times allotted to maintenance) has reversed the roles: production has regained its primary status at the expense of repair work. This inversion sorely affected the repair technicians, who understandably resisted any move towards preventive or anticipatory maintenance.

To counteract this resistance, workshop managers resorted to three very rational methods.[7] As a first measure, they decreed that the maintenance personnel did not form part of any specific service, parallel to or placed over the manufacturing process – they were now attached directly to it, and functionally depended on it in an increasingly hierarchical manner. Second, the workers in the manufacturing section were themselves to take charge of the first level of maintenance: greasing, changing tools and minor repairs. This transfer of their functions disturbed maintenance technicians ever further: not only because these semi-skilled workers were acquiring new skills (which until then had belonged rightfully to the maintenance crew), but also that this transfer drastically reduced their role as 'saviours' by greatly decreasing the downtime – the 'repairmen' were always present on the spot. In return, the maintenance technicians could look forward to a re-evaluation of their position as they retained the higher levels of maintenance (complex repairs and the preventive maintenance of entire installations). For their part, the operators, who were once classified as semi-skilled workers, saw their field of work expanding and their responsibilities multiplying. Though this was no small addition, it did not entail anything much deeper, and they remained confined to subordinate operations while the jobs that required initiative or creativity remained beyond their grasp.

Third, manufactures and managers of workshops began to make greater use of more or less automated systems to keep track of breakdowns and their causes. These 'manufacturing aids' not only helped the production workers in their diagnoses, but more importantly facilitated the planning of the preventive maintenance. In some cases, the data generated by these computerized information systems were used by the planning department, which then introduced newer methods of curative, and in particular preventive, servicing. This further reduced the role of the maintenance technician. It also often happened that the only remaining creative function, that of burning-in and upgrading, was entrusted to some other department, further eroding the technician's professional identity.

Considering that the concept of preventive maintenance required a profound change in mentality also meant that a need arose for methods to bring about such a reversal. And once again, it was Japanese industry that provided the required toolbox in the form of the 5Ss. Used as preliminary or as accompanying measures, the 5Ss stood for:

- *seiri*: clearing up (removing all that was not needed);
- *seiton*: organizing (everything in its proper place);
- *seiso*: cleaning (no rubbish or dirt in the workplace);
- *seiketsu*: standardizing (maintaining rules and regulations); and
- *shitsuke*: discipline (discipline, commitment and constant improvement).

The essence of the 5Ss can be summed up as a drive towards inculcating a strong sense of responsibility in workers regarding the work, and a complete involvement in the whole manufacturing process. The change in the mindset advocated by the 5Ss can be seen as a clearer and more binding summary of all the 'job station instructions', procedures, recommendations and standards issued by the plant managers and the process planning department. Both *seiketsu* and *shitsuke* brought an element of constraint and checked the initiative and freedom of workers, who were now required to follow more strictly the rules and regulations imposed on them from outside. This is not to say that other avenues of autonomy did not arise, such as, for example, from 'complexification' of the manufacturing process and the need for personal reactivity.[8] Nevertheless, the 5Ss, a necessary condition for the implementation of TPM (and of 'total quality'), must first be seen, as a director of a French firm's Karlsruhe factory put it, as 'social training' – social training that standardized responses regarding the increasingly precise and exacting demands of the planning department.

The transformation in attitude engendered by the 5Ss also meant that workers were left without some of their usual points of reference. For example, they were asked by management to adhere strictly to procedures which at one time they had habitually avoided, sometimes even, according to them, in order to be more efficient. In the Spanish factory of a large French motor vehicle company, the workers had resisted the implementation of the 5Ss. As this factory was susceptible to the hazards of demand and volume variations, and the danger of layoffs weighed too heavily, there could not be any explicit opposition. And so the workers resorted to derision. The system implemented required that every production unit must go through the five stages, with the completion of every stage being marked by a sticker on a poster. The idea was that an inter-workshop competition for the most displayed stickers would motivate everyone and accelerate the implementation of the 5Ss. But workers got hold of the stock of stickers and immediately filled up all the posters, claiming triumphantly that all the work had been accomplished. While this little incident does not do justice to the fundamental changes in the workers mindset that were wrought elsewhere, it does give an idea of the resistance to this change. Workers saw in this transformation the loss of all their normal power in a production system that they had come to know well – without knowing where they were headed or whether they had any guarantee of compensation.

From the 5Ss to TPM, the work was remodelled through a reallocation of tasks and the extensive use of micro-electronics in the automation process. This led to an improvement in the qualifications of employees through the diversification of the tasks as already discussed, or even simply by the ever-increasing use of computer terminals. But at the same time, although their qualifications improved, we also see that the differences between the field operator and the repair technician or the process planning department have remained, if not in fact increased. A number of authors have contested this because they have been interested more by the study of the processes than by the actual work done by workers and salaried personnel. A similar debate rages over the transformation of work stemming from the implementation of policies dealing with quality issues.

The total quality process

To ensure the continuity of the flow, every part or service delivered downstream had to be of the required quality. In keeping with the concept of tight flow, the quality was not enforced at the end of the production line, but all through the process, and in fact formed its very core. This meant that every operator was required to declare defects occurring upstream that had percolated down to him or her, to adhere strictly to the quality required, and moreover to inform and propose amendments to management (via the suggestion system) if any defect did creep in.

The quality drive led to a streamlining of the work based on ever more stringent work procedures. Quality memos were generally drawn up in the following manner: operators described in detail the work done in the course of their time on duty. Quality specialists then compared this description to the existing job station instructions and then streamlined the work so as to avoid defects – sometimes also in the name of productivity gains. The revamped operating manual, with highly detailed new procedures, was then returned to the operator, who was then required to adhere to it strictly. By the magic of inter-department relations within the enterprise, the 'I write what I do' of the first step was transformed into 'I do what is written'.

The first step, which required creativity and stimulated intelligence, brought these operators together in a bid to co-ordinate their activities, avoid duplicating jobs, improve the process, and so on. In the course of these meetings, the workers shared their hard-earned know-how, their personal tricks and secret techniques they had learnt in the course of their job. But why did they do it? Why did they share their private and exclusive resources with others? Largely because they had no choice. Management's clear injunction ('I write what I do') and the general feeling that the survival of the enterprise depended on satisfying the customer by improving the quality meant that there was little resistance (who could declare themselves to be against quality?). Moreover, the write-ups required were mostly on an individual basis, while the meetings brought collective pressure to bear on the few remaining pockets of resistance. To be effective, the resistance to the publicizing of personal know-how and to its standardization in the form of procedures would need to be collective and organized – which hardly ever happened: operators found themselves helpless when faced with managerial injunctions. On the bright side, we can show how these meetings and quality circles brought in freedom of speech and highlighted to the operators channels for new suggestions and innovative proposals outside any question of claims or demands (which were banned in these cases). For certain groups of salaried workers who performed under suffocating conditions, to have found their voice in the workplace created an opening and a window of opportunity that management could well use to further its own objectives.

The last step, during which positions were redefined and enriched with new procedures so as to 'do well right from the start', generally went ahead under favourable conditions as it came at the end of the whole process, with general consensus and participation. On the other hand, the long-term implementation of these stringent procedures quickly led to drudgery and weariness. The interest taken in their creation dissipated very quickly in the course of their repetition. As always, the operator remained the one to blame for lack of quality, whose possibility and genesis s/he had demonstrated her/himself just a few months before! Based on the universal dictum of the satisfaction of the final customer, quality processes were at the heart of work reorganization from the beginning of the 1980s,[9] accompanied by a battery of certification.

Rapid change in tools and production

Downstream management, which had for its first objective to reply immediately to the demands of the client or the stations downstream, required, in the absence of buffers, an extremely rapid change in production. This was the essential core behind the production in job lots, or as Ohno put it, 'job splitting'. In fact, changes in production had become so frequent that they hardly lasted longer than the time taken for the production itself! Engineers at Toyota had thus to systematize the process to reduce the time taken to change job runs and, more particularly, the tools, such as the single minute exchange die (SMED), which married industrial techniques to organizational reforms. For example, changing the original moulds of cup presses in the can industry required, in the past, between six and eight hours, and engaged two to four qualified tool and die workers. Today, with the aid of some relatively sophisticated techniques and rigorous pre-setting, this work requires only eleven minutes for most manufacturers in the world. In the course of this magical ballet, mother moulds weighing several tons are removed automatically on trolleys from the five presses, and another set of moulds is simultaneously put in their place. In most cases, even the first few pieces moulded by these new moulds turn out to be good – in stark contrast to the old system, where it used to take hours of adjustment before acceptable pieces could be produced.

To cite the example of a manufacturer of motorcycles and scooters: previously, a change in the job run for sectioning tubes required professional workers who would appear in their own time. Today, the women operators can do the same job on their own. While the SMED ousted many tool and die workers, it greatly improved the overall productivity of the enterprise. It reduced machine and operator downtime while decreasing the number of technicians (the tool and die workers). To top it all, by shortening changeover times between different job runs and thus allowing a larger variety of products to be manufactured on the same line, SMED boosted the overall flexibility of the entire production apparatus.

Though we have taken some examples from the manufacturing sector, since it is more striking, and also because that is where SMED was born, the same principle also dominates the service sector today. In the field of data processing (in banks, insurance, administration, for example) or the service industries (catering, tourism, generally any distribution), the need to meet the varied demands of customers immediately imposed a similar dexterity and the same rigorous methods of organizing work. The needs of both service and manufacturing industries converge from the moment we combine downstream management (customer satisfaction) and tight flow (the flow of goods or information) against a backdrop of drastic cost reductions (manpower in particular).

In other words, the intense competition prevalent in almost all areas required fast response capabilities in terms of the need for rapidly-changing job runs, products and services offered. Traditionally, one would think of the necessity of reactivity only when faced with the constantly varying demands of the customer. But in fact the number of enterprises in direct contact with the final customer is very small. Today, this responsiveness concerns the small and medium enterprises (SMEs) more, and the SMEs that have to meet the demands of the large enterprises, be they through just-in-time deliveries, or through what we term *business* or *industrial services*. In this case, it would do well to meet as quickly as possible the widely varied and constantly changing demands of the large enterprise, with the same need to maintain tight production flow (of goods or services), since in turn, it had to face the final customer.

This requirement for a tight flow had its own effects (SMED on work), just as *kaizen* influenced the socio-productive (a combination of social and technical logic as being inherent in the system) techniques which accompanied the just-in-time revolution.

The continuous improvement of production

Kaizen is usually translated as 'continuous improvement'.[10] A visit to the Toyota engine factory in Toyota City, Japan, surprises visitors because of the obsolete nature of the equipment and the lack of staff in the workshops. Machine parts are transported from one place to another by means of chutes and gravity, aided only by rudimentary automatic material handlers and elevators. In the West, the most common interpretation of *kaizen* is of continuous and global improvement of production equipment in terms of competitiveness: reliability (no more breakdowns); faster response; and a reduction in the costs of raw material, energy and staff. Similarly, to the general public, this improvement was a result of a conscientious implementation of all the suggestions that management had encouraged workers to make. But in fact, this Western interpretation of *kaizen* seems somewhat incomplete. The concept of *kaizen*, as it was first conceived at Toyota, had as its first objective the reduction of costs, and initially, the cost of manpower. In effect, the Toyota Production System (TPS), which gave birth to tight flow, was at the beginning, a comprehensive system for 'cost planning' from the concept of the product (simultaneous engineering) up to its manufacture. TPS[11] was based on the rigorous planning of cost reduction over the entire life of the product. Even though in this book we concentrate more on the technology of tight flow, its relation to work and its subsequent transformation, the reader must always associate tight flow with *cost reduction* – the two essential components of the TPS: completely interlinked, indissoluble and which have created fortunes all over the world.[12]

The drive towards cost reduction cascaded down to every work team, with management needing to find bottlenecks in order to remove them. Even when there did not seem to be any, 'it could happen that the section leader tried to bring one to light by speeding up the flow. The section would then embark upon an improvement drive by calling in a *kaizen* team and/or engineers from the technical office of the factory'.[13] According to the widely accepted view, the work team would normally find solutions on its own by means of internal staff suggestions, and its autonomy regarding its functioning and resources allowed it to make local modifications or produce a better piece of equipment. Thus we see the justification behind the ideas of autonomy, initiative and participation so often associated with the

Japanese work team – ideas which found widespread acceptance, particularly in the 1980s, through the efforts of Piore and Sabel.[14] In truth, the suggestion system was primarily a means of mobilizing labour and technicians, but had only a small role to play in this – most of the improvements came mainly from *kaizen* teams and management, both of which were greatly concerned with reducing costs, especially in terms of manpower. Finally, when the changes envisaged required large investments or in-depth studies, the work was taken up by the engineers from the technical department. According to E. Ogawa, as quoted by K. Shimizu, 90 per cent of *kaizen* activities were effected by autonomous *kaizen* teams, or by management, with workers' suggestions having only marginal influence.

It is this, we feel, leads to the misinterpretation of *kaizen* in the Western minds. Rather than simply focusing on manpower savings, it was interpreted as meaning the efforts taken towards overall improvements – simultaneously taking into account the quality, responsiveness and global productivity of the plant.[15]

Effects of socio-productive techniques

Preventive maintenance, total quality, the SMED and *kaizen* combine with each other perfectly to maintain the flow of material or information (services) with ever-decreasing costs. The coherence between these four socio-productive tools rests on their common objective and explains the fact that an enterprise or a consultant could begin on the transformation of the production facility equally well through any one of these four tools – that is, for the introduction of tight flow at minimal cost. There exist implementation methods and specialized books for each of them. The objectives being identical, apart from the specificities of the programme, the changes induced would essentially also be identical, whatever the starting point. It would be difficult to implement preventive maintenance fully without being confronted by questions regarding rapid changes in production and in quality, and the continuous improvement of equipment very soon becomes an absolute necessity. Similarly, it would be impossible to talk of quality without passing through TPM and then, necessarily through *kaizen*, in order to reduce the costs that were incurred by the original quality drive.

The most common point of entry remained quality, at a reduced cost – with this last item rarely being mentioned. This was because, initially, the producer being himself a consumer, saw quality as having a universal appeal and a feature that management could easily make employees relate to. However, it must be said that this universality had no sound basis, nor was it an absolute – in fact, quite the reverse – a scientific definition of quality very quickly descends into the quagmire of convention and morality.[16] Nevertheless, no one could oppose a drive for quality, and it thus turned into a universal watchword which brushed aside or overcame all opposition.

As these socio-productive tools were created to produce tight flow, their implementation necessarily meant the realization of a manufacturing system which produced goods or services at low cost and without interim or final stocks. The central aim of tight flow (at minimal cost) was, at the start, the primary objective of management. This signified that when the operators shared the objectives of the socio-productive tools already described (and how could they declare themselves against quality or the reduction in cost or in delays?) they identified their immediate objectives (for example, implement the SMED, quality) with those of management as regards tight flow and cost reduction.

Thus these socio-productive tools were also, apart from being purely technical aids to production, an important means in the hands of management for mobilizing labour. This had already been foreseen in a Toyota manual that enumerated three indirect effects of *kaizen* and the suggestions system:

- Educational effects. By trying to make suggestions, the employees learnt to think about their work, to solve the problems they faced and thus enrich their know-how.
- Effects on human relations. By forming groups to make suggestions or by being advised by their superiors, they improved their communication skills, horizontally as well as vertically, and enlarged the circle of co-operation.
- Effects on participation. Making suggestions gave them a community feeling within the company and increased their participation in the aims of the company.[17]

Over and above their purely technical functions, these socio-technological tools also played a fundamental role in the general acceptance of all the obligations linked to tight flow. They were in fact a means of making junior employees participate in the objectives of the enterprise. It was thus that the *economic* objectives of the company were packaged and transmitted within *technological* concepts in the course of quality circle meetings, progress groups or discussions regarding suggestions. Broad-spectrum objectives as well as the demands of shareholders were translated into local micro-objectives adapted to the field of employees who were themselves confined within narrow social, corporate and technological bounds; to proclaim broad objectives that had no link to day-to-day work would have had little effect. They had to be made concrete and tangible by creating directly linked and immediately achievable practices. 'There is no ideology without practice', wrote Althusser.[18] In this case, TPM, *kaizen* and TQM constituted the practices that corresponded to the ideology of globalization and its demands.

Moreover, these practices, which transformed relations between junior employees, technicians and engineers as well as management, brought alive the concept of *participative management*. This time, however, it was with some real substance: the close ties that arose between these corporate levels meant that union representatives could be bypassed and, in fact, rendered superfluous. To say that these socio-productive tools were also management tools should take into account freedom of speech ('write what you do') and the transformation of workers into a force for suggestions and proposals – or at least, that is what was claimed. Not only did freedom of speech give rise to discussions regarding technical aspects and other issues shared by the management, but by that very fact, it also meant a shifting away from questions of differences and protests. Moreover, the contact with (and sharing of issues with) white-collar workers (technicians, engineers, auditors and so on) gave lower-level employees a kind of kinship with these higher categories. A similar trend can also be seen in retail business and the public sector. Also, such discussions, which involved and captured the imagination of workers, kept them from dwelling on other preoccupations such as fixed production rates, stress, fatigue and quality of working life issues in general.

Tight flow, work and time constraints

To remain tight, the flow required that certain conditions be met, and it was the socio-productive tools that met these demands. At the same time, they also had an integrative role to play as they led the junior employees to accept management's larger objectives via the means of local micro-objectives which, by and large, satisfied their aspirations.[19]

In the Taylorist–Fordist system of production, the primary function of the group leader was one of discipline – through which the group leader made sure that the work (the job assigned) was done as required. This explains why this job was often handled in the mass production industry by ex-servicemen – group leaders who guaranteed discipline. In the case of tight flow, there was no longer any need for a disciplinarian: discipline formed part of the tight flow itself. The moment an employee accepted the principle of tight flow – that is, of its having to remain unbroken, s/he was controlled by the flow and had to confirm all his/her actions to the maintenance of its continuity. To accept the principle of tight flow was to accept the discipline it imposed, and there was no longer any need to maintain any other discipline. We have thus the profound significance of the paradoxical concept of 'constrained involvement'. Once caught by the surge of tight flow, the employee was completely swept up by it and had no choice but to use all his/her faculties to maintain the tightness of the flow. We could note that this mobilization of the workforce by tight flow goes hand in hand with the mobilization wrought by the socio-productive tools that have already been described.

On the other hand, these constraints (regulations, procedures, time pressures, deadlines – all with minimal manpower) seemed 'natural' to the employee, in the sense that they were no longer imposed by an individual (the boss) but rather formed part of the requirements to maintain the process of production in a tight flow. Thus the constraints were felt to be something external to the economic or corporate world, something that formed part of the neutral flow of material – just as men or women look upon all matter and nature – something outside themselves. This made the constraints seem 'natural', that is, independent of any human volition and therefore to be respected. In effect, either one accepted tight flow and its attendant constraints, or one walked out of the enterprise. Such a naturalized acceptance was markedly different from the relationship employees once had *vis-à-vis* management. We could even talk of the advent of a new relational fetishism at born out of the functional dimensions of the technological work involved in maintaining tight flow.

The end of the need for supervisory staff meant a shortening of the hierarchy well beyond what management had promised. It was simply a question of mechanical cause and effect: as discipline was now very much an integral part of the flow, the supervisory staff took on another function – controlling things instead of humans. Thus arose the concept of *reporting* – the monitoring of the production of goods or services in terms of quality, and quantity with an eye on production conditions and with a view to improve productivity constantly. Management could no longer, as before, isolate itself from the flux; it had constantly to anticipate and keep one step ahead in order to avoid any break – management was itself dominated by the dictates of the flux and its intrinsic constraints of time and deadlines. Also, once freed of its disciplinary function, it could participate increasingly in 'human resource management' within its department or workshop by evaluating workers and embarking on an anticipatory policy of recruitment or training.

All these time constraints on the work were contained within the paradigm of tight flow. In our opinion, the main reason behind the spread of

Table 2.1 The development of work under time constraints

Proportion of employees who declare	1991 (%)	1998 (%)
Having frequently to abandon work-in-progress for another which had not been foreseen:	48	55.7
and that it disturbed their work	n/a	48.2
and that it is a positive aspect of their work	n/a	14.6
Do not take their eyes off their work	26.3	31.9
That a mistake in their work could result in:		
an adverse effect on quality	60.2	65.2
financial costs to the company	43.8	50.2
sanctions against them	46.0	59.8
a serious breach of security	30.7	37.8
Who felt that their relations with the public were strained	34.4	47.7

Sources: *Enquêtes Conditions de travail*, 1991 and 1998, Paris, Ministère du Travail.

this new production paradigm to all manufacturing sectors was its capacity to systematize the work through time constraints. Our generalization is supported and borne out by statistics published by the French Department of Labour and Manpower in the 1990s (see Table 2.1).

Historically, the systematization of work under time constraints was first adapted in the production lines of large industries such as motor vehicles, furniture, household appliances and consumer electronics. Theoretically, just-in-time and its corollary, tight flow, are just a extension and development of the Fordian flow.[20] By eliminating stock between production stages, not only along the line itself, but from the entire production system of goods and services, tight flow turned time pressure and deadlines into management tools to deal with human activity during working hours.[21] Being objectified within the requirements and exigencies of tight flow, time constraints were 'naturalized' and accepted as unavoidable. This allowed a reduction in the number of supervisory staff.

The reduction in costs was the result of both rising competitiveness as well as the drive to maximize profits. The effort at cost reduction entailed the implementation of tight flow, which put an end to idling material by eliminating stocks and buffers while at the same time significantly reducing labour costs by means of socio-productive tools, as shown above. Thus, if the search for lowered costs leads to tight flow, it too in its turn brought with it a system and the necessary tools to reduce costs. With the whole process based on stock market and financial considerations – which brings us back to the necessity of increasing productivity, especially that of work (the fact that a rise in the stock market is associated with a rise in unemployment is proof of this elementary observation). Every day, news of price wars, hyped by the media, jump at employees from the pages of their dailies, justifying the constraints under which they have to work and which are the natural outcome of tight flow. The success of Womack *et al.*'s book on *lean production*,[22] which has been translated in all the major languages, is due mainly to the fact that, under the guise of a scientific approach, it deals mainly with the question of cost reduction. No wonder, then, that it captured the imagination of managers and shareholders worldwide.

The difference between the traditional Fordian flow and tight flow (the fact of its being 'tight') rests on the latter's extensive use of information and communication technology (ICT) with the capacity to handle large amounts of data. In fact, it was only the ICT that made it possible to combine meaningfully the activity of men and machines; that is, to co-ordinate their activities in *real time* and *over distance*. There exists a very close tie between time savings (a characteristic of capitalism) and the use of ICT. An integration and instantaneous (also over distance) sharing of the correct information – that is, of data that reflect accurately the current state of stock, a machine or a process, greatly enhances the efficiency of both men and machines. Such quality information allows the automation of certain decisions, or at the least helps when making rapid and effective decisions, and thus maintains the 'tightness' of the flow. At the same time, while automation and tight flow led to a reduction in the number of employees linked directly to production, they also required other, newer ones (albeit in smaller numbers) – especially in the industrial service sector. In effect, tight flow and its heavy reliance on ICT resulted in an increasingly complex production system that also entailed further fragility. The number of monitoring and repair staff needed to oversee the flow of information went up steeply and sometimes ate into a significant portion of the productivity gains realized. Whether it was a flow of material or information, the overwhelming emphasis was on it being at its 'tightest'. This was the case with both industrial goods and the service sector. Of what use would be a three-month-old bank statement or a weather bureau that offered the weather forecast for the day before yesterday? But at the same time, the requirements of tight flow needed, in their turn, radical changes in the organization of work.

The advent of teamwork

The maintenance of the flow needed a *collective* effort. By definition, tight flow was a linking, a putting into direct contact of the different machines and/or different segments of the production apparatus. It created permanent connections between all the elements which up until then had remained more or less isolated by the interim stocks, which acted as buffers and helped to absorb any difficulties that arose – in other words, they allowed the process as a whole to continue even if a part of it fell behind for a time. Today, to have independent workstations would be unthinkable as they would never be able to keep the flow tight. Only close co-operation between employees (read *collective work*) can keep the flow tight with a reduced labour force. We see here the implementation and illustration of Marx's thesis on co-operation, according to which, 'Not only have we here to increase the productive force of the individual, by means of co-operation, but to create a new force, namely, a collective force.'[23] In fact, collective work increases efficiency not only by the coming together of individual forces, but because it has eyes and hands at the back as well as in front, because it sees all and is everywhere. To top it all, profit from this extra efficiency that stemmed from the collective nature of work did not have to be paid to employees as it did not belong to them:

> The special productive force of the combined working-day is, under all circumstances, the social productive force of labour, or the productive force of social labour. This force is due to co-operation itself ... The co-operation of wage-workers is entirely brought about by the capital that employs them ... The capitalist pays each of the 100 workers the value of 100 independent labour-force, but he does not pay for the combined labour-force of the hundred.[24]

This sort of collective work required by tight flow is termed *teamwork*. Japanese in origin, it has been widely popularized by Womack *et al.* (1990) and by major consultancy firms worldwide. Teamwork is made up of (at least) four essential characteristics:

- the collective responsibility of the group;
- the versatility of the group members;
- a self-organization of the group with ambivalent consequences; and
- the creation of the *team leader*.

Some of these may be seen in embryonic form in a movement that went beyond Fordism–Taylorism but ran out of steam in the late 1970s. A few pioneering companies such as IBM, McDonald's, AXA, Carrefour, for example, also came up with a few scattered elements. But it was the large, post-war Japanese firms, especially in the motor vehicle industry, that created the *team concept* as a mature and complete model which now finds itself being implemented in the production industries of all sectors.

Collective responsibility

Just as tight flow linked machines and activities (or groups of machines and activities) by eliminating the individual, isolated station, it also made it impossible for a single group to manage the entire flow. Consequently, it was divided into productive segments which were, wherever possible, homogeneous or logical within themselves and in their contribution to tight flow. A working group was assigned to each of these segments, which, as the management would have it, acted as clients to the preceding one and as suppliers to the one downstream. This client–supplier relationship was the crucial rule of engagement and the linchpin of tight flow.

Each work group was *collectively* responsible for the quantity and the quality of the goods or services it supplied. The concept of the flow, especially in continuous process industries – which all would like to become[25] – meant that production was not calculated in terms of volume or quantity of pieces produced, but rather in the amount of time a work station was up and running. This led to a synthetic estimate of the productivity rate which took into account both the causes of a breakdown as well as the reasons behind any dip in quality.

Collective responsibility remained at the heart of the model, and it is only natural that the image of a sports team was used so often in training sessions. A sports team, just like a surgical team or a managerial team, comes together with a single objective: to meet a challenge.[26] This was not a competition between the different teams within an enterprise, but between the company as a whole and other such enterprises. The team, even a local one, fought beside management to win the competition war. The local challenge – the attainment of an objective that had been more or less fixed in agreement with the management team – was part of a larger challenge, which encompassed and shaped it.

The development of versatility

As employees became increasingly versatile – that is, they could, and were required to, intervene at any point in the segment whose responsibility rested with the group. The best of them were even able to work on other segments when the necessity arose. Versatility, in others words, implies the ability to carry out different jobs at the same work station, with the help of the team leader, or better still, after a brief period of training, individually and independently. It was the foundation that made the rotation of jobs possible, thereby reducing the monotony and repetitiveness that so often led to musculo-skeletal problems.[27] At the same time, versatility – without which the skill required to do a job well would deteriorate rapidly – was itself encouraged by job rotation.[28]

This versatility, along with job rotation, meant that the knowledge (special know-how) that each worker had gathered from his/her personal experience, was now made public and accessible to all. This 'publication' was quite in keeping with the socio-productive tools mentioned earlier (TPM; TQM, *kaizen*), since these formed their support and were their instruments. The employees' versatility also meant their interchangeability. In fact, the gathering and implementation of every employee's personal know-how into a public knowledge base naturally weakened their individuality. The increase in internal (in fact, external) mobility is illustrative of the growing 'replaceability' of employees in general. This explains the rather strong resistance put up by the more experienced workers to job rotation and the acquisition of multiple skills. They not only wanted to keep to themselves their hard-earned expertise and thereby assure a certain autonomy for themselves, they also did not want to be posted to other jobs where their former skills were of little value and they would be obliged to learn new skills and gather other proficiencies.

Versatility generally meant more broadening of activities (multiple job stations) than any deeper development (an enhanced qualification). Though this was no small matter, it nevertheless did not prevent the monotony and repetitiveness of jobs that were increasingly coming under time constraints (see Chapter 3). In some situations, especially in the monitoring of the production process, every employee's versatility was also accompanied by a specialization in a field of their own choosing. This supplementary specialization, added to each one's versatility, created a collective qualification that went well beyond the sum of its parts. The capacity, and especially the speed of intervention, greatly surpassed traditional versatility by solving the toughest problems in-house. But, for this to exist, the collective qualification required that at least one condition be met: the group had to remain stable.

Self-organization and peer pressure

The collective organization and responsibility within the work group increased peer pressure on every individual. Lack of punctuality, repeated leave of absence, fatigue or poor performance were no longer commented upon or dealt with by the manager, but by the group itself. The group was committed to maintaining the average standard that had been set for the group by the group itself. This *average standard of work* was not established 'scientifically' in a Tayloristic manner. On the contrary, it was settled informally between colleagues. This is the crux of the active debate at present on suffering and harassment faced at work. But the ostracization, stress and harassment were very often the result of the organization of work within the group rather than a result of the behaviour of an irate manager towards a hapless underling.[29] It was the direct result of the 'naturalization' of the constraints that weeded out weaker individuals to allow the survival of the group and enabled it to face these constraints, which were by definition unavoidable.

In this case, self-imposed group discipline was far more efficient than any other kind would have been in weeding out those who fell below the standard. Conceptually, we could say that the *heterosuggestion* derived from the work standard – the compartmentalized standard described in Chapter 3 – which had been created and imposed by the group. It resulted in a self-subordination of the subjects to its rule. Moreover, this satisfied the productivity requirements and conditions of tight flow.

Ultimately, such a transformation of the subjective conditions of work was possible because the old work groups that had been formed by affinities and solidarities slowly gave way to groups formed primarily for functional reasons, to meet the demands of tight flow by ridding themselves of these very solidarities.[30] Such was the new role, among others, of management in dealing with local human resources.

The creation of the team leader

Chosen by management or the group itself (in Scandinavian countries and sometimes in Germany), the *team leader* was a colleague and a peer, generally without hierarchical powers (the chiefs of the Basic Work Unit at Renault and at Fiat being exceptions). The team leader's role as the prime mover of the team had much in common with the group leader of the past, except that the team leader did not form part of the company hierarchy. We have shifted from command (sometimes peremptory in tone) to communication – which convinces and persuades rather than restricts and controls. This form of management was a result of the rise in the level of training of employees and the failure on the part of the old industrial engineering approach, which did not recognize the salaried executive as a subject. The team leader thus helped to motivate the team by re-establishing vertical communication between management and workers (see Figure 2.1 on page 52). The *team leader*, who normally arrived before his/her colleagues and left after them, divided his/her time between the functions listed below:

- The distribution of jobs among the different operators. Through this function of the allocation of resources, the team leader organized the rotation of job stations (at a pace which varied between two and four hours a week, depending on the nature of the work: assembly, monitoring automated procedures and so on) and at the same time diversified repetitive tasks, thus creating or maintaining versatility.

- The preparation of training plans for the permanent members of the team in order to increase their versatility as well as a test of their efficiency and as a basis for the interchangeability of operators (which would help with the replacement of absentees). In the rest and meeting area allocated to every team, a noticeboard juxtaposed the rate of absenteeism and production figures in terms of quality and quantity, together with a versatility chart highlighting an individual's skills in relation to those of his colleagues. The obvious aim of this *social transparency* was to rouse the ambition of at least those who were aspiring to a higher post to escape the pressure of tight flow. At the same time, it could also be hoarded and used for other ends by employees whenever they found that the road to promotion was becoming unaccountably narrow.[31]

- Welcoming new arrivals to the team with an introduction to work, the principal objectives and the difficulties encountered. The team leader also had the responsibility of training new arrivals if no other training location was available.

- Filling-in for short-term absences (medical leave, injuries, visiting the lavatory, reunions, short training sessions and so on), which in fact reinstate the team leader into the flow s/he thought s/he had escaped. This is why every team leader was always looking for external resources, especially from management, by using the argument that other, equally important, jobs had to be completed.

- The control of product quality or services at the outlet of his zone of responsibility – that is, the self-monitoring inspection carried out by the operators. In cases of persistent deviation or a repetition of defects, the team leader did not need to correct the problem there but rather go back to the root of the problem, which often meant looking somewhere upstream.

- The monitoring of the quantity and quality of production by means of a statistical report based on more or less comprehensive charts. In the best cases, these results were commented on by the technical department and management to find ways of improving them.

The attributes of the *team leader*

Thus the role of *team leader* forms part of the same logic of rationalisation of unpredictable social relationships. Team leaders organise both horizontal communication within the group and vertical communication with management (hence the designation 'spokesperson' adopted for team leaders in northern Europe). Because they are the pivot between these two systems of communication, they help them to communicate with each other.

So the position of team leader brings together two functions which were previously heterogeneous, exclusive, even antagonistic, those of horizontal communication and those of the management prerogative. Each person derives some advantages from this situation, from the operator who no longer has permanent direct contacts with supervisory staff, to managers who re-establish communications with operators and the heart of the production process, and the team leaders themselves whose dedication to carrying out their contradictory functions is enhanced by their knowledge that they have been chosen for possible promotion. There remains the question of the costs for the team leaders themselves, placed in a contradictory situation, with all the consequences in nervous tension and stress which may follow (hence the frequent resignations of team leaders in certain work areas). The category of team leader is a category with ill-defined roles, that is to say roles which are multiple, centrifugal and heterogeneous and which are difficult to hold together. Not only is the position ambivalent, but its legitimacy is questionable. The latter depends largely on the methods for designating team leaders, and especially on who designates them. Thus, although the team leader's role is defined in broad outline, the way in which it is carried out depends to a great extent on the origins of its legitimacy. If team leaders are nominated by management (without any rotation of leaders) and if in addition they receive a bonus, they obtain their legitimacy from management and have to win acceptance from their peers. If they are elected by their peers, they must continually prove their loyalty towards management without losing the confidence of their peers. Moreover, if they are the candidate of the trade union, the likely confusion over their status makes the function impossible to fulfil (hence, for example, the frequency of resignations at Saturn or at least the non-renewal of team leaders' mandates). Where trade unions are strong (in Sweden, Germany and older factories in the United States), they confront management to ensure that they are the source of the team leaders' legitimacy, hoping thus to promote their point of view and to defend workers' interest more successfully. But there is no indication that in most cases the 'double bind' which characterises the position of team leader does not work out to the advantage of management, simply by defusing potential crises which would have blown up in traditional situations.

In all of these cases, the function of team leader disperses throughout the team the tasks arising from the technical requirements imposed by tight flow, and it secures external communication while maintaining a strong internal social cohesion. It contributes to softening the constraints and reducing awareness of the rigid discipline associated with tight flow, through obtaining if need be employees' consent to this discipline. Thus it is one of the cornerstones of teamwork. Teamwork, in turn, both satisfies the intrinsic requirements of tight flow and, in a social context which is quite restrictive, makes discipline at work appear neutral, a product merely of technical necessities 'naturalized' by tight flow. In this way, it is an inherent part of the new employee relationship and the new conditions for employee involvement.

Figure 2.1   The attributes of the team leader
Source: J.-P. Durand *et al.* (1998), pp. 26–7.

Team leaders chose to take on the thankless task of belonging to the group and remaining equal while at the same time pushing and directing their peers, for several reasons – the least of them being monetary considerations (they were paid barely 4 per cent to 6 per cent more). Becoming a team leader, first, meant breaking away from the immediate pressure of the tight flow, especially in instances where the work dealt directly with materials. Even though tight flow remained very much present, it no longer ruled every action, as it did in the case of an assembly worker in the motor vehicle industry, the telephone operator in a call centre, or a cashier at a large bank. This was the first motive we came across in our analysis, especially in the case of the 'young people with potential', who abhorred the idea of being confined to a routine job. The lure of this freedom had a profound effect on their motivation as operators – they were the most efficient, the most hard working and, in spite of the criticisms levelled at them by older members – the most demanding in terms of versatility or diversity of jobs within and between teams. In fact, the degree of versatility was the first criterion considered in the choice of team leaders, the others being communication skills and leadership abilities.

Chosen from among peers, who were also very often competitors, the team leader accepted this ambivalent position in order to escape the constraints of tight flow and because it was the first rung on the professional ladder that led to being a supervisory officer, or to some other technical function. In order not to disappoint his/her peers, who would otherwise ostracize him/her, nor to displease management, which demanded results, the team leader has to dig deep and use capacities and resources going well beyond those of others. To be able to command without having a formal authority while at the same time having to hold several jobs and keep up with one's peers meant bridging an almost impossible divide. And to have such an example so close to them meant that the other workers could not but be impressed and inspired to imitate them. Conceptually, the creation of the team leader contained a central component of the post-Fordian drive – the close proximity of the team leader to the other workers made the example of the work ethic so alive to the other operators. The effect was so obviously for the good of the whole group that they could not but succumb to the exemplary manner of working.

In spite of all the criticisms we could level at the social relations and organization of work in the motor vehicle assembly factories in Japan and the USA, the function of the team leader and the effect on the operators seems to be the basis of their high productivity.[32] At the same time, and this being not the least of the paradoxes, the shortening of the hierarchy – itself due to the constraints of tight flow – meant that the chances of promotion remained slim for the team leaders aiming for a managerial function. A number of them who failed to break into management even after years of effort, had to return to the constraints of tight flow, with all the attendant feelings of disappointment. This led the directors of large corporations in Japan, as well as in the West, to design easier vocational schemes than the traditional lifetime employment.

The past should not be confused with the present

The four essential components of teamwork (that is, collective responsibility, versatility, peer pressure, and the role of the team leader), stand as evidence of the clear break that this signified with the traditional, Fordian–Taylorian organization of work. The end of individual job stations, with relatively meagre and specialized qualifications (in the USA, semi-skilled workers had been divided by up to ten classifications in some branches), the softening of the authoritarian nature of management, and the emergence of a new actor on the stage in the form of the team leader, all combined to create a new kind of work organization under a salary structure that had itself also been transformed. Hence the necessity of making a clear distinction between Japanese teamwork and the traditional, Fordian system of group working. On the other hand, a second confusion consists in taking teamwork and group work to mean the semi-autonomous Scandinavian-style group work which was conceived in the 1960s and later spread to Germany and, to a lesser degree, to France and Italy. In the Northern European countries, the lack of skilled manpower had led management to invent newer, more attractive forms of work, such as, for example, in the Swedish *new factories* or the *humanization of work* in Germany.

In the latter cases, the objectives of the group, which had more or less been negotiated with management, could be achieved by a certain autonomy of the group and a mobilization of complementary resources such as training, materials and goods. In the meantime, the leader of the group, the spokesperson, was elected. Strictly speaking, teamwork and the semi-autonomous group did resemble one other, but they diverged on at least three essential points: (i) in a social context there was no longer a shortage of manpower,[33] – on the contrary, there was underemployment; (ii) objectives were in no way negotiated; and (iii) in teamworking the organizational autonomy was rather restricted because it was bound by processes that stemmed from the socio-productive tools (TPM, TQM, the SMED, *kaizen*). The promoters of lean production and teamwork quietly passed these off under the guise of the semi-autonomous work group – thereby hiding the intrinsic differences that exist between these two kinds of work. By subverting the term 'group work' by a conceptual substitution ('teamwork' replacing one more favourable to the employees), the organizers introduced a confusion which was maintained for a long time by the unions themselves because they had neither the thinking non organizational power at a time when they were fully occupied in dealing with the massive lay-offs in Sweden, followed closely by those in Germany.

To summarize, there arose a new concept called teamwork, which encompassed a novel system of work organization. Because of the lack of an adequate vocabulary, a terminological and semantic confusion prevailed and resulted in a paucity of debate regarding its introduction. This organizational innovation was implemented almost unnoticed in France and over most of Southern Europe, while in the Scandinavian countries and Germany, the changes were greatly mitigated, mainly by the unions. It was only in the USA, with the movement surrounding *Labor Notes*, and in the UK, which saw the publication of a number of books on the Japanization of industry and a relatively strong union movement, where the organizational innovation of teamwork was resisted. Persisting with terminology, we also note that the English language has the advantage of having four terms (*shift*, *gang*, *group* and *team*) to qualify the exact organizational approach, with team and group directly specifying the Japanese innovation, while the other two correspond to traditional organizations (though it must be noted that the first two are also present in the Fordian vocabulary under certain conditions).

The first coherence of the *combinatoire productive*

Tight flow at reduced cost has two fundamental requirements that distinguish it from the traditional system: on the one hand, it needs new and specific production technologies, and on the other, a holistic and collective approach to the organization of work that would help in incorporating these new elements and in facing increasing organizational complexity.

The first requirement was effectively met by the socio-productive tools which, helped in the elimination of stocks and buffers by minimizing the time required to change job runs, could better anticipate and forestall breakdowns or quality lapses, and ultimately reduce the cost (*kaizen*). The second requirement was met by teamwork. It placed the responsibility of an entire production segment on the whole group, which in turn was motivated by internal competition (peer pressure) and the ambivalent status of the team leader. The versatility and the interchangeability of personnel that went with it meant that it could cope comfortably with the absence of a team member, and the resulting work overload.

It could have been that the two (satisfactory) answers were incompatible; that is, proved to be contradictory by having effects that were opposed to the objectives sought. But, as it turned out, the socio-productive tools and teamwork meshed together beautifully:

- These tools could only be implemented collectively as they involved, for the most part, a sub-set of the flow – that is, the machines and people who formed part of it. At the same time, it should be noted that the set of people interested by a socio-productive tool did not necessarily constitute a unified group responsible for a single production segment. In general, those interested in a particular socio-productive tool formed a larger sub-set than the work group because it involved a technological and intellectual co-operation between people spread all along the flow.
- Versatility, defined as being skilled at a wide range of jobs, was indispensable for handling the tools referred to, while the specialization that went with it increased efficiency. As a matter of principle, the solutions suggested by more versatile workers were less likely to be discarded, as they would take into account a larger number of variables regarding any particular job station.
- The respect for the average standard of work for the group. Linked to collective responsibility, this brought the group closer together and discouraged any deviation that might jeopardize the preventive maintenance, total quality or rapid transformations required.
- Finally, the presence of the team leader, clearly on his/her way up the professional ladder and thus highly motivated, prevented or defused any failure in the implementation of the available tools or in keeping the flow 'tight'.

The efficiency of the productive combination depended, on one hand, on the quality of the solutions proposed to resolve the problems that cropped up in day-to-day work, and on the other, the coherence between these solutions. But there was more: all the solutions provided, including the teamwork and socio-productive tools required to keep the flow tight, contained only part of the solution to yet another problem – that of involving the employees completely in this model, of getting their complete approval, and thus extracting the best performance possible from them. Yet it was absolutely indispensable to have the entire and heartfelt collaboration of the employees if the enterprise was to succeed. This final piece of the puzzle was put in place by the *'competency model'*,[34] which replaced the qualifications inherited from the post-war period.

3
The Competency Model

The transformations of work, which are at the very heart of the new and emerging '*combinatoire productive*' introduced in Chapter 1, revolve around three essential components that together make up a single system: tight flow, teamwork and the 'competency model' – this last being one of the linchpins for the mobilization of the workforce. In effect, while the capitalist wage system meant the buying of employee time by the employer, the contract said nothing regarding working conditions or workload (except in the case of piecework systems). Consequently, the efficiency of the enterprise, according to the theory, required that work contracts be completed by the addition of a clause regarding the involvement and motivation of employees.

In the 'Golden Thirties', the Fordian motivation system consisted of granting a bonus or salary rise to compensate for any inconvenience incurred by work or its environment. Problems such as noise, heat, cold, distance from home, night shifts, health concerns and so on were all rewarded in terms of money. All discontent, so often the fundamental cause of a strike, or the threat of one, was often averted by showering bonuses all around, for, come what may, production had to go on, since the sale of all goods produced was guaranteed. This *involvement by salary* was consistent with the spirit of accumulation based on mass consumption. The rules of the game were clear: the Fordian system lessened social inequalities by paying for any inconvenience through monetary reward. However, this system of involvement by salary began to fall apart at the beginning of the 1970s. On the one hand, repetitive and monotonous work began to take its toll on semi-skilled workers (in the form of absenteeism, sluggishness and strikes, for example), with obvious consequences for productivity. On the other hand, once primary needs were more or less met in the industrialized countries, demand began to falter and brought the curtain down on what some have called the second economic cycle – that of mass consumption.

After two difficult decades, the emerging production model that succeeded Fordism had, in its turn, to search for new ways of mobilizing labour. To be effective, it had to work on at least two levels: on the more abstract plane it had to provide the motivational mindset required to make employees accept their status, while on the other, more concrete level, it had, by means of immediate, practical measures, to factually support and give credence to the grand promises made.

Constrained involvement and forced co-operation

The fact that Toyotism, with its tight flow and its corollary teamwork, has spread throughout the world's industries, implies logically that its system for mobilizing the workforce must have been a success. What, then, is the nature of this method, which was first seen to such great effect in mobilizing the Japanese labour force?

In Japan, all new labour market entrants, whether educated to higher secondary level, or armed with more imposing diplomas, wanted to enter the large corporations on a long-term basis. This was hardly surprising considering that the firms offered 30 per cent to 35 per cent higher salaries than those paid by small and medium-sized enterprises (SMEs). Moreover, while direct salaries played a large part in their decision, there were also other important perks such as medical insurance (including cover for one's family), a pension, housing, subsidized loans, paid holidays and so on. At first sight, this seems little different from the Fordian involvement by salary that is so familiar in the West. But here it was implemented by means of a specific technique, a biannual individual evaluation of all employees by their immediate superiors (who, in turn, were also assessed by *their* superiors). As can be seen in the evaluation chart shown in Figure 3.1, in order to remain in employment in a large corporation and to climb the corporate ladder (towards teamleadership and further – into managerial and technical levels), all employees were obliged to strain every sinew to live up to the diverse company expectations.

The first section of this chart deals with the results of work and, we might suggest, the evaluation of objective and almost quantifiable facts. On the other hand, the second section, labelled, 'Attitude towards the firm', deals essentially with behaviour. The variable 'Co-operation' encompasses the essential points regarding dual collaboration – co-operation with management and co-operation with colleagues and peers. It is instructive to note the elegant manner in which the contradiction between individual

CONFIDENTIAL

Date: ....

Name	Department/Section	Grade	1st evaluation	2nd evaluation

Name		Criteria	Notes	Coefficient (%)		Points 1st half	Points 2nd half
				For grades 1 and 2	For grades 3 and above		
Attitude towards work	Quantitative results	• Achievement • Quantity of work • Growth in efficiency	2nd half 100 80 40 60 15 1st half 100 80 40 60 15	15	20		
	Quantitative results	• Achievement • Quantity of work • Growth in efficiency	2nd half 100 80 40 60 15 1st half 100 80 40 60 15	15	20		
	Objectives set by the party concerned	• Are the objectives being extended? • Have the objectives been reached?	2nd half 100 80 40 60 15 1st half 100 80 40 60 15	10	20		
	Creativity and inventiveness	• Number of suggestions • Value of suggestions	2nd half 100 80 40 60 15 1st half 100 80 40 60 15	10	10		
Attitude towards the firm	Co-operation	• Control over self and own feelings • Obedience to superior • Respect for discipline at work • Co-operation and collaboration with others rather than attachment to own opinions and interests	2nd half 100 80 40 60 15 1st half 100 80 40 60 15	10	5		
	Initiative	• Willingness to develop as an individual (participation in training) • Attitude toward *kaizen* (suggestions) • Attitude to challenges beyond required work	2nd half 100 80 40 60 15 1st half 100 80 40 60 15	10	10		
	Responsibility	• Responsibility toward work • Does s/he face up to his/her responsibilities? • Can s/he be given work to do in all confidence (work autonomously)?	2nd half 100 80 40 60 15 1st half 100 80 40 60 15	10	10		
	Absenteeism	• Number of days absent (other than for holidays and during menstruation) • Number of days arrived late or left early	2nd half 100 80 40 60 15 1st half 100 80 40 60 15	20	5		
				Total points			

Figure 3.1   Evaluation form A (for workers)
Source: Information from a large motorcycle company.

evaluation and collective work has been so neatly resolved. It involves the assessment of every employee based on 'co-operation and collaboration with others rather than attachment to personal opinions and interests'. Co-operation with management does not require elucidation and promotes, just as those that follow do, emulation and competitiveness among the employees. Over a period of time, absence and lack of punctuality – just like 'co-operation', begin to lose their importance for established employees in large enterprises. For them, the most important aspect of behaviour was loyalty and keeping to the norm – that is, conforming to the behavioural norm and keeping to the mean labour norm established by the group (as we have seen in relation to teamwork). This mobilization of manpower can be seen as being *incited involvement*, to differentiate the obligations and constraints contained in this dependence of salary on behaviour. We prefer the term *constrained involvement*, to underline the workers' lack of choice and the pressure on them to toe the line if they hoped to remain in the large corporations providing the famous Japanese 'corporate welfare'. At the same time, constrained involvement highlights the paradox between involvement that is normally voluntary, and the social and institutional constraints that obliges everyone to accept allegiance to the large corporation in order to benefit from the advantages conferred.

The crisis of capital accumulation in the 1980s and 1990s destroyed a large number of jobs in the USA and Europe, and the subsequent productivity gains that accompanied the economic recovery forestalled the creation of new jobs. The nature of employment itself underwent a change in the course of the crisis, with job security fading into the background and part-time jobs rapidly taking their place (in the USA, part-time jobs generally meant that the employer did not have to provide social security cover). Thus, in the West, underemployment and a lack of job security played a role similar to Japan's 'corporate welfare' environment, in which people were forced into accepting work and employment conditions. Therefore, all the prerequisites were in place for the mobilization of manpower in the form of constrained involvement – whose efficiency had been one of the pillars of success in the Japanese model. And, as in Japan, global and general pressure was applied in a concrete manner through behavioural evaluation. Systematized into competency charts by the MEDEF,[1] they were introduced gradually in France, with little controversy which was odd, given the whole point of these individual evaluations – what are they looking for, and why?

But before we delve deeper into this question, we have also to take into account another type of pressure, closely associated with underemployment and job insecurity. We are talking here of the financial pressure exerted by the shareholders, who would like to see ever-increasing profit margins – pressure that had a direct effect on the day-to-day work of the employees. In fact, shareholders were constantly threatening to close or sell off (with consequent and inevitable restructuring) any unit or subsidiary that did not perform at the expected level. This was one of the results of the globalization of trade (and of capital in the first place[2]), and pitted all the units of a group against one another in the race for increased profitability. Management and directors made full use of this threat to mobilize employees because, as they put it, 'we are all in the same boat'. The only way to survive and thrive was to do better than the next unit – to the great benefit of the major shareholders.

Moreover, it was not merely the greater dividends offered by a highly profitable enterprise that made it interesting to shareholders; it was more important for its stock market impact. The stock exchange had an effect on the price of the quoted shares, depending on the companies' financial results. By the end of the 1990s, the value of the stock market had increased thirty times faster (depending on the year and the stock exchange) than declared dividends. It should come as no surprise, then, that the owners were more interested in the *market value* of the enterprise than in its actual results.[3] Every employee thus kept a wary eye on the CAC 40, the Eurofirst 80, the Dow Jones, or the trading rates of his/her company's shares to reassure him/herself of the continuity of his/her unit and job.

Thus the development of the stock market, a macroeconomic phenomenon, turned into a lever for the mobilization of the workforce on a day-to-day basis:

> Under certain ideal conditions, the capital market can serve as a *collective cognitive system* which can give to management of an enterprise a realistic indication of the level of the maximum productive efficiency. And jointly with the labour market, it could also act as a disciplinary device to goad employees to collectively attain the objective under the threat of not only losing the prize, but even their jobs. In short, if employees know that only by working as a team would they be able to achieve the target, then they would cooperate in 'communicative action'.[4]

Even though the employee did not live quite like Damocles, with the sword of the stock market price hanging over his or her head, the term collective cognitive system says a great deal about what it meant for the engineers and the executives who had to pass on this culture to their subordinates. For their part, the employees – at least the white-collar workers – saw it used in magazines and on television, and it was so much easier for them to relate to something that they met both at work and at home. Listed enterprises, if shares are spread too thinly, are in danger of falling easy prey to a more or less hostile takeover. To escape this, and keep its independence and jobs, the only way was to increase profitability and, through high market capitalization, reject any hostile bids. Market pressure compelled management to develop new marketing strategies, and lay greater stress on bringing out new products and especially new services – while increasing, day by day, pressure on employees to produce increasingly improved results. No wonder that, according to T. Coutrot, 'it is the financial market which directly fixes the performance level to be attained at any cost'. And that, 'the tyranny of financial criteria is not an aberration which should be replaced by proposing better, more "realistic" ones to the management – on the contrary, they are completely rational because they constrain workers into cooperating in order to achieve the highest performance standard possible, which translates directly as "highest profitability" '.[5]

The concept of *forced co-operation* of employees by the pressure of financial logic converged with that of *constrained involvement* of the same employees because of a lack of job security (particularly in the large Japanese enterprises). These two concepts embody the paradox within the contradictory situation that is the hallmark of the capitalist wage relationship. We still prefer the concept of constrained involvement, because it expresses much more sharply the outcome of the whole process and its objective: to mobilize employees into an active and aggressive participation in the management's (and shareholders') objectives, thereby continuing to provide ever-improving results.

While the determinants of employee involvement are more macro-social (competition, globalization, market prices and so on) its implementation, effects and evaluation derive from the micro-social. In fact, this post-Fordian system of mobilization needs to be compatible with the requirements of tight flow (and its socio-productive tools) as well as with a work organization that corresponds best with it, including the concept of teamwork. While the reorganization of work and production processes had been accepted practically without a murmur (see Chapter 2), and later, more or less 'naturalized' by the fact of its being seen as a solution stemming from the economic conditions of the period, the same did not apply to the new mobilization drive.

In order to break the resistance of employees and their unions, the CNPF – later the MEDEF – launched a massive drive in 1997 to educate workers regarding these competencies by means of plant visits within France as well as to other industrialized countries. It seems that France was the only country in which employers took such a step to redefine the wage relationship on the political, ideological and managerial planes, notably by shifting from past definitions of qualification to a univocal definition of competency.

Defining competency

There is no universally accepted definition of competency, and this absence itself is an indication of the problems and difficulties underlying its evaluation – let alone any discussion regarding recognition or remuneration. We could say that competency cannot be observed directly – only its manifestations can be observed in the course of work; or, that competency is a composite, linked to a combination of different elements. A simple, though not unreasonable solution could lie in first defining qualification as the collection of knowledge (generally confirmed to by diplomas or certificates) and know-how – which is always linked to the former, but garnered in the field. Competency could then be defined as qualification plus a certain 'know-how-to-be'; that is, the behaviour and attitude regarding work, the environment (for example, the supervisory staff, colleagues, company) and vis-à-vis oneself (do I want to progress?). Thus defined, competency is larger than, and encompasses, qualification as one of its components.[6]

From qualification to competency

This definition of competency as the addition of '*savoir-être*' (literally 'know-to be') to qualification is contestable, because 'it involves the judgement of individuals, based not on their *doing*, but on their *being*, opening the doors to arbitrariness or the recognition of aspects which have no place in the labour contract'.[7] But, these risks and cautions have been disregarded by the MEDEF in its definition of competency: 'Professional competency is a combination of knowledge, know-how, experience and behaviour within a specific context. It can be observed and validated at the time of implementation in a job situation and is therefore left to the enterprise to find, evaluate, validate and further it.'[8]

By retaining behaviour as one of the components of professional competence, and promoting a system which not only rewarded qualification (knowledge, know-how, experience) but also the modalities of its implementation (how diligently), the MEDEF took a clear stand on the side of the employers. We should also note here that only the enterprise was qualified to evaluate this competence. This forms a major point of contention in the long-standing debate between French employers and the national education board, in which the former denied the latter the exclusive right to evaluate knowledge and know-how. MEDEF's definition declared the enterprise to be the only institution that could legitimately evaluate competence – but what about its recognition; that is, its classification and remuneration? The best that MEDEF could do was to validate, which in no way meant recognition. It was a completely new type of wage relationship, where the increased qualification and diligence of the employee (acceptable behaviour) was demanded in exchange for job security. The ongoing general deregulation (especially financial) also affected labour relations, with the labour market reflecting it accurately by placing the individualization of labour relations at the heart of the new system, far away from the conventional protection of collectivity.

Competency is generally understood as the quality that both sits astride and completes qualification – it is the manner in which qualification is implemented (the 'know-how-to-be', including behaviour). But the MEDEF developed a different definition of competency and its relationship to qualification. According to the MEDEF, competency was specific to an enterprise, while qualification was the entire set of personal resources that could be mobilized to meet diverse requirements:

> competency is the implementation of the resources of an individual, in keeping with the means provided by the enterprise, in a given work situation ... Competence is therefore at the heart of the enterprise. To think of validating competence externally makes no sense as it is implemented only within the enterprise. On the other hand, an individual acquires knowledge, know-how and professional grooming at school, in his personal or social life and from his previous work experience. When he quits the enterprise, he does not take with him his competence, he goes with his knowledge, know-how and grooming which he was able to enrich thanks to the situations and experiences that he shared with others during his tenure. We feel that professional competence validates these resources. We therefore make a clear distinction between two levels: competency arises within the enterprise while qualification belongs more to the whole branch. Competency lies in the work within an enterprise, qualification is a potential, a capacity to be developed.[9]

In the definition of competency given by MEDEF and detailed in this long quote, the individual employee occupied the central position – a subtle bypassing of the old Taylorian labour division,[10] which had always been promised, but never realized.

From the job to the individual

By generalizing the concept of individual evaluation (and the resultant job loss for some and the promotion of others in large corporations) the Japanese had already put into practice in the 1950s and 1960s the revolution that later swept over the Western world with the widespread acceptance of teamwork. This was possible in Japan, which was then riding high on an economic boom and capturing new markets – a trend that lasted well into the 1990s. In this new system, the employer did not pay for the job. To be more precise, the employer did not give equal pay to all those occupying similar positions. Every individual was paid in keeping with how well that employee performed. In fact, the Japanese salaries, apart from the many perks and bonuses, were made up of two major components: the job or the function itself, and the individual – that is, the manner in which s/he did his/her job, and ultimately, the manner in which s/he served the enterprise. The evaluation chart shown in Figure 3.1 served as a basis for both gradation and promotion.

To no longer remunerate the position (that is, not to 'pay for the job') at the very time that the individual job was giving way to the collective effort of teamwork was indeed fortuitous, and perfectly matched the spreading concept of tight flow. It was also in keeping with the idea that paying individuals/meant not only paying for their qualifications (knowledge and experience) but also for the manner in which they applied them in the service of the enterprise – that is, with the ability to co-operate and share knowledge and know-how.[11] All this matched quite perfectly the socio-productive tools of tight flow, which required the collectivization and spread of personal know-how and acquired skills.

The placement of the individual at the centre of the competency model allowed the MEDEF to pass it off as a social development: 'for the employee [the notion of competency] presents the opportunity to show his contribution to the performance of the enterprise and to showcase his know-how, independent of his certificate. The latter had long been a cherished hope and demand by all the unions.'[12]

As part of this system that placed the individual at the centre, employees were asked to manage their own competency portfolios: first to create one, then to complete and finally look for ways to increase the number of entries (competencies). As a further step, there was even talk of 'competency capital'[13] which an individual could manage just as s/he would a share portfolio. On a more sober note, one of the authors adds: 'The management of competencies based on the individual and no longer on the position he holds, leads, by that very fact to an involvement on the part of the employee. Moreover, it renews the social dialogue, the search for replacing the lifetime employment with an aid for the development of employability.'[14] All of this is fairly obvious, if unpleasant – employees who are considered to be less efficient have to leave the enterprise, since it no longer provides lifetime employment. In fact, we do not know how those unfortunate souls who have been labelled second-rate would be able to increase their employability. Neither is it clear what resources the enterprise could mobilize to help these weaker employees.

Evaluation of competency: behaviour first

As far as the promoters of the competency system are concerned, the individual is greater than the job, and behaviour is more important than the outcome of the work. Here, 'the attitude of the employee is decisive. First of all, such a system can only work if the employee takes an active part, if he gets involved, if the proposals made to him meet with his own motivations, his personal projects. It assumes that the employee is taken up by a "sense of competency" '.[15] Thus, to talk of developing an employee's potential means to base oneself on and begin with the knowledge, motivation and projects of the individual: 'it is the individual himself who is the main character in the development of his own competencies and the first to look for ways of using and furthering them in actual work situations and in the field ... In other words, in the competency system, the role and motivation of the individual is an inescapable *sine qua non*.'[16]

From here onwards, we enter into a discussion that is as complex as it is of strategic importance for the future of wage relations in France (and elsewhere). Either we accept the premise that a relationship of trust can be established between employer and employee and we proceed towards a positive definition of behaviour and its constituent parts, whose evaluation would help both parties, or, we could take a stand and state that this evaluation of behaviour is just another avatar of the old inequality between employer and employees, and that the latter have nothing to gain. For the French trade unions, the substitution of qualification by competency 'amounted to the evaluation of the employee's capacity to adapt himself to any particular position, or the work itself'.[17]

But the employees' adaptation to their jobs, their behaviour, their attitude, and their loyalty or dedication all belong to their own personal domains – the employer's buying rights pertain only to an employee's *work time*. It is true that it is up to management to make this work time as efficient as possible, but does that mean that a lacuna in the work contract should be filled by deciding peremptorily that over and above the work time bought, the attitudes and subjectivity of the employee belong to and can be controlled by management? Is purchase of personality, mixed with purchase of work time, acceptable? 'It is possible that a hidden aspect of the competency model has been overlooked – namely, that the individual now has to learn to regulate, on his own, a large part of his professional interactions, just as he does in his personal life.'[18]

The placement of the employee's subjectivity at the disposal of the employer is very much part and parcel of the competency model, with the demand for his/her wholehearted participation in sustaining a new high in the employee's involvement at work. But what does the employee gain in return for this involvement? On the one hand, the gains in economic performance (with a rise in market capitalization), and on the other, more interesting work. The question of sharing productivity gains did not seem to arise. Lichtenberger (editor of the 9th volume of summaries proposed by the CNPF at the International Training Days at Deauville) has attempted (with difficulty) to answer these questions. On the one hand, he condemns all that constitutes 'behavioural competencies', all judgement regarding the 'being' of an employee that is open to arbitrariness or leads to outcomes that cannot be part of the labour contract.[19] On the other hand, he defines competence as a *responsibility* in the face of a given work situation. The latter is based on knowledge (including know-how), ability to do (that is, the provision of adequate means by the enterprise in a well-defined field of responsibility) and a will 'to hold and assume the responsibility conferred'.[20]

But can we really separate behaviour – which the author removed from his definition of competency (as opposed to the CNPF, which put it at the very heart) – from the commitment, the will and the assumption of responsibility that together form part of professional competency and the professional qualification in occupational skill, according to Lichtenberger and Zarifian?[21] Such a split seems to us to be unreasonable.

The second coherence of the *combinatoire productive*: measuring the involvement

For anyone who has researched workplace life, there is no doubt that the definition of competence as given by the MEDEF is the prevailing one, with ever-increasing stress being put on behaviour, and particularly its evaluation. The guidelines set down by human resource managers for interviewing personnel should be sufficient proof of this trend. For example, a copy of an evaluation chart seen by us and used by a motor vehicle equipment manufacturer is a perfect example of this trend towards evaluating competencies based on the definition given by the MEDEF and the actual needs of enterprises using tight flow. The first evaluation criteria in this chart attempts to assess the outcome of work (production, quality, security), its minimum conditions (assiduity, order and neatness), the actual qualification used (versatility), and to derive from this some relatively objective facts linked to both production and outcomes.

On the other hand, it is not the same with notions such as *initiatives*, *availability* and *sociability*, which evaluate directly the behaviour, commitment and degree of involvement of workers. 'Initiatives' corresponds to the 'assumption of responsibility' proposed by Zarifian and Lichtenberger, in which we can see clearly how behaviour itself is taken into account. The excellent worker (with a top score of 5) who 'looks for and finds solutions on his own to the problems encountered even outside the boundaries of his work' is contrasted to the attitude of the mediocre worker, who 'passively waits for orders' (scoring 1). 'Availability' is in fact an evaluation of the 'acceptance of the flexibility of work' which, initially, is the immediate acceptance of overtime in addition to mobility within the workshop – thanks to the interchangeability made possible by versatility. Finally, 'sociability' is based completely on behaviour, with the good worker 'being extremely polite', while the mediocre worker has 'no respect for the hierarchy' and the aims and reasons that motivate him or her – that is to say, management objectives.

Similar causes resulting in similar effects, tight flow and teamwork induced the directors to steadily increase and depend on the evaluation of employer behaviour and loyalty. It would be naïve to believe that this concerned only those employees who were assigned to monotonous and repetitive tasks. On the contrary, the more complex production and organization became, or dealt with the service sector (especially corporations) the more it became difficult to judge the result of work because of the increasing number of intangibles. Further, now that it was almost impossible to evaluate the results of work, management began to shift controls upstream to assure itself of the proper execution of work; that is, to ensure the full collaboration of the employee. We have thus gone from an evaluation of work or its results to a judgement of the worker and his/her behaviour.

Which is exactly what the unions were against. For the CGC[22], 'the question of competencies arises within the enterprise and the unions must ensure that its evaluation concerns only the work and not the individual'.[23] Moreover, the unions called into question the means provided by the enterprise to the employee for achieving its objectives – an interesting point we have not come across in all the evaluation processes studied, or in the evaluation charts given. As a matter of fact, during all the negotiations regarding the objectives to be attained by the employee, the means themselves were never negotiable: the employee was required to tolerate whatever was set by management. According to Lichtenberger, the evaluation of competencies can never be unilateral; it had to be 'a comparison between the means supplied by the organization and those mobilized by the employee'. Thus we come to a need for mutual trust between the two parties:

> Competence is a quality of the relation between the individual and the enterprise, which can only exist on the basis of reciprocal trust. The enterprise must have the confidence in the loyalty of the employee regarding the use of all the means at his disposal to fulfil his professional duty. The employee must trust his hierarchy regarding the impartiality and goodwill in its evaluations concerning him and of its support and the means provided to him for fulfilling his professional duty and for the stability of his employment.[24]

The prospects of such mutual respect and confidence are extremely alluring, but is that the impression that most employees have regarding their company? Has the enterprise really become such a balanced organization, without any conflicts or contradictions, working equally for the good of all, shareholder as much as employee? How nice it is to dream of such a harmonious world – but alas, it turns out to be just another impossible, utopian dream. The very existence of trade unionism brings us squarely back to earth: a unionism that is clearly afraid that the system of competencies is more than just an evaluation – it is a means of selecting some employees and excluding those who perform less well.[25] From this standpoint, this system could work as part of the training process, which, by eliminating those employees who perform below par and are seen as not worthy of investment, excludes them gradually from the enterprise before labelling them 'unemployable'.

The often generous representations of the *competency model* should not hide the fact that it is a new system of involving the employee that goes hand-in-hand with the idea of tight flow and the concept of teamwork. The question is how to interpret this method, which seeks to motivate the individual through the meaning given by his or her work. Other things being equal, this discussion regarding the interest, motivation, involvement and mobilization of competencies for the benefit of both parties is similar to the ideas of Taylor, who wanted to boost work productivity in order to increase the income of both employee and employer. At the time of writing, the development of competencies aims at increasing overall performance and helping individuals to grow to their full potential (by encouraging initiative, creativity and autonomy). Of course, for Taylor, the increase in productivity, which was measurable, led theoretically to an increase in salary, which was equally quantifiable. By contrast, in the *competency model*, the benefits for the employee are subjective, and not at all measurable. Moreover, it is unfortunate that nowhere is there any mention of the fact that work now falls increasingly under the rule of time constraints with, in the name of competitiveness, an ever-decreasing stock of resources and tools – conditions that explain why all statistics point to the general perception that workload and stress have increased.

In other words, it would be difficult for us to see the competencies system, which acts as the handmaiden to tight flow, as a just and egalitarian work contract. In this we beg to differ from Lichtenberger, who argues that:

> More than the mercantile or commercial aspect of this labour contract, the competencies system brings to mind its reciprocal, bilateral aspect, that is to say, in perceiving the contract not as the buying of merchandise (the qualification used and the time spent), but as an exchange of services wherein, while it is possible to depict for each one the purpose and the objectives, it is much more difficult to foresee the actual modalities.[26]

In this interchange of services, and in particular in the concrete modalities of its implementation, the two parties do not have similar resources. The inequality in exchange, which is a characteristic of the capital–wage relationship, persists even when management accepts some risks by encouraging free thinking regarding the work, and offering greater autonomy.

Social control over activities remains very much in place, even if under other, gentler guises (such as group work and collective responsibility), or exerted more upstream in relation to the negotiated–fixed objectives. Moreover, by imposing a behavioural norm and obliging employees to adhere to it by means of individual evaluations, the managers proved, if proof is still needed, their power over salaried workers. It is the same relationship of inequality all over again, though it is true, this time it is in another form. This new model attempted to assure itself, by evaluating employees' loyalty to the enterprise, that they had taken on board the paradigm of the tight flow system, with its physical, intellectual and temporal demands. It requires workers to give freely of their knowledge and know-how that had been acquired over the entire length of their professional career. What, then, was the situation on the other side of this *competency model*?

Competencies and vocational training

In France, vocational training was the only area where unions and employers arrived at a quick and easy understanding, as is evident in the Law of 1971 on continuing vocational training, the declaration of 1982 on *congés individuels de formation* (CIF) (individual training leave – ITL), the Law of 1997 on the *Bilan de compétences* (Assessment of competencies), and so on. In fact, the convergence was merely superficial, as each side had its own agenda to fulfil. On one side was the desire for individual development and the growth of the employee, while on the other, the impetus was more for an improvement in technical (or managerial) performance.

There is yet more. While the amount of money set aside for vocational training was considerable (€22 billion per year), the benefits proved to be rather meagre. The major portion of these funds benefited the more highly skilled, protected and stable employees, such as white-collar workers and management. On the other hand, the less-qualified, those working in smaller enterprises, women, and in particular the unemployed – those who needed it the most – received only a small portion of these subsidies. Almost a quarter of the training took place during employees' free time, and individual training absences generally amounted to only 20,000 per year. Contrary to any expectation regarding proper management planning of job descriptions and competencies, the training followed more often than preceded the promotion of employees, and generally did not entail any significant salary rise. Finally, the large majority of training courses were of short duration, which went on to become even shorter – the average length being only some 15 hours per year per employee – equivalent to only about two days in the whole year!

It may be that a regard for MEDEF's definition of competence, or the conclusions of the Deauville Days of 1998, would bring about a change in vocational training in France. But the problem is massive – only 10 per cent of the money goes to the national education board: in other words, almost all the funds collected are absorbed by the enterprises whose only *raison d'être* is profit. In keeping with the definition given by the MEDEF, and for a realistic development of the employees' competencies, 10 per cent of work time should be reserved for further training – amounting to four full years over the span of a career. We thus have the specialized training institutes which promoted the concept of education and training throughout life 'something not only of longer duration, but also larger and wider in terms of diversity of capabilities and specialization (for the young who are in school, employees undergoing vocational training, the unemployed, retired people, etc.)'.[27] For the French trade unions, the most urgent matter is to gain the right to negotiate around continuing professional education – that is, to end the monopoly held by employers who, at best, simply inform work committees about plans regarding training.[28] It also follows that qualification, and not just competence in the field, should be given due recognition. Most of the trade union confederations agree that training should take place during working hours and not in employees' free time.

Since the mid-1990s, the concept of continuous training has turned into a point of discord between the confederation of trade unions and the MEDEF because, after the development of competencies, there arises the question of the recognition of these new acquisitions – that is, the cast of the more recent, more sophisticated labour. Keeping to the classic view, according to which labour is always an expense and never a producer of value, the MEDEF refuses to accept the consequences of its own definition of competence – as can be seen by the endless negotiations that took place at the beginning of the 2000s.

In fact, discussion regarding competencies often hide certain characteristics of tight flow that are not always seen clearly by analysts. All too often it is claimed in the name of some 'evidence' or a development in society, that the demand for highly qualified employees is rising continuously. Even if this is partly true, it conveniently overlooks the continuing high demand for less qualified (and, more importantly, lower paid) workers in the workshops, offices, stores and so on. While tight flow needs qualified employees for its conception, monitoring and maintenance, its day-to-day running does not need any high qualifications, only that its basic principles and constraints are accepted. Certainly, the *competency model* forms very much part of, and is indispensable to, this 'constrained involvement' and the emerging *combinatoire productive*.

4
The Reshaping of Labour: Tight Flow and the Mobilization of Employees

The advent of the tight flow regime in most sectors and the consequent reorganization of labour, considerably modified work itself – its rhythms, the manner of approaching objectives, its relations with employees, and ultimately, the perception that men and women had of their work. In a certain sense, the necessity of keeping the work tight meant that employees had to put up with its constraints at any cost. Acceptance of the principle of tight flow automatically entailed the 'natural' acceptance of these pressures – what we term 'naturalization of constraints'. The employees were obliged to meet all the demands positively, be it by using their competencies and commitment in the face of chance hazards, or by their presence at all times – which signified availability of time and flexibility of working hours.

As a union representative declared: 'we are hostages of factory events'.[1] This chapter aims to show how tight flow held employees 'naturally' to its exigencies – that is, how they were made to satisfy its requirements with, in the name of competitiveness, ever-decreasing resources. It was a cost competitiveness brought on by the share market and financial pressures. Tight flow has spread to become the almost universal mode of reorganizing work in most branches of the economy and its influence can be seen on almost every activity. We shall examine the effects of tight flow by citing examples from the air transport industry, retail business and through the concept of *groupware (white-collar employees working together as a team)*. We hope to study its effects on work and the methods for the mobilization of employees, which form part of these very changes, in conjunction with the competency model that completes this new work paradigm.

A closer analysis of tight flow reveals that there are two distinct kinds of work situation that can and often do link together – as for example, in the fast food industry and call centres. There are two types of constraint depending upon the relationship of the employees to the tight flow situation: either the activities of the employees form part of the tight flow itself and they are compelled to meet its requirements, or the tight flow is outside the employees' field of work but nevertheless influences fundamentally the rhythm and nature of their work. The queue of clients in retail stores, public services and call centres is an example of the latter. In both cases, it is tight flow that applies pressure on employees, who are then required to meet its demands in a positive way.

Employees as part of the tight flow

Being part of tight flow, employees have to ensure that there are no breaks in continuity. The absence of buffer stocks and with each employee acting as the supplier to the next, who is *already there and waiting*, means that they find constraints at both ends: both upstream and downstream. Examples of such just-in-time systems, whether in the workshop, or between supplier and client, include the system of air transport hubs and shuttles, hypermarket supply chains, the management of information in banks and insurance companies, groupware, simultaneous engineering and so on. In such a system, the involvement of the employees could take one of two forms: either they work directly on the material (for example, working on an assembly line, transporting, record processing in insurance, baggage handling at airports, data processing in groupware) or they monitor the flow of work (such as in the maintenance of automated tooling processes or, for example, the role of computer technicians in the service sectors). The actual work undertaken differs significantly between the two situations, with a greater reliance on the intellectual aspect in surveillance and monitoring. But, in both cases, the absolute necessity of keeping tight flow in operation determines the work from moment to moment, and the individual or the group is evaluated largely by the ratio of productive work per unit time.

Labour organized by an external tight flow

Second, tight flow creates pressure without making workers become part of it. In this case, tight flow is organized scientifically in such a manner that it automatically maintains pressure on employees – essentially, it is customers queuing, be it in retail stores or fast food outlets, for buffet meals in hotels, at public service counters or waiting for a response from call centres. While the productive model may differ from the traditional idea of tight flow, work situations are practically identical because employees are faced with the now familiar and imperative demand of tight flow: under no circumstances should continuity be broken. This keeps employees bound solidly to their immediate activities, which could not be changed with regard to either schedule or content. What we would like to show here is that, just as in the manufacturing industries, the service industries also rapidly adopted tight flow – which is perhaps as it should be, because Ohno (1988) tells us that it is from the service industries that he borrowed the idea in the first place.

'Just-in-time' in the industrial sector

In the twenty-first century, the effects of tight flow on work in workshops are well-known enough for us not to need to go into too much detail here. But this does not mean that labourers have disappeared from industry – in fact, at the time of writing they still represent a full quarter of the active population in France. Moreover, the number of people working under time constraints – that is, under the constraints of tight flow, is continually rising. The vast majority of consumer goods produced today are assembled manually by labourers on assembly lines, and it is no wonder, then, that the labour force is most concentrated in this sector. In the motor vehicle industry, the traditional Fordian flow with its stockpiles has been replaced by a single, continuous assembly line, sometimes several hundred metres long, which does not allow any stoppages as this would immediately render hundreds of assemblers jobless. Such a willingness to 'fragilize' the line in order to push workers towards zero fault tolerance regarding time constraints epitomizes the manner in which tight flow pressurizes and coerces labour. In the French literature there have been a number of studies that have attested to this form of labour subjection by tight flow, embodied in the stock-free (or with minimal buffer stock) assembly line.[2]

While, in general, management shared the conclusions arrived at by these researchers and seemed to regret the inhumanity of an arduous workload, they pointed to rising international competition before continuing to reduce cycle times (to less than a minute) in a bid to further increase efficiency. The principle of tight flow needs no comment in respect of its ability to organize working time and to dispense with a hierarchy that had become superfluous. There are at the time of writing some optimistic publications that talk of the humanization of work in the Toyota factories, especially the one on the island of Kyushu. But how can we argue that splitting the assembly line into six sections, while keeping to the one-minute cycle time and placing some green plastic plants along the line constitutes a humanization of assembly work?

It would be misleading to conceive of tight flow as having some kind of physical embodiment in the assembly line. In the manual welding section of a motorcycle manufacturer in France, simply positioning workers in a 'U' rather than a straight line allowed each of them to supply the pieces one by one to colleagues downstream for the next operation.[3] In such a system, no one could afford to slow down – anybody who wanted to take a breather had first to speed up their pace for a time, to create a small, temporary buffer stock.[4] While co-operation between workers helped to tide over any temporary difficulty at any given post, the main function of tight flow was to impose cycle-time-based discipline with minimum staffing. Such was the objective of the Toyota Production System (TPS) as described in Chapter 2, especially when associated with tight flow.

Even workers and technicians who were charged with keeping track of the continuous tooling process and monitoring assembly lines found themselves caught just as tightly in the exigencies of tight flow. In fact, many of them not only claimed that they had more work to do now with the added pressures of preventive maintenance and total quality control, but they also felt that the Taylorian division of labour was still in place and as strong as ever. And no wonder – maintenance work had risen significantly, with quality checks, standard replacements, dismantling and assembly activity. While the need for preventive maintenance increased strongly, maintenance personnel found themselves losing their status, identity and autonomy.[5]

The redeployment and reallocation of work among employees was much more for tight flow continuity at minimal cost than for the loudly proclaimed motive of enriching the work of semi-skilled workers.[6] The fundamental objective was to add the other categories of workers, such as supervisors and monitors, under the constraints of tight flow:

> This subtle form of harnessing the workers took a step away from the old Taylorian system – from the more concrete and confrontational 'face to face' to a more discreet control which formed part of the individual's own self. Parallel to the economic side of the tight flow was its psychological aspect. From an external, tangible constraint, it turned into a subjective pressure whose power was there for each to feel within himself. The operational ambiguity, vagueness in work allocation and the general fuzziness of the whole system meant that the worker had to fall back upon his own resources in order to attain the required results – results which not only remained crystal clear, but now widened to include the whole production apparatus. Thus, having to fix one's own objectives, take decisions, anticipate and react, pitted the subject against himself and actually worked out much better than having to execute or accomplish an externally imposed, prescribed task.[7]

By thus 'internalizing' the demands and pressures of work objectives, tight flow brought about a change in the employees' perception of work itself. While the main objective remained something external, belonging to the employer, the sub-aims were internalized. Such are some of the fundamental behavioural changes that we have attempted to portray by the term 'constrained involvement'. This new way of reacting to work was the direct result of perceiving it not as something enforced 'face to face' but rather internalized and 'natural'.

Tight flow in intellectual work: groupware

As mentioned earlier, the coming together of white-collar workers as a team is called *groupware*. It integrates three computer and telecom related applications:

- messaging (that is, communication, including forums);
- sharing of resources (database and information); and
- co-ordinating the work and activities of participants through computer and telecom networks; sharing agendas and synchronizing work.

Specific software such as Lotus Notes and MSMail were used to integrate these diverse functions. Also, custom-built software, provided it integrated all required functions, could also serve the groupware through an intranet (enterprise resource planning). We could define groupware as: 'the set of techniques and methods used to realize a common objective of a group of people, be they close or separated by time or distance, with the aid of any manner of communication, using computers and/or telecommunications, to achieve interactivity'.[8] Thus groupware is a tool generally used for collective work to be done by widely separated workers (geographically as well as separated by time zones). While computers and telecommunications are essential in this concept, they are only tools to bring people together on a common project.

The project as a collective activity

Groupware is a tool used in the management of projects, especially in those where sequential flow has been replaced by the *simultaneous* – this it does by integrating immediately the input from diverse sources. As the term itself indicates, in groupware (*collecticiel* in French) the group or the collectivity takes precedence over the individual. At the same time, the question of time remains at the heart of the system. This means that every individual is required to furnish, within a specified time, the information absolutely essential for the collective project. The whole project rests on the employees being able to supply the information in a tight flow. And as each worker typically participates in a number of such projects, groupware and its derivatives prove to be very efficient tools in the hands of management for managing employee time. Even here, while the collectivity clearly dominates the individual, it does not mean that employees find nothing in it for themselves. The collective sharing of resources means that the individual has the opportunity to widen his or her autonomy – obviously within the limits set by the project.

As a co-ordinating agent, groupware formalizes all that remained until then informal as regards inter-group interchanges and exchanges. At the same time, it also helped to demonstrate the experience, knowledge and know-how of everyone by integrating them within a common knowledge-base. Such a publication of personal know-how and the formalization of collective work were new, powerful methods for streamlining intellectual labour, which before that had remained untouched. The efficiency of collective work increased 'by codifying the interactions between the different actors, rendering behaviour more predictable and thus reducing uncertainties and behavioural risks'.[9] In fact, the drive for co-ordination itself, which was partly automated by the software itself, imposed a certain normalization of behaviour by codifying its expectations. It thus added to the control of subjective behaviour – a control that, as we saw in Chapter 3, had already been initiated by the system of competence.

In other words, does this not amount to 'bringing some people together who share neither their values nor their aims?'[10] Should we then talk of 'group work' or simply 'working in a group'? According to B. Faguet-Picq, while co-ordination is achieved mainly through networking, 'groupware directly linked the individual to the enterprise, without creating, as was done in the Fordian system, a stable workgroup which was all too ready to form a coalition against any managerial decision which did not please it'.[11] Thus co-ordination is based purely on an 'instrumental' relationship which created certain constraints arising out of tight flow: to deliver, in a stipulated time period, the information required to complete the project, which in itself lay well beyond the control of the individual employee. Moreover, this heteronomy took place against a backdrop that gave precedence to the sharing of knowledge through the use of knowledge bases. This gave rise in turn to versatility and interchangeability, including that of experts. Groupware can thus be seen as a sort of 'instrumentalization' of the individual's intellectual activity for the attainment of a collective result whose objectives are far removed from the individual, together with the means of achieving them individually.

Co-ordinating and streamlining work

Groupware, and in general the ERPs, revolutionized the work of white-collar employees by changing their perception of products and services, and by the use of new decision-making systems. In the first place, group-ware was a tool 'for a new system of coordination which simultaneously combined hierarchy and contract, rule and negotiation and fundamentally changed the hierarchy established at the beginning of the century which was based solely on obedience and surveillance'.[12] Groupware thus gave to tight flow the advantage of a 'natural command'.

Second, the organization assured by groupware was more than just a simple matter of co-ordination – it was a systematic and coherent gathering of the output from dispersed and often far-flung individuals. Craipeau puts it well with his wonderful oxymoron 'working together separately'. It gives a good idea of the double innovation it intrinsically contains: on the one hand, it creates a virtual collectivity by mobilizing employees who are otherwise occupied; and on the other, by bringing them together to work on a single project, though they might be widely dispersed geographically and/or working at different times. Groupware was thus the means of overcoming the limits of time and space in order to put together a project under fixed conditions.

Just as the Taylorian system brought together and organized scattered and divided work, groupware brought together and organized dispersed *intellectual* work. To say that groupware (and ERPs in general) were tools for co-ordinating work signified two things: first, that, contrary to what was so often claimed regarding the restructuring of jobs, work remained very divided and specialized; and second, the employees were not paid for this co-operation – or rather, for the effects of this co-operation. The benefits of groupware and ERPs were cumulative. They not only helped to streamline intellectual work, which as we know is so difficult to implement, but they also brought about a co-operation between widely dispersed workers – for the sole benefit of management.

Further, the greater use of software and ICT meant that management had more information at its disposal regarding the functioning of the organization, as well as the reactions of the employees. We can thus talk of a reflexive, even a *cognitive management* to highlight the extent to which it depended on the information gathered regarding the organization.[13] As before, we see here that this system of organization (tight flow based on the rapid data processing power of ICT), along with the resulting labour management, tended to become part of the productive system itself and thus was felt to be more 'natural' and unavoidable.

An analysis of groupware shows the extent to which its implementation led to a form of 'permanent constraint' through newer ways of 'reporting' and the resulting transparency in the activities of employees. Similarly, a shared agenda (and the mobile telephone which assisted collective work) also meant that everyone knew where to find anybody else at any given time. Are we not getting uncomfortably close to control of the personal 'how' of private behaviour? To top it all, this control was synchronized – thanks to the telecom network and high data-processing speeds – with the operational flow, which led workers to feel that it formed a 'natural' part of the activity itself:

> With such systems at their disposal, enterprises readily embarked upon a drive to streamline their activities. Instead of only formalizing the jobs (which was what had been done before), they now also formalized inter-faces between activities. This was another way of defining the relational aspect of these new devices. By shifting their hold, they changed the very nature of their control. By defining presentation, they also deter-mined to some extent areas which had up to now been implicit. Henceforth, control was no longer purely external, as it had been in the traditional system.[14]

The principal function of groupware was one of co-ordination. It also brought the individual component of collective work out into the open, which brought the concept of transparency into play: as nobody could hide delays or weaknesses from anybody else, there was no option but to perform. Control thus passed from being external to becoming internal, even *interiorized*. A subdued and repressed individuality seems to be one of the significant results of groupware. We can now understand why, wherever there was any close-knit collective work involved, the intro-duction of groupware met with resistance and elicited more or less loud protests. Its reorganization and method of control were quickly seen to be of little profit to workers.[15] The difficulties encountered in the imple-mentation of the ERPs, and especially of the SAP ('Systems, Applications and Products for data processing' – one of the most popular ERPs) were not only a result of methodological problems within corporations that had bought the software, but also (and mainly) caused by employee resistance, including resistance from junior management.

The hubs: airports under tight flow

Invented by Delta Airlines in 1978, the concept of the *hub* was originally a commercial idea. As it was becoming increasingly uneconomic to service multiple sectors with planes flying half empty, each airline chose for itself an airport, its hub, through which the airline serviced all its destinations with fewer aircraft. As the very term suggests, the hub was the centre of activities, an interim airport in which, by definition, passengers wanted to spend as little time as possible. The time between connecting flights had to be reduced to the minimum or risk customer dissatisfaction. Finally, the hub was also an aggressive commercial tool used to capture new clients from competitors by offering a range of diverse destinations available from this hub. The greater number of passengers per aircraft meant a reduction in the cost of each flight and, added to the air deregulation of the early 1980s, meant that running costs in the air as well as on the ground were falling continuously.

The policy of the hub

Air France organized its principal hub at Charles de Gaulle 2 airport around five time slots (6:30–8:00; 9:00–11:30; 12:00–14:00, 15:00–17:00; 20:00–21:30) during which passengers transited from one aircraft to another in less than an hour.[16] It was planned in such a way that (for long haul flights) every aircraft took off after a maximum of 90 minutes on the ground. The aircraft stayed parked only long enough for the luggage to be off-loaded, the air-worthiness to be checked, refuelling completed and finally re-loaded with new passengers, luggage and freight. In this manner, the restructuring of air routes for commercial reasons also became an organizational tool for managing work and personnel. On the one hand were the aircraft, all lined up, so any delay affecting one departure would have an adverse effect on all the following and connecting flights. On the other hand, and intimately connected to the first, was the hectic work involved with every stationary plane. Moving the freight and the luggage, cleaning, maintenance checks and minor repairs all had to proceed in a tight flow which squeezed work time,[17] even as the number of employees continued to be reduced. (When the concept of the hub was implemented by Christian Blanc, chairman and CEO of Air France, the productivity of the ground personnel went up by 15 per cent).

Before the implementation of the concept of hubs, the different jobs were completed by a large number of specialists from different departments working under various hierarchies. There were three main functions:

- The movement of the aircraft on the ground was the responsibility of the 'pull–pushers'. Whether it was to pull or to push the aircraft to a parking lot or towards the passenger bridges – the entire manœuvre was done by two line mechanics, one sitting in the cockpit and the other in the tractor. These mechanics required some kind of qualification,

mainly for security reasons, and even though their work was completely different, it came under the same hierarchy as maintenance
mechanics.

- Aircraft maintenance was then carried out by maintenance mechanics
who were themselves divided into three categories: cockpit mechanics, who regularly replaced the equipment inside the cockpit; electricians, who were called only when needed; and ground mechanics,
whose responsibilities included the 'stick approach' (visual guiding of
an aircraft towards its parking area), refuelling, visual checks of the
aircraft, chocking the wheels, and so on. They were in charge of all
ground operations and were in constant touch with the crew.
- The loading and unloading of luggage and freight was handled by a
team graded into three categories: the co-ordinator prepared the
loading plan in order to balance the weight; the deputy chiefs were in
charge of the loading and unloading; and the baggage handlers did
the physical work. In reality, the deputy chiefs were also required to
join their subordinates in lugging the freight into the cramped cargo
holds – laborious work, tough on the joints and the back. All these
personnel were also trained to navigate the runway in motorized
vehicles. This luggage handling service was completely independent
of the maintenance section and was distributed over several zones in
order to get closer to the aircraft. It was directed by team leaders.

Versatility and time constraints

As a result of this functional specialization and the consequent time-bound
exclusiveness (one cannot unload a moving aircraft!), many workers
found themselves unoccupied during some part of their shift, and had to
remain idle within specific areas reserved for each of the services detailed
above. The reforms of the 1990s, and the concept of versatility, brought an
end to all that. As is now evident, it was more for economic reasons than
any idea of 'job enrichment' that drove management to implement this
new concept. In effect, it meant the elimination of idle-time during working hours, and a reduction in the number of employees – the ones who
remained would be constrained to finish more work (demonstrating versatility) in a time fixed by the tight flow determined by the arrival and
departure of aircraft.

The first step was the merging of the work of ground mechanics and
'pull–pushers'. This was soon followed, in the mid-1990s, by complete
versatility – which meant that all operations could be undertaken by
everyone. A flight operations officer would allocate work and announce
aircraft arrivals to two teams. The one in front of the aircraft was responsible

for parking, refuelling, and loading and unloading the forward cargo holds. The other team, stationed at the rear of the aircraft, looked to the loading and unloading of the rear cargo holds. The idea of off-time disappeared – quite the reverse, in fact, as personnel were now held by a time constraint imperative imposed by the principle of the hub. There is no doubt that their workloads increased along with the number of jobs that each employee could handle. But, according to management, this increase in workload was accompanied by greater variety, so work became much more interesting.

However, versatility did not prove to be as popular as management would have liked. While the luggage handlers of yesteryear, on the lowest rung of the hierarchy, had everything to gain by becoming more versatile (interesting new jobs, career prospects), the tractor drivers were none too keen. By replacing promotion by seniority with promotion by qualification, the new system brought in another form of hierarchy within the work teams, with the most versatile employee taking charge as a kind of team leader. At the same time, the hierarchy above became shorter, with executives occupied more and more with administrative work and dealing with issues of regulation and co-ordination.

Concurrently with the phasing out of specialized tasks, the work of loading and unloading freight, especially bulk cargo, was also undergoing a major transformation. While container cargo was handled by permanent employees of Air France, the bulk cargo had long been in the hands of temporary workers. At the time of writing, however, the handling of bulk cargo has been entirely sub-contracted. The work does not require any high qualification (the load balance being ensured by Air France personnel), is hard and back-breaking (cargo holds are never more than 1.3 m in height) and subject to intense time pressure (sometimes more than five tonnes have to be moved in under thirty minutes). Poorly paid and ill-supported by non-airline unions, these handlers also have to live with major mobility issues – they are called on only for specific requirements at precise time slots. Though the uncertainty regarding this work was roundly criticized and rebuffed, the sub-contracting of bulk cargo had a significant effect on Air France personnel, since this alternative model could be used as a means of pressurizing them into accepting new working conditions.

We have dwelt at length on versatility and interchangeability because they represent the shortest route for resolving two different yet convergent issues:

- to deal with the constraints of the hub, which by definition introduced a tight flow in triplicate: aircraft, passengers and freight. The diverse nature of the jobs involved meant that a radical solution was needed that would unify the required skills in order to meet time constraints; and

- to decrease the amount of down time experienced by mechanics, tractor drivers and goods handlers by training the same individuals to perform diverse jobs (versatility). This resulted in an increased work output and well as reducing the number of ground personnel. The next step was to increase the mobility of Air France employees, modelled on the sub-contracting of bulk cargo (with the threat of outsourcing).

The tight flow model, with its methods of the work organization (versatility, interchangeability, team leader) and its handling of human resources (competition and meritocracy) was admirably suited to the new requirements created by the concept of hubs in the air transportation sector. In the other sectors, while the employees might not be directly involved in tight flow itself, they learnt to depend on it so much that they were just as much slaves to it, as is the case with supermarket checkouts, fast food restaurants and call centres.

The checkout and customer flow

Work at a supermarket or store checkout is completely dependent on and sensitive to the queue of customers lined up to pay for their purchases. Whether it is in supermarkets or hypermarkets, selling food, tools, CDs, DVDs, books, music systems or computers, all checkout activities revolve around customer flow. In order to sustain pressure on the cashier, the aim of every manager is to maintain at any given time a queue of at least two customers at every checkout.[18] On the other hand, too long a queue would put off clients, who might even (God forbid!) go to a competitor. The constant pressure on the cashier to pass goods as efficiently and quickly as possible over the barcode reader is very reminiscent of the Fordian vehicle assembly line. This fact was not missed by the cashiers themselves, one of whom, employed at FNAC (the equivalent of 'Virgin' in France) said, regarding her colleagues at the food checkout: 'First, she does not even look at you, it is assembly line work – it is as though they were at the Renault factory, passing the pieces – it's exactly the same thing.'[19]

The customer is king and king–client determines the flow

In fact, the relationship between cashier and client has seen a reversal. There was a time when the cashier could refuse a mode of payment or even to impart a piece of information if the behaviour of the client did not meet with expectations. Today, because of cut-throat competition, king-client rules the roost. To ensure quality service, management transferred all power to the client, including that of organizing the cashiers' work rhythm and tempo. The client could complain verbally or via a complaints book. This also helped to speed up the processing of individual articles (*x* per minute) as well as clients (*y* per hour). And just as it happened in the traditional Fordian system, there arose a number of procedures to ensure the quality and speed of processing:

> In an effort to become more efficient and to minimize the time taken for every transaction, the cashier began to resemble an automaton – repetitive gestures, the rejection of anything out of the norm and the depersonalization and artificiality of the dialogues. This was even more pronounced when there was a crowd and speed was of the essence. All personal gestures had to be eliminated. She disinvested herself of any human trait to retire into the safety of anonymity within the ambit of her machine.[20]

But this led her into a vicious cycle: her impersonal attitude, the lack of any genuine feelings in her relationship with clients made the latter feel as though they were simply objects and they reacted by becoming aggressive. Faced with this aggression, the cashier retreated even further into the safety of her machine-job. It was only when the sarcasm or the insults overstepped a limit that she reacted in some manner: the vacuous smile, some derision, or sometimes, seeking the help of an executive to remove the disgruntled client from the scene.

The cashiers solved the contradiction between the quality of service (including a soft, human touch to please the king–client) and speed of service by their skill and professionalism. They represent the last remaining scrap of humanity left in the working of large retail stores. In fact, today, the technology that allows the shopping trolley itself to scan the products as they are placed inside is already developed and reliable. Other ideas using the required technologies are also available, which could give cashiers a run for their money. But they will have to wait until the difference in operating costs becomes large enough to make up for the possible risk of losing customers. That is the challenge behind increasing cashier efficiency while keeping their all-too-human customers happy and loyal.

The elimination of the second copy (which was at one time mandatory for accounting purposes) and the installation of faster, bioptic barcode scanners helped to speedup the process: 'The cashier is no more than an adjunct to the checkout desk.'[21] As in other sectors, the work of the cashier too came under time constraints: 'It is as painful a task as it is repetitive and no different from any assembly line work' said a cashier at FNAC. The relative body positions of the clients who 'stood over' the seated cashiers also showed how work rhythm was clearly determined by client flow. The cashier was positioned lower than the customer[22] (except at Ikea) and had to submit to the latter 'naturally'.

There was also the very real sense of an absence of autonomy at work: 'Whenever there is a problem, one has to always call someone ... We can't take any decisions. I'm not free, that's not just an impression, it's a fact. I'm not free because I'm not entitled to take the least decision.'[23] As for team spirit, it was more like that of teamwork and felt closer to peer pressure: 'If you make a mistake, there'll always be someone too who'll rub your nose in it'.[24] This sense of the absence of autonomy was also related to the number of tasks involved after SBAM (the French acronym for 'Smile, Good morning, Goodbye, Thank you' – *Sourire, Bonjour, Au revoir, Merci*): the return of the change, the collection of company checks, to begin the job with the opening of the cash register, and so on. While these tasks were very necessary to minimize errors, there was also an effort made to streamline work, speed up the processing of goods and thus meet the demands of customer flow.

New clients are always available

The pressure of tight flow meant that cashiers at food checkouts in hypermarkets had to handle tons of goods every day in awkward positions (such as holding and shaking a pack of six 1.5 litre bottles at arm's length in front of the scanner until it goes 'beep'). Though not acknowledged, work-related health problems multiplied:[25] back-aches and MST (musculo-skeletal trauma) – the problems encountered by assembly line workers in motor vehicle plants. In order to minimize the risks, Carrefour management published the following guidelines:

> To perform better as a cashier, ensure frequent alternation between standing and sitting positions.

- In the sitting position:
  - sit as erect as possible,
  - sit as close as possible to the conveyor belt,
  - adjust the foot rest,
  - support your back by placing the lumbar support of your chair against your kidneys.

- In the standing position:
  - stand balanced firmly on both feet,
  - lean against the counter (support point).

On the other hand, client flow pressure sometimes proved insufficient for optimum performance. Some cashiers could cheat by overlooking some articles or, by engaging in other, external, activities to slow down the whole process. In order to prevent such cashiers (mainly students and part-timers whose future lay elsewhere) from taking too much liberty with the flow, several kinds of surveillance techniques were implemented. In the first place, the average number of articles passed per hour was calculated, and norms established, and the cash over/short of every cashier was also retained. These figures could then either be used to reprimand the under-performers on a daily basis, or serve to help management conduct the annual individual interviews. Second, while video cameras were installed primarily to stop theft, they could also be used to keep an eye on the behaviour of the cashiers, whether with a client or among themselves.

As the flow of customers was never constant during the day, nor in any given week, month or year, the core group of permanent, full-time cashiers was always surrounded by a host of contracted workers. While most of these were on open-ended contracts (as well as the temporary workers recruited at specific times of the year), they were mainly part-timers. At one end were the working students who – for example, at Carrefour – worked for 8–16 hours per week (mostly in the evenings and on Saturdays) while at the other end were the senior cashiers who worked full-time as receptionists, in the planning department, and so on. The others came somewhere between these two extremes, with a working week of at least 23–28 hours being the minimum required to attain full-time status (less than a quarter of the personnel) and, more importantly, to escape the pressures of client flow. The requirements necessary to achieve full-time status have been decided and integrated into the system itself: to be available at all times and without complaint.

Though strictly speaking it was illegal, in some countries, such as Belgium and Switzerland, cashiers were summoned by telephone. This 'employment on call' or 'minute employment' (known as 'zero-hours' contracts in the UK) was similar to another system, in which the cashiers waited between shifts in a cafeteria or in a hall equipped with a TV set. In all these cases, only the time spent working was paid – without any consid-eration as to the effects of the work schedule on employees' social lives. On the other hand, the 'integrated' cashiers, and even those on the way towards integration, did enjoy a certain amount of autonomy. The former because they were sometimes given, in recognition of their seniority, jobs outside the tight flow, such as collecting the merchandise clients have left behind at the checkout. The others could negotiate their work schedules to some extent, with students filling the empty slots.

The use of students offered multiple advantages. Contracted on a weekly basis, with light work schedules, these students were more willing to put up with degrading work conditions (though sometimes it did create some ill-will between them and the 'permanent' cashiers – as at FNAC and the Bazar de l'Hôtel de Ville), changing work schedules and widely-spaced work shifts. Another advantage for management lay in reducing rest periods. While a full-time worker took about an hour off, part-time employees needed only a quarter of an hour. On the scale of 150–200 checkouts in a supermarket, the differences became significant. Finally, knowing that this work was only temporary, students did not complain much about work conditions, including schedules.

Checkout work was tiring, both physically and emotionally, especially as client pressure was scientifically organized and reinforced with the use of statistical tools and surveillance equipment. Cashiers within the retail business depended on their individual management. On the one hand, most employees at 2/3 or 3/5 of full-time schedules acceded to behavioural norms in the hope of becoming full-time employees, and on the other, students easily accepted the widely spaced working hours and the pressures of client-flow because they worked for only a few hours a week, and because they knew that they would be leaving comparatively soon. Funny system this, which managed permanent employees by institutionalizing part-time workers! But the retail business was not the only place that adopted such methods.

Tight flow in call centres

In the first part of 2002 this new form of business created over 200,000 jobs in France alone. Then, as now, call centres can either remain in-house or be outsourced.[26] If retained in-house, employees enjoy all the advantages of being full-time employees of a large company. Many companies have, however, begun to move this part of their business to countries with lower labour costs, such as Ireland, the UK, Morocco, India and Mauritius, provided, of course, that language problems can be resolved. There are basically four types of telephone conversations (of which parts are beginning to be replaced by email):[27]

- B to B (or B2B) signifies *business to business* calls;
- B to C is designated telemarketing (*business to consumers*);

- C to B is for calls from consumers to enterprises, when setting up their computers, asking for operating instructions, buying air or rail tickets and so on (*consumers to business*); and
- B to E (*employees*) for calls from businesses made to their employees.

While the business to business calls (B to B) and customer support (C to B) remain mostly in-house, telemarketing (B to C) has been widely out-sourced. In fact, even C to B calls are increasingly being pushed offshore: buying, setting up and maintaining PCs, software or any other high-tech home appliance.

Completely dependent on human resources (machines are not as yet versatile enough to tackle the diversity), call centres have one major preoccupation – reducing manpower costs. On the one hand, the qualifications required have been set as low as possible so that salaries may be kept to the minimum, and on the other, there is a constant push to increase productivity – enter the tight flow paradigm, the continuous flow of calls from consumers leading tele-operators to answer questions 'naturally' or to follow prescribed procedures for pushing a kitchen, a car or a dream holiday. Supervisors have only to see that the routine is maintained. The operators either have to go with the flow or leave the job.

The degree of pressure exerted by incoming calls (and consequently by work conditions) depends on the technical nature of the responses and the amount of information exchanged. A rise in either would mean a lowering of the pressure because, on one side, quality service requires time, and on the other, the lack of appropriately qualified personnel who accept/work in call centres means they have to be used sparingly.

In a Level 2 call centre[28] of an internet service provider (ISP), 150 technicians take calls every day from 8am until 9pm. The average duration of a call is around 15 minutes. At peak times, less than 60 per cent of calls are processed, the rest being deferred. Apart from their technical expertise, tele-operators also have what they call 'mastery over the call technique' which could be summarized as:

- taking a call (the accepted gap between two calls is 15 seconds, but technicians can, within narrow boundaries, adjust this somewhat);
- call up the client file from the database (to use what was written by the Level 1 tele-operator while at the same time making a summary in case of possible errors);
- ask a structured set of questions to arrive at a diagnosis; and
- give the solution after the question–answer session has confirmed the diagnosis.

In fact, technicians do much more than this. They keep track in a rough notebook of all the answers given, so as not to repeat a question, they might go to another computer terminal in order to access the database, and they may even approach a supervisor in case of a difficult problem. Finally, they insert details of the main conclusions into the client file. This whole process is going on at the same time as the operator is keeping a dialogue going with the client.

If the co-production of service has any meaning (see Chapter 6), it is in this exchange between consumer and tele-operator. The latter, though, remains on top: the first requirement is to assess the client as quickly as possible – the caller's technical knowledge and emotional state (Is s/he angry for being kept waiting? Is s/he furious at being charged for a service s/he thought came as part of the internet package?). By asking four or five technical questions, the operator can evaluate the technical level of the customer as well as their mood. According to these operators, the biggest problem in their job lies in these 'customer relations', for which they have not been trained. Some clients slam down the phone, others heap insults on the operator. Such bad behaviour accounts for some 10 per cent of the calls, and operators have to try very hard to bring about an amicable solution. Globally, some 90 per cent to 92 per cent of calls taken are eventually resolved.

From the operators' point of view, their working days are full to overflowing. Not only are breaks kept short (only five minutes every hour, to be taken with their supervisor's consent), but the mental load is also considerable: two monitors; simultaneous completion of the client file; solving the problem under the added pressure of the client who is paying for the telephone charges; establishing a fruitful communication with the client; and sometimes coping with their ill-humour. In contrast, the work of supervisors is quite light: they must see that things are proceeding normally, and intervene mainly regarding technical matters. They can and do sometimes listen to dialogues, mainly for two reasons: to improve the quality of the service (a short briefing may follow the completion of a call); and to evaluate the performance of new recruits, put the finishing touches to their training and confirm their job placement. The main work of management lies in keeping technicians within the tight flow – that is, working at the telephone and attending to the next call – because there a number of ways through which they can avoid activity, all detrimental to the company.

In the first place, the operator could choose to remind a client to answer complex questions that were left pending, or simply process those calls that had not been attended to immediately and were left on the answering machine. In order to avoid any misuse, it was only with the permission of the supervisor that the operator could make outgoing calls (the reminders). Such reminders were always much more comfortable to handle because, on the one hand, it meant that they were outside the tight flow pressures, and on the other, customers were naturally in a much better mood because they had been remembered and considered.

In the second place, operators could reduce the pressure by dragging out the time. For example, they can ask their customer to reboot their computer repeatedly without it being really necessary. The operator can then switch off the microphone and use this idle time for personal purposes such as a short conversation with a neighbour, chatting over the internet, web surfing, putting on some music, and so on. These methods for letting off some steam and getting back some sort of autonomy make working conditions somewhat more acceptable.

As in the case of the worker stuck on the automobile assembly line,[29] the prime preoccupation of the telephone operator at these call centres is to find ways of escaping tight flow pressures. Outlets are limited in number, however – becoming a supervisor (but there are few vacancies in spite of the growth in the sector), becoming a Level 3 expert who works on the knowledge base and on the most difficult cases, or to use the experience gathered over one or two years to jump into another, computer-related enterprise. It comes as no surprise, then, that less than half of the personnel at these call centres had been there for more than a year (of which a large number were supervisors or Level 3 technicians), and that more than 40 per cent were in rotation in spite of the advantages (relatively higher salaries, 35-hour weeks with only four working days and so on). The principle of tight flow played havoc with the idea of company loyalty.

Thus we see how tele-operators in these call centres, cashiers in supermarkets, workers in fast food restaurants and workers in major industries were all subjected to the constraints of tight flow which dominated their work while mobilizing them at the same time. These detailed studies should shed some light on the universal appeal of this work paradigm, because it has as its essence the constraint of time on work. In this sense it is the ideal capitalist tool – an instrument for *economizing less time*, which is just another term for capitalism itself.

It must also be noted that these emerging businesses in the tertiary sector (retail, fast food, call centre and so on) have practically solved a problem that the traditional industries of the West could never quite satisfactorily resolve, that of managing manpower adequately within time constraints. Semi-skilled workers in the motor vehicle industries,[30] in banks and insurance companies found themselves more or less stuck, with very few options regarding their mobility or other job opportunities. On the other hand, these new businesses in the service sector had kept the major portion of their labour force (the young, students, for example) fluid by presenting work as only being provisional. And their involvement lasted only as long as their time in the company, without there being any deeper commitment to the enterprise or its objectives.

But what was it like elsewhere? Especially in those businesses requiring a certain stability in the workforce? In the first place, employees in such companies were held by the tight flow itself. The client–supplier relationship needed initiative and the involvement of the whole group. At the same time, these constraints alone were not sufficient to keep employees glued permanently to the objectives, and consequently to the work. This was particularly true of the continued obsession with reducing running costs – this was a pressure imposed from outside the tight flow itself (though economically linked to it very closely) and thus was not shared by everyone.

Clearly, what is happening is that a different sort of social control is developing. Traditional methods, such as simple hierarchy, are no longer sufficient, for two main reasons: first, they are expensive, but more important, the complexity of the production system (tight flow, greater dependence on ICT, more complex products with shorter life-cycles) render these social controls ineffective for organizing immediate work. Direct control has lost its power, and the performance of workers depends more and more on results. We have gone from external control to auto-control as felt by every employee. This changes everyone's outlook radically, including that of the company itself. Social control exerted by the management still exists – but now, more typically it has taken the form of a meta-control of the attitudes and behaviour of employees implemented by the 'competency model'. Still, for this *combinatoire productive* to function, some social and economic conditions have to be met. There must be a certain pressure, either the threat of sub-contracting or job insecurity, to push employees into 'behaving' themselves. Such is the nature of work in this post-Fordian era.

5
The Fragmentation of the Labour Market and the Mobilization of Employees

The labour markets are not just *there*, to be taken for granted – on the contrary, they are social and economic constructs that develop gradually, and change with the requirements of industries at any given time, while depending largely on the prevailing labour law (the government) or power plays between the labour unions and employers' associations. Thus, while the general outlines are consistent within the OECD nations, each country has its own way of dealing with employment issues, especially the 'atypical' kind. For example, the UK has a much larger ratio of independent workers than the rest of continental Europe, which depends more on interim employment. For a long time, the labour market was seen as being divided between two distinct levels: on one side were highly qualified employees, with degrees and diplomas from universities and the French *grandes écoles*, and on the other, the poorer cousins, mainly from Third World countries, who had no qualifications to offer. There was also talk of it being split into the primary and secondary markets, or of being internal or external to the enterprise. In fact, the labour market is much more fragmented than that, and in truth should be talked of in the plural. The fragmentation of the labour market was not just the outcome of some incidental changes, but was in large part the result of the different ways that individuals reacted to the policies set down by their employers and the government.

If the fragmentation of labour markets was a result linked to the demands of enterprises, we then need to study the different functions assumed by these labour markets in relation to the organization of the enterprises themselves. In other words, *what were the different needs of the company that necessitated a fragmentation of the labour market together with the consequent labour flexibility?* Companies related to and managed their workforce depending on the economic context – that is, whether they found themselves in the middle of an economic expansion or recession, the openness of markets, the extent of protectionism, whether or not the conditions were conducive to the accumulation of capital and so on. Depending on such prevailing conditions, they could either find ways to attract and keep their employees (or only those of a certain category) or create internal or external flexibilities such as *functional flexibility* (mobility between jobs and functions), *numerical flexibility*, for example. How did the fragmentation of the labour market, which has been systematized since the 1980s, respond to the new demands of the enterprises, and what were these demands in the first place?

The first of these is the reduction of the costs of manpower. By using the available flexibility, management sought to ensure that employees were paid only for the period they were actually working. Moreover, the work period itself was reduced to the minimum, to extract the maximum amount of work possible. Work shifts offered by retail stores and fast food chains are a good example of making use of the labour force to meet managerial objectives exclusively. But this labour market fragmentation also has a second, more subtle (though strategic) role – that of fostering competitiveness among employees waiting at the periphery of production centers, and thus to be better able to select those required in these manufacturing or service industries. Consequently, labour market fragmentation played a major part in mobilizing employees towards company objectives. This is exactly what we hope to show by a detailed analysis of the evolution of corporate structures, and the coming of age of the cross-linking between independent companies (which constitute the company organized in a network: a dominant company provides direction and control for the network of subcontracting SMEs). Before this however, it might be well worth taking a quick look at the organization of traditional enterprises in the 1960s and 1970s.

The structure of the Fordian enterprise and traditional flexibility

In the post-war decades, large enterprises used to create a value addition of around 70–90 per cent and bought only standardized parts from the market. But as industrial products became increasingly complex, there was a greater reliance on sub-contractors for accessories and parts that could not be manufactured in-house quickly enough or at competitive rates. Gradually, sub-contractors grew in number, size and strength. Their manpower increased to the extent that one could speak of a double labour market, or of the primary and secondary labour markets. The large enterprises employed the more qualified ones and gave them full-time, secure jobs with relatively higher salaries. The subcontracting SMEs kept the low-qualified and unqualified personnel (producing goods of less added value) in insecure jobs and in particular with significantly lower pay scales. Though this polarization of enterprises and the division of the labour market should be taken for what it is – that is, a representation that reflected only a part of reality – it has all too often served as an accurate description of actual situations. It is true, though, that there have always been in the large industrial enterprises (motor vehicles, household appliances, electronics) jobs that required practically no qualifications and were relatively badly paid, while some mid-sized enterprises (first-tier and sometimes even second-level sub-contractors) had openings for qualified technicians who were rather well paid (in order to retain them), and even provided with some kind of job security.

This dual or polarized model had two essential characteristics: the large-scale enterprises enjoyed an easily organized flexibility, while employees in SMEs were constantly on the lookout for job opportunities in the large enterprises. During the upswings in the economy, the large enterprises recruited more labour (some of which came from the SMEs), and which they subsequently found difficult to lay off because of strict labour laws (at least in continental Europe) and stringent corporate rules regarding lay-offs. So, to adjust for the reduction in work, they re-appropriated some of the jobs that had previously been subcontracted and thereby passed on the recession-related employment issues to mid-level sub-contractors. In their turn, the sub-contractors, who were not bound by having to maintain a social image and enjoyed convenient labour contracts, reacted by laying off workers. In other words, the heart of the production system (the large enterprise) transferred the negative effects of a recession on to the periphery (the sub-contractors). The requirements of industrial flexibility were largely met by the sub-contractors and their labour force, which grew or shrank to meet the requirements of the large enterprises. No wonder, then, that people were so keen to get jobs in these large enterprises – it would ensure job security while at the same time bringing in a larger salary. Strictly speaking, this core–periphery relationship cannot be called a dual model because it depended on constant hope and a persistent tendency to cross over from one sphere (the SME) to the other (the large enterprise). On the contrary, it was a systemic, coherent function, in which the SMEs took upon themselves the burden of labour inflexibility faced by the large enterprises while the latter benefited from the trained manpower available in these same SMEs.

Eventually, however, this model gradually lost steam, especially under the pressures exerted by the crisis of accumulation that destabilized the

Fordian production system and brought about a number of changes in the structure of enterprises, in the manner of handling flexibility and in the mobilization of employees.

From the 'small is beautiful' to the centrifugation model

Once the more mundane responsibilities (such as the maintenance of buildings and manufacturing equipment, plant security, logistics of production flow, managing wages and so on) had been delegated, it was now the turn of the other, more intellectualized, services to be outsourced. The resulting tertiarization of the industry, and of all economic activities in general, was accompanied by the outsourcing of data processing jobs, accounting, auditing and consultancy, the design and conception of non-strategic sub-systems, marketing and promotional activities and so on.

All these activities were generally sub-contracted to young and small-sized enterprises[1] (which does not mean that they were not themselves motivated by the tendency towards incorporation). A major restructuring wave swept through the entire business landscape, accompanied by a significant change in its activities, which became increasingly service-orientated. At the same time, because of the competition engendered by the crisis of accumulation, there was a big push towards innovation, and a major portion of jobs were relocated from the large enterprises towards SMEs. It developed to the extent that the SMEs accounted for two-thirds of the entire workforce and began to create the vast majority of all new jobs. But this corporate restructuring did not entail any dispersion of the power centres – on the contrary, the fragmentation of enterprises was accompanied by a concentration of capital at the global level by means of mergers, agreements and buy-outs. This is exactly what J. Allen also argued, though in different terms:

> it is certainly preferable to regard the large modern company as an entity which controls its activity through a variety of ways (the property belonging to these establishments, franchises, granting licenses, sub-contracting, etc.) on a variety of markets and which employs people at different locations and installations. Therefore, the fragmentation of the large enterprise must not be seen to be a fragmentation of control.[2]

In fact, even though each sub-contractor or the supplier of parts, sub-assemblies or services is legally independent (that is, has independent capital), it is no less subordinated to the large enterprise or the reticular enterprise, as described in Chapter 1 of this volume. Large enterprises dumped the hazards of a fluctuating market with all its incertitude on to the SMEs, who could not but accept with good grace. The structural fragmentation of the reticular enterprise not only reduced the size of workgroups, but also broke the power of labour unions and allowed the development of job flexibility.

Moreover, whenever the sub-contracted work came close and was physically juxtaposed to the core of the work process, as happened with computer maintenance or industrial processes, it radically changed the working conditions themselves. The outsourcing of maintenance meant that personnel from the home company worked on the same equipment and shared the same workspace with employees of other service enterprises.[3] In such cases, the core–periphery relationship did not play itself out simply by a lesser or greater subordination of one to the other depending on the contract, but was lived on a daily basis by employees brought together from different companies, with different statutes, salaries, work conditions and working hours. The different company policies regarding labour and work conditions, at one time done in physically separate locations, now came together for all to see. For the employees involved, the core–periphery relationship was lived on a daily basis – with employees of the large enterprises often being envied for the advantages afforded by their employers, such as job security (at least better than in the SMEs), higher salaries, generally lower working hours (with one or two extra weeks of holiday), various corporate perks (holiday centres, better social security and retirement options) and so on.

Finally, to this enterprise fragmentation in which the larger controlled the smaller, and the employees lived as though they belonged to two different worlds, was added employment variety. Without getting into too much detail, we could say that on a day-to-day basis (or on the basis of time slots, as in retail and fast food businesses), management could resort to two basic kinds of employment to meet any anticipated work demands: temporary employment (interim or fixed duration contracts) and part-time employment.

This core–periphery model could also be called a *centrifugation* model because the big business corporations, including the large enterprises that controlled many smaller ones, were constantly discarding activities that were no longer profitable. As the technology behind these activities had matured and could not tolerate further innovation, opportunities for any significant value addition ended. Also discarded along with them were the lowest types of employment, such as part-time and temporary jobs, which had no guarantees and were meagrely paid.[4] What interests us here is the generalization of the core–periphery model which had until now been seen only as the relationship between the ordering agent and the sub-contractor. At the time of writing, this centrifugation model has percolated into all types of commercial activities (industrial as much as service-orientated) within all kinds of enterprises, whether engaged in the manufacture of goods or in providing services. Moreover, this model penetrates the very core of these enterprises, touching even those activities considered strategic to the company. Activities that do not generate enough value added are quickly sub-contracted. They are then either handled internally – that is, on the company's own premises, by personnel employed by a sub-contractor, or externally, by shifting the whole activity to a location that provides a cheaper work space and labour force.

The only reason to fragment an enterprise through this system of centrifugation was to reduce costs by adjusting the management of manpower to suit its strategic importance and its unavoidable characteristics. Only the activities that required – for the moment – highly qualified personnel, remained protected at the heart of the enterprise, while all others were slowly but inexorably pushed towards the exterior. Even those activities that had evolved close to the centre but were not of strategic importance were marked for externalization. The centrifugation model thus became more and more complex, refining itself with every opportunity to reduce costs while maintaining the efficiency of the productive system.

Naturally, this model had its limits. For the moment though, it was the dominating force and each day saw it being pushed further and implemented more fully – fuelled by the competition between SMEs (in fact, between the SMEs and the internal services) to reduce costs. What remains to be seen are the actual methods used to reduce costs, especially of manpower. For that, we propose a short detour to look briefly at the work by John Atkinson,[5] who formalized these transformations.

Atkinson's model of the flexible firm

Atkinson's model takes into account both company flexibility and labour market fragmentation. He starts with the core–periphery dichotomy and builds on it by analysing actual situations and the types of employment available at the periphery. We shall present here a slightly modified version of his model to take into account the situation in France,[6] and then build on this to create a general theory.

According to Atkinson, employees at the heart of the company are hired full-time, paid high wages and given a comforting security blanket, in return for which they are required to execute a wide variety of tasks, well beyond the traditional divisions of labour. Functionally, they must be extremely flexible, and capable of adapting themselves to market variations by being widely qualified. In fact, by being so highly qualified and versatile, these employees begin to blur hierarchical distinctions and are often assigned managerial functions. The most distinctive feature of this group is that they hold qualifications that are not easily available on the labour market. The company thus goes to great lengths to retain them, and also to isolate them from the external labour market.

This core of the company is surrounded by several layers, each corresponding to an increasingly 'peripherized' level of employment. The first and closest of these is made up of employees who also work full-time, but with lower career prospects and lesser job security. Often poorly qualified, they are hired from the external labour market and occupy specific posts. Somewhat bleak career prospects meant that they had a high rate of turnover and provided the company with some flexibility regarding manpower. The next level comprises non-standard jobs (employees on fixed-term contracts, part-time workers, government-aided recruits, specialized trainees) and routine jobs such as cleaning, caretaking and security. Around them is the final layer, made up of those not employed directly by the company and who hold a wide variety of posts (either industrial or service orientated, operational work or conceptualizing) – this is especially so at the time of writing, when the principle of centrifugation has penetrated to the very heart of every enterprise (apart from, of course, the financial heart of the business corporations!). Atkinson has also shown that a company can achieve numerical flexibility by sub-contracting, offering temporary jobs, hiring independent workers and obtaining supplies externally.

The generalization of the core–periphery model

The theory we propose has a dual aspect: to retain and refine Atkinson's model, and to show that this concept of core–periphery is applicable not only to the relationship between the ordering agent and sub-contractor, but is found increasingly within these two sub-sets themselves (core/ ordering agent and periphery–sub-contractor). In other words, the core–periphery paradigm needs to be seen to be working at many different levels. Questions regarding sub-contracting, temporary work (especially interim jobs), and independent workers, which traditionally arose at the periphery, are now brought into the very heart of the production systems themselves. When thus generalized, the model is seen to be a 'fractalization' of the principle of centrifugation between hierarchically structured 'molecules' as well as within each of them. This model also takes into account that the traditional form of employment (full-time, open-ended contracts) constitutes 85 to 90 per cent of the active employed population – that is, that non-standard jobs (fixed-term contracts, temporary, partial and various kinds of supported jobs) make up 10 per cent to 15 per cent of the global employment market.[7] At the same time, around these 10–15 per cent that make up so-called precarious jobs, there revolve some 20 per cent to 25 per cent of the active population. In other words, almost a quarter of the population within the legal working age finds itself faced with the spectre of job insecurity. The proposed model takes into account the systematic development of this lack of job security (see Table 5.1) and shows how it has become a means of controlling employee behaviour.

The twin levels of centrifugation

Figure 5.1 shows the twin levels of centrifugation. On the one hand, it shows the relationship between the core and periphery within each work group of a company (in a service, a workshop – anywhere there is a team), and on the other, the relationship between companies and the work groups themselves, whether within or between companies. Every group represented by an encircled nucleus indicates the ratio of the different kinds of employee (see Figure 5.2 to zoom in on one such employee ratio). Every work group belongs to a specific bona fide company, with the one at the centre normally dominating the ones around the periphery, and controlling their activities. This does not mean, for example, that there cannot exist within Company A, and especially along its walls, independent

Table 5.1   Unemployment and non-standard employment in France

Items	March 2002
Unemployment rate (ILO)	9.7%
Unemployment rate of those below 25 years of age	25.3%
Percentage of long-term unemployment	31.7%
Percentage of part-time employment	18.3%
Short-term employment (000s) compared to the 22 million people who are employed full-time:	
Fixed term contracts	897
Temporary workers	513
Apprentices	273
Financially-aided contracts	420
Number (000s) of recipients of RMI (financial aid)[8*]	1 088

* The RMI (*revenu minimum d'insertion*, a form of financial aid) was instituted by the left-wing government in 1991.
Source: INSEE, *Enquête Emploi*, March 2002.

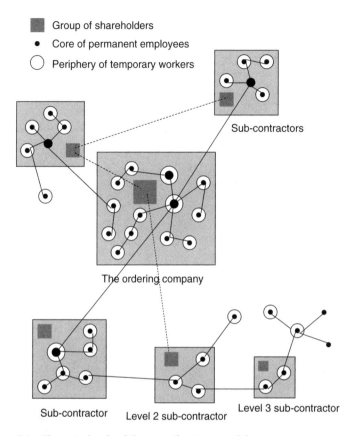

Group of shareholders
Core of permanent employees
Periphery of temporary workers

Sub-contractors

The ordering company

Sub-contractor   Level 2 sub-contractor   Level 3 sub-contractor

Figure 5.1   The twin levels of the centrifugation model

employees or temporary workers who do not depend on Company A (while working for Company A, their salaries are paid by Company B, which could be a sub-contractor or a short-term employment enterprise). The thicker lines connecting the nuclei represent the functional and organic links between the service centres within the same company, or the functional links between centres belonging to different corporations (or establishments) that have a relationship of domination.

This representation of the centrifugation model is somewhat complicated because it has to take into account two relatively distinct dimensions which still interact closely with one other:

- the productive structure of the enterprise which delegates its problems to the periphery via sub-contracts and external supplies. Though it is true that this system can be found within the enterprise itself, and in fact has come to characterize the very core of the reticular enterprise – that is, the company at the centre (often wrongly called the large enterprise) that controls the entire production process; and

- the management of the manpower that grades employees by their qualifications and grants them guarantees of employment, higher salaries and various other privileges.

In this centrifugation model, every molecule functions according to the principles set down by Atkinson (as shown in Figure 5.2). Here, the nucleus at the heart of every work cell represents the permanent core of full-time employees and gives the system its functional flexibility. These full-time employees are highly qualified, with secure jobs and good salaries – everything to ensure that they apply themselves fully and use all the resources at their disposal to meet the objectives of the company.

The first band around the core represents those employees who are a little less qualified. It contains two distinct kinds of workers: the young newcomers freshly out of training and gathering experience on their way up, and the older ones who find themselves doubly disqualified – by their age (physically worn out, in the case of manual labourers) and by the absence of any continued training (the newer technologies and processes used are well beyond their grasp). Though they work full-time, they do not have, nor will ever have, a guaranteed job. They do the jobs

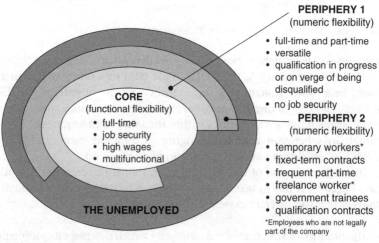

Figure 5.2   The core–periphery continuum

that require lower qualifications and are more routine. They also give the enterprise a dual flexibility: a functional flexibility through their ability to help the core whenever required (after all, they have had some training and were, until recently, versatile) and a numerical flexibility because their lower salaries allow them to fill in for employees of the second peripheral zone.

The next band around the centre (the second peripheral zone) includes all employees with more or less insecure jobs: temporary workers, those with fixed-term contracts[9], independent workers (who have mostly chosen to be so under pressure of their ordering agent-cum-employer), home workers and trainees subsidized by the government (qualification contracts and employment solidarity contracts, for example). They are given lower-level jobs at the periphery of the production process (loading and unloading machines, equipment or trucks, various type of manual labour and cleaning) and are often hired on a part-time basis according to need. Even if they have some kind of degree or are qualified, there is no way they can make use of the qualification in these work situations. Promised jobs are also slow in appearing. This second zone is illustrative of the theories of disaffiliation,[10] as well as new ways of bringing the work under the sway of capital – not unlike eighteenth- and nineteenth-century capitalism.[11] Some commentators might be tempted to see in this return to the infant stage of capitalism a kind of senility, and consequently its possible demise – unless, of course, this centrifugation turns out to be just another stage in an infinitely progressing capitalism.

To better express these structural changes, experts have sought to go beyond the present-day model of employment which makes a distinction between, if not directly opposing, typical and non-standard jobs (all those at the periphery and the unemployed share these non-standard jobs). After an analysis that places more importance on changes in work than the deregulation of the labour market, A. Supiot has proposed an active adaptation of the labour law that would *reinstitutionalize work relations*: 'Here reinstitutionalizing means: to fix rules, open avenues for renegotiating the rules and allow a collective group to intervene efficiently ... To the status of the employee, which links his subordination to his security, should also be added a new professional status, founded on a comprehensive approach to work and capable of including the requirements of liberty, security and responsibility'.[12] The shift from employment to professional status remains moot. Though we agree in large part with A. Supiot's analysis, the principles which he would like to see implemented do not take into account restructuring elements that have led to the present situation, and that lie at the basis of the analysis itself. By this we mean the new forms of capital appreciation that depend, among other things, on the accumulated imbalance between capital and work (for example, the acceptance of the paradigm of tight flow with a reduced workforce, and the resulting consequences on work itself), while at the same time cut-throat competition has led companies to make ever-increasing demands on their employees. Therefore, we feel that the principles proposed as foundations of professional status are too tenuous in the sense that they do not take into consideration the present situation and the existing relationships of power between employee and employer, as well as the current condition of trade unionism across Europe as a whole. Even in countries where trade unions have a strong base and a hefty presence, can they really initiate anything? (We are not talking here about their capacity for resistance.) While these principles seem to be well-founded, they do not pertain sufficiently to the actual situations regarding the re-institutionalization of the wage relationship, because the stated conditions do not exist in most parts of Europe. Moreover, creating these conditions would mean a readjustment of the balance of power between employer and employee, which the former would naturally oppose. What is more, in the present situation, this new professional status[13] would be more likely to destabilize the nucleus of standard jobs which represent the mainstay of all employment than to stabilize the 10 per cent to 15 per cent of non-standard jobs (which occupy some 20 per cent to 25 per cent of the active population). By bringing labour laws into the domain of job security, the remedy could well prove to be worse than the malady itself. The notion of professional status is indeed laudable, as it covers all the stages encountered in an individual's professional career, from work contract to vocational training, including the periods of forced inactivity (job hunting, switching careers, community service, parental leave and extended sick leave). But nothing will be gained by plunging headlong into such a proposal without making sure that the benefits will be shared by all, in particular all the different categories of employees.

At the same time, in the present situation, we would like to remove the dual aspect of the labour market and replace it with the idea of a *continuum* between the core of every cell in the centrifugation model and the two layers around it that represent the two major kinds of employment status (see Figure 5.2). The absence of any clear boundary forms one of the bases of this proposed new model, with the continuum signifying mobility, under some conditions, of people in both directions: from the core to the periphery and vice versa. The diagram shows how it is relatively easy to move from one zone to another, while it is more difficult to 'jump' over any. This is why the approach going from unemployment to the core has been made so narrow. On the other hand, the route leading towards unemployment, though not shown specifically here, is much wider and frequented whenever the enterprise undergoes a restructuring, which normally results in massive lay-offs.

Two examples to illustrate the core-periphery continuum

There exist a number of examples that could serve to illustrate this core–periphery model of work cells. We give here two of these – one from the industrial sector and the other from the tertiary sector. On a motor vehicle assembly line, the old system consisted of lining up a group of poorly-qualified and poorly-paid workers who toiled away at more or less fixed posts (this was the heart of the Fordian model). At the time of writing, the production team (called the basic production unit (BPU) or basic work unit (BWU in France) consists of some thirty people. A permanent core of sixteen to twenty qualified, full-time workers are employed directly by the company – leaders of small groups or versatile and established assembly workers – and they enjoy good salaries and job security. Around this nucleus revolve some six to eight different kinds of worker: usually, young men under training or freshly transferred from some other workshop, older workers or those with some medical restrictions (posted to specific jobs), the young and the not-so-young on their way to some promotion outside the workshop, and the 'super' – that is, the highly versatile workers who, for example, can take up any job on the line. These workers change their teams (BPUs) whenever they feel like it or to meet the needs of production. The team is completed by a few workers who are on trial or, as more often happens, temporary. If circumstances permit, they can remain as temporary workers for up to two years in the hope of being hired permanently. The judicious combination of different types of employee within the enterprise and those on temporary assignment results in a high numerical flexibility as well as a ready functional flexibility (replacements for absentees and the assurance that difficult jobs will be completed by qualified personnel).

The work in a warehouse supplying electrical household appliances to a chain of supermarkets consists of receiving the material, arranging it by location, preparing the orders and executing them. Management, employees, supervisory staff and assistants make up the nucleus of the workforce. Full-time workers with open-ended contracts are versatile (the principal requirement for assistants), and each have to shoulder a specific responsibility. Around this nucleus there are a large number of temporary workers acting either as fork-lift drivers or sundry assistants. To ensure contract renewal, they have to meet three conditions set by management: to be available – that is, to accept overtime without question, be productive (keep to the norm of preparing 700 packages per day) and respect the hierarchy. A closer inspection reveals subtle undercurrents of conflicts and alliances between the permanent and some categories of temporary workers. P. Stéphanon lists three types of temporary workers[14]: *waiting* temporary workers – mostly the younger ones who take a temporary job while looking elsewhere for a long-term contract; the *negotiating* temporary workers – composed mainly of older workers, who negotiate their salaries and work pace; and between the two, the *salarial* temporary workers, who negotiate only their salaries. Some within the negotiating category see their status as stable (their contracts often continue for years) and even boast about it. They can refuse any job they feel is not lucrative enough, and define freedom as the option to quit any job at any time to take up another which might be better paid or simply more convenient. They take pains to build special relationships with employees in other companies and with the supervisory staff, to gather two types of resources: a certain control over time by being able to accelerate or slow down (slowing down allows a full working day to be filled even when there is little work) and, by procuring strategic information, to know the anticipated workload as well as the actual locations of misplaced items. Moreover, the choice of being able to take up congenial work at odd hours allows them to further supplement their salaries – there is no need to resort to bank loans, unlike the situation with other temporary employees. Enterprises welcome them because of their adaptability and flexibility. Being closest to the core and often perceived as being more efficient than the assistants themselves, they can easily land full-time, open-ended contracts wherever they want to (which generally happens after their mid-thirties).

One of the reasons for the very existence of the core–periphery continuum is the mobility of manpower it creates. For there to be mobility, there must be differentiation (different advantages for the core and the periphery within every cell). In its turn, this mobility becomes a motivating factor for each employee (promotion or demotion).

Mobilization of employees in the core-periphery model

The first effect of the centrifugation model was a reduction in the production cost of goods and services: the larger the portion of the work done by employees at the periphery, the lower the cost, because these workers are paid less. In fact, the pressures of cost reduction on this segment of the workforce are numerous: whether within a large enterprise or spread widely, this labour force was almost never unionized. Neither labour unions of large corporations nor local branches of national unions[15] succeeded in drawing these employees into any sort of a union movement. Although often concentrated at the same premises, they came under a wide variety of contracts (belonging to different activities with different collective agreements) and were hired by several different employers. Managements of large enterprises thus could take advantage of an ill-protected and functionally dispersed workforce by handing out rather meagre salaries while offering none of the advantages (social cover, other privileges, holiday centres, for example). Moreover, they also paid most of the workers only for the time actually spent working. On the other hand, they 'scientifically' assured for themselves the flexibility of their workforce by giving work to only those who made themselves available at all times. Until now this had been the practice for domestic work[16], where the employer kept only those who worked most efficiently and never complained. Today, such a practice exists in the retail business in Belgium and Switzerland in the form of so-called 'work on call' already mentioned in the previous chapter.

Social mobility and 'constrained involvement'

The second effect of this centrifugation model was to break all resistance to the new work conditions (any-time availability, low wages and heavy dependence, if not complete subjection). Faced by the splitting of the workplace and the fragmentation of the labour market, employees could not put up any organized or collective resistance. If there was any resistance or adaptive strategies, they were limited to the individual, and in fact went along the lines set by the employer. For their part, corporate administrative boards encouraged systematic competition between employees to identify the best and to integrate them within the large enterprise, and more, within the core of the centrifugation model – with all the advantages discussed earlier. Every individual thus sought to attain to what S. Paugam called *assured integration*[17], which brings with it job security, high wages, social rights and, in particular, work satisfaction (interesting work and recognition through work). By holding out this carrot of assured integration on the one hand, and brandishing a whip on the other, corporate administrators gradually developed yet another method of managing the labour force: *access to the core*. We must also add to this a second goal that has proved to be at least as important: *staying at the core*. Once in the core does not in any way mean always in the core. There are a number of reasons for being removed: physical age, difficulty in adapting to different technologies, delay in acquiring new know-how, unacceptable behaviour, and so on. We have thus an extremely efficient system for mobilizing workers with, on the one hand, promises of entry to the core, and on the other, threats of expulsion. By now it must be clear why we call this the centrifugation model: for many (young and old, women, and especially those with few qualifications) the chances of remaining at the periphery or of quickly being thrown out are far greater than the chances of gaining entry to the core. On the one hand, 80 per cent of the jobs created are located at the periphery, and on the other, there is a constant outward push from the core in order to reduce its size. These core–periphery exchanges lie behind the geographical, professional, social and statutory mobility within large or reticular enterprises. And it is this mobility, which now effects every category and statute of employee, along with its rapid increase, that we feel has not been explored sufficiently deeply by researchers. In fact, if one were to frequent work places often enough, one would be surprised at how often these changes take place at every level. This mobility within the enterprise was also the result of methods used by the management *vis-à-vis* the workforce. The movements of ascension towards the centre or of regression towards the periphery were clearly the result of a rigorous selection process that evaluated not only work results, but also behaviour with just as critical a perspective. This is not just the competency system discussed in Chapter 3, but also includes the underlying methods of employee mobilization (see Figure 5.3).

The centrifugation model encourages constant competition between employees (of the customer enterprise as well as the sub-contractors), and between the core and periphery of every production segment, be it in conception, manufacture or distribution. Moreover, this labour market fragmentation – created by the different requirements of different production processes – creates a manpower surplus for every production segment. This means that the unemployed reservists are not just those who have neither jobs nor qualifications, since this section of the labour market has layers made up of qualified individuals. It contains a whole range, from the unqualified (often young) to the highly qualified engineers in all sectors (for example, engineers above the age of 55 who were dismissed because they had become too expensive), including all categories of workers and technicians. In the race to get a job (there was practically no question of any collective resistance movement) and in order to have any chance of attaining the status of assured integration, all have to conform to the employer's expectations or, more importantly, to those of recruiting agents.

Employees pushed out of the nucleus (generally ageing workers) and wanting to return, together with younger people who, with or without

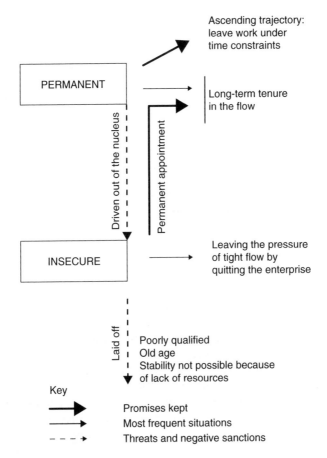

Figure 5.3 The emerging system of mobilization

qualifications, want to climb out of insecurity to enter the core of the process and attain assured integration, have to conform equally to strict behavioural norms. This trial period often lasts for several years, with workers being on their best behaviour and striving mightily with great zeal. No wonder, then, that management tries to lengthen this period of observation wherever possible!

Thus we see that this centrifugation model goes very well with the *combinatoire productive* previously described. In fact, it meshed beautifully with some of its elements, such as the 'naturalization' of the constraints of tight flow (which compelled employees to accomplish tasks without any supervision) and the competency model which formed part of the concept of teamwork, in which individual evaluations were fundamental to the selection and retention of all personnel within the work group.

Continuity of the core–periphery model and the fragmentation of the labour market

In conclusion, we could ask ourselves, can this centrifugation model last? Is it not the imbalance between the number of unemployed and the number of available jobs that makes such a system possible? Can we not then imagine a time when a return to full-time employment would lead to the disappearance of this system? That would also create difficulties for the new *combinatoire productive* because then each employee could, without becoming part of any dissenting collectivity (union), resist individually the demands made on his or her behaviour. Is it not to combat this very risk that the competency model tried to assure enterprises of their employees' loyalty?

For us, an eventual return to full-time employment does not pose a threat to the essence of the centrifugation model:

- In case of any strain on the least qualified segment of the labour market, there always exists the possibility of importing any number of unqualified workers. This is what has been done in the USA since the 1980s, and has resulted in a growing population of the *working poor*, who sometimes have to take on two jobs at the same time in order to survive. In France, some branches (particularly public works and civil engineering) and enterprises within certain areas (motor vehicle factories in eastern France) that did not want to raise salaries, clamoured for a new wave of immigration to provide the required manpower.
- Because the labour market is so fragmented, pressure on the least qualified segment has little effect on the other sections. The ready availability of workers at the periphery of every segment of the labour market who aspire to enter the core and achieve secure integration has meant the implementation of a selection process along the lines already detailed. Only a few segments escape this fate, such as that of computer experts and, in particular, network specialists.
- It would seem that in the USA, labour market fragmentation associated with the centrifugation model has led to a great elasticity regarding employment volume in every segment as well as the size of salaries. A stable economic growth rate of 3–4 per cent per year would affect all labour market segments and result in a significant increase in revenue. This is exactly what happened between 1996 and 2001, at the end of which a comfortable social cover was instituted (the famous Plan 401k).

But, as soon as the growth rate fell, it precipitated a snowball effect that caused a dramatic drop in salaries, as occured in California in 2001. The end result of the centrifugation model is a yo-yo movement whose amplitude is as yet unknown and whose frequency has set alarm bells ringing for employees. But this serves to reinforce the model itself, because it is based on the unequal sharing of resources (not least of which is job security).

Thus, while non-standard jobs and the dichotomy between core and periphery are often studied as social and economic responses to the requirements of an enterprise (with employees refusing or adapting themselves) they could also be seen as coherent and integral parts of the new *combinatoire productive*, which is one of the tools for the mobilization of employees.

6
Information Technology and the Service Industry: White-Collar Work

In the more developed countries, the service industry has grown to such an extent that it has all but eclipsed other sectors. Having begun with the manufacturing industry, now agricultural activities have also come to depend so much on information technologies and the service industry that no clear demarcations can be made and we might have to abandon the model of three distinct sectors.[1] In this chapter, we shall first deal with the question of how to define a service, then suggest some interpretations of the nature of the ongoing social transformations linked to the explosion of this tertiary sector. Along the way we shall also study the concept of a service relationship and try to deduce the possible changes in wage relations.

The information and communication aspect of the tertiary sector leads us to question the very nature of work performed by the various services in their diversity. We shall need to revisit the definitions of information and communication, especially in relation to work. Has the present dependence on the ICT transformed work? If so, what are the characteristics of it that allow us to draw such a conclusion? And what are the dominant paradigm(s) to which both information and communication find themselves subjected? What are the changes wrought by them in work? How can we qualify and interpret them?

The explosion of the service industry

Certain activities which had long been part of domestic routine and chores have gradually been externalized because they had become too specialized or required highly specific qualifications. The hair stylist, the shoe repairer, the dry cleaner, the garage mechanic and the teacher now all live off their qualifications. Added to the finance sector (banks and insurance) and public works, these activities explain why providing services has come to occupy more than a quarter of the entire population of Europe and North America (with a much greater proportion in the developing countries) since the beginning of the twentieth century. When we talk of the explosion of services in the more advanced nations, we must take into account that each country has its own agenda – not only in the development of new activities within previously established domains such as education, research, health, social security and the social services in general, but more importantly, in the emergence of a host of new and rapidly growing activities, such as:

- tourism (tour organizing, the hotel and catering industry, air transportation), leisure and recreation, the restaurant business (fast food and otherwise), the retail industry and/or shopping, banking, insurance, and so on;
- telecommunications (mobile telephone services, internet, and so on) and media (television, magazines, films, video games, advertisements and so on); and
- outsourcing of jobs that previously had been done within the enterprise itself (for example, cleaning, catering and, especially, logistics, data processing, accounting and personnel management) – that is, business-orientated services.

The first of these categories, which seeks to substitute traditional in-house work by externalized services, depends also on the growth of new job opportunities that have now sprung up outside the domestic circle, such as tour operators, accommodation and inter-client social relations. Maintenance of houses and gardens has now been handed over to specialists. Banquets and parties are handled and arranged professionally, while in a growing number of homes, fast food has come to replace the family meal and get-together on Saturdays and Sundays. A large part of all domestic activities has been slowly but inexorably commercialized, and an increasing number of employed men and women find themselves wooed away from domestic chores under the triple lure of the services available, lack of time at home, and very often, physical or mental fatigue after a hard day at work.

The second category (providers of information and communication services) is also a support and substitute for social communication and a substitute for individual creativity. Telecommunications and the internet have to a large extent replaced face-to-face interactions. As these devices minimize the physical effort of travelling, it has been shown that they increase the time spent communicating and in fact more things are said than in a direct, face-to-face conversation. It still remains to be seen whether this leads to deeper and more meaningful relationships or simply to greater superficiality. The growth and widespread use of these communicating media could be a great help in reinforcing all that makes us human, the development of our sensibilities, our aesthetics and our power of reflection. But while there are some sections of the media that do try, it is painfully obvious that the vast majority have their fingers on the pulse of the people and an eye on sales figures. This obviously leads them to flatter the public and to avoid taxing it either intellectually or emotionally – a sure way of reducing their financial prospects.

The third category (business orientated services) appeared as a result of the growing trend in the large enterprises of externalizing activities towards SMEs – which sometimes could even belong to the holdings that include the large enterprise itself! This outsourcing consisted of pushing towards the periphery all that did not provide any significant value addition and did not form part of the enterprise's core activities. We shall deal with the specifics of these services at the end of this chapter.

One of the ways of looking at the service industries would be to note the extremely rapid increase in the volume of employment in this sector, which first came at the cost of the agriculture sector and then affected the industrial sector from the 1960s. This is illustrated clearly by Figure 6.1 which charts the percentage of the staff employed in each of these three sectors in the USA – perhaps the most advanced country in terms of the growth in the service industries.

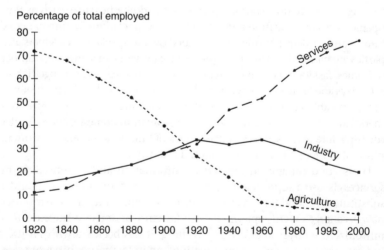

Figure 6.1   Employment growth in the USA
Source: J. Téboul, *Le temps des services*, Editions d'Organisation, 1999, p. 9.

While an inter-service analysis does not show anything as striking as the explosive growth of the entire sector in general, there are three statistics that do stand out: a massive growth in business services, a strong showing by the public services,[2] and the recent blossoming of information services (part of which is obviously targeted at enterprises).

Definitions and types of services

Over the years, various analysts have proposed a bewildering array of definitions. Should we look at their usages or the importance of these services in the national budget? Should we give precedence to their non-commercial side and their role in the development of our society? Should we evaluate them merely by their productivity? Are they to be measured by the number of jobs they create or value produced?

The service triangle

A viable definition of service has been proposed by Gadrey:

> a service is an *operation* undertaken by A, which aims at *transforming the state* of a reality C, in the possession of, or utilized by a consumer (or a client or a user) B at his request which stops short of producing any object which can be circulated commercially independent of C.[3]

While this microeconomic definition might not cover all possible service-orientated activities, it does show how service belongs to the sphere of social relations and that, while immaterial in itself, is linked to a point of application that has some physical reality. This definition makes it clear that service has as its objective the transformation of the state at the point of application C, which refers to theories regarding communication and informational content of services. Gadrey illustrates his definition with the diagram shown in Figure 6.2.

As regards the classification of services, Singlemann's[4] analysis remains at the base of many diverse approaches. Apart from extractive industries (agriculture, mines) and the processing industries (for example, construction, agri-food, manufacturing), Singlemann proposes categorizing services into four sub-sections:

- Distribution: transport, communications, commerce;
- Services targeted at the intermediary producers (the *proservices*): banks, insurance companies, real estate, services to enterprises;
- Social services: health, education, social security, public utilities; and

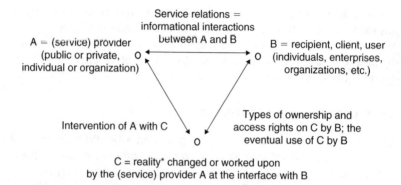

Figure 6.2 Definition of a service

Note: * We understand *reality* to mean here: objects or material systems (transportation, repairs, maintenance, etc.); information; individuals, according to some of their characteristics (physical, intellectual); and organizations, according to some of their characteristics (technology, structure, collective knowledge base, etc.).
Source: J. Gadrey, *L'économie des services* (1992).

- Personal services: domestic help, hotels, restaurants, repairs, painting, leisure activities.

The reader might have noticed that there are a number of difficulties in the implementation of such a classification because the distribution services such as the *proservices* take on completely different characteristics depending on whether they are targeted at the individual or the enterprise. That is why we feel that a better system would consist of a table with two columns that would categorize the services by their destination and their sub-set (see Table 6.1). It would then be possible for anyone to choose which met one's own aims. From the sociological point of view, we would rather go by the service destination – the 'client' being different, we feel that the type of relationship is also markedly distinctive, not so much in nature as in form, and depends greatly on whether it is directed towards an individual or an enterprise.

From purchasing an item to accessing a service

Another way of looking at the vast majority of services is to think of them as a means of using a physical product or accessing a source of information. According to the theory of the advent of the *age of access*:

Success depends more on long-term commercial relations than on individual market exchanges. During most of the industrial era, the

Table 6.1 Classification of services

Sector	Destination of the service	
	Individual	**Enterprise**
Distribution	Shipping and parcel delivery service, courier Passenger transport (train, plane, bus, underground train) Commerce: retail business Telephony, media, video games, advertisements, internet	Transport of goods, delivery service Transport of personnel (staff bus) Wholesale trade, import/export Telephony, telecommunications, internet/intranet
Insurance Real estate Services to enterprise	Monitoring of individual bank accounts Insurance of private goods Estate agent, notary	Corporate and merchant banks Building insurance, transportation insurance Corporate real estate Outsourcing of services: data processing, logistics, accounting Security and cleaning
Social services	Health: hospitals, doctors, pharmacies Education: schools, colleges, universities Retirement/social cover Public administration (central and regional)	Occupational health, work-related injuries Further training Social security/pension funds Public administration (taxation, subsidies, grants)
Personal services	Fast food and leisure restaurants Tour operators, hotel and catering Motor vehicle repairs Dry cleaners, hair stylists	Company catering Security Cleaning

most important thing was selling a product – the free service offered to the consumer in the form of the guarantee was nothing more than a sales pitch. This relation has now been effectively reversed: more and more companies are giving away their products practically for free in the hope of keeping their customers over the long term and having them return for all kinds of services.[5]

In this context, the most striking image that comes to everyone's mind is the mobile phone. The service provider literally gives away the handset for free (or for a pittance) so as to subsequently sell an ever-widening net of services: telephonic communication, of course, messaging services, internet access, sending images and so on. Though taken to an extreme in this case, this example is by no means unique; Rifkin has shown similar trends in the sale of motor vehicles, air conditioners and wall-to-wall carpeting, among other activities.

The primary aim of opening up the access to and radically transforming the use of a product or an information source is to attract clients who feel that they only have to pay the minimum required for the precise amount of service consumed. Rifkin has shown how this phenomenon is accompanied by the merchandising of all interchanges, including human relations, to the extent that 'access becomes a life-style'. Possession is no more an aim in itself, only the usage in all its forms is of any value – such as access to a service; that is, the relationship of a client to the availability of a service.

The rapid expansion of services has thus seen a parallel decrease in the manufacture of physical goods, agricultural as well as industrial. What is more, the increasing efficiency in the manufacturing process of these goods continues to lower their prices, and consequently their relative importance in the family budget. In other words, a virtuous circle has been formed: while more time can now be spent on developing services (industrial products taking up less time), the reduction in the cost of material goods means that, at the same time, more can be spent on these services.[6] In addition, decreased working hours in the more socially developed countries means that employees also have more time to devote to these often time-consuming services.

The hectic pursuit of material goods, which had dominated all social interaction in Europe, Japan and the USA during the twentieth century has now lost its hold, and physical objects no longer occupy their erstwhile pre-eminent position in the pantheon of well-being, comfort and social status. These new services have brought in some sort of *dematerialization* in the lives of people. Consumption has now changed from being dominated by the discovery, availability and spread of new material goods to the availability of and access to a variety of intangible services. This has had a double impact: while these new activities are in general more time-consuming, they take up far less physical space than does the acquisition of physical objects. Consequently, it has helped to check the growing congestion in homes, and particularly in urban agglomerations. In addition, a large part of these activities, transportation notwithstanding, are much more sparing of our natural fossil reserves and less detrimental to the ecological balance of the planet. In this sense, 'information services' has marked a real break from the Fordian brand of consumption, and it is tempting to envisage a time when humanity will begin to live more in harmony with its natural environment by shifting requirements towards less destructive pursuits. But this conveniently forgets the fact that almost two-thirds of humanity do not have the material goods considered as the bare minimum in the OECD countries. Nor are we any closer to understanding the fundamental causes behind this paradigm shift in our 'pursuit of happiness', and of its becoming more subtle and insubstantial – neither the wisdom of men, nor God, nor the nature of production relations give any satisfactory answers.

Services as a purchase of work time – defining the service relationship

Time holds a central and paramount position in any capitalist economy, and obviously we cannot afford to neglect its importance in the rapid expansion of the tertiary sector. From the time of David Ricardo (reiterated by Adam Smith and more recently by Karl Marx) we know that the cost of a product is directly linked to the time spent in its manufacture. To buy a physical product is to buy the time spent working on it – crystallized in a physical form. Moreover, apart from the cost of the time itself, the value of such an object also depends on the qualifications of its manufacturer. If we define qualification as a shorter or longer period of acquisition knowledge, know-how and experience, then it too can be reduced and quantified in terms of time-units. The qualification of the work team is transferred to the product in the form of the quality (practically defined as user satisfaction against the expectations and/or the claims advertised), the price (the lowest possible for the same quality) and variety offered.

Services and time

To buy a service is to buy work time, not in the form of some material product, but the *qualified work time of an individual or an institution that is placed at the disposal of a private individual or organization.* As such, the customer buys him/herself, for a fixed period of time, one or more of the following:

- the rights to use a material product (which itself is an embodiment of a quantity of work time);
- someone else's time (personal service, tourism, the restaurant business, consultancy);
- a way of saving time (retail shopping, telephony); and
- someone else's qualification (health, education, leisure activities, television, journals and magazines).

The services targeted towards enterprises have the same elements, except that here, the prime objective is the purchase of a *potential for productivity gains* – that is, the purchase of more-or-less qualified work time from outside the enterprise at a price lower than would have to be paid internally, and might at the same time prove to be more efficient than the internal workforce.

This purchase of more-or-less qualified work time brings into force a service relationship, which also entails face-to-face contact between people. Though as yet in most cases it takes the form of a direct face-to-face meeting, the telephone and the internet are becoming ever more important in effecting this relationship. There can also be service relations without there being any real relation of service in the sense of 'face to face' contact (except at the time of purchase) such as in the purchase of all types of media, and in transportation, banks and insurance companies. In all these services, back-office work dominates the face-to-face relationship.

From an anthropological point of view, this purchase of others' time can be perceived as being closely linked to the never-ending struggle against the passage of time, against its wear and tear and its ravages – it is the eternal struggle of all mankind against fate itself. In some situations, though, this purchase is more of an anticipatory (preventive) measure. Thus one of the foundations of the theory underlying the services offered is the question of time. Most of the services targeted at individuals (health, home maintenance and household appliances) and at enterprises (cleaning, general maintenance) stem from this struggle against the wear and tear of time. In one form or another, it consists of making *repairs* to the damage caused by the passage of time.

On the other hand, insurance (especially social security and pensions), bank loans, and in a certain sense even education, can be seen as anticipatory actions taken as precautions against, or in anticipation of, future eventualities. Insurance against damages hope to cover potential risks and hazards, and contributions to retirement funds are a bulwark against certain inevitable eventualities, including old age. Bank loans and purchases on credit depend on an anticipated income. Other services, such as transportation, retail, telephony and business computing save time by bringing people closer together or by increasing data processing speeds. The remaining services depend greatly on manipulating information (particularly the 'cultural industries' such as crafts, film, sound recording and book publishing) and on communication, which is the second pillar of the theory of services (see below).

The cost of these services lies along a continuous line which goes from being given away free ('rendering service') to being extremely highly priced, in the case of rare information. Public services are free only in appearance – they are in fact the result of a complex redistribution of tax revenues. Other services, such as banks and insurance agencies, function by sharing risks and financial needs based on fund availability. A number of services continue to be attached to industrial products, such as the maintenance of household appliances, computers and their peripherals, video and hi-fi equipment, and motor vehicles. These services are all justified by the financial advantages they represent when the alternative would be the replacement of the entire piece of equipment. Consequently, the maintenance or repair of cheaper products is not viable and, in fact, fast disappearing. On the other hand, the cost of services to enterprises (consultancy regarding policy issues, finance and computer systems) can reach dizzying heights when it becomes a question of the very survival of the company and its directors.

In each of these cases, the qualification (or the competency) of the serving personnel forms an intrinsic part of the service relationship and is included in the service itself. In fact, it *is* the service (for example, to diagnose and repair a broken television set or give the correct train schedule to a passenger). This is what distinguishes it from the purchase of an industrial product – the collective qualification that went into the product loses its worth at the very instant it is bought. The moment something is bought, it is only the qualification or expertise of the buyer that can in future meet any subsequent needs. For example, success in making a delicious sauce does not depend on the manufacturing quality of the mixer or utensils used, but on the talent of the buyer. On the other hand, the success in a service relationship depends primarily on the competency of the service provider. Primarily, but not entirely – as the service relationship brings together, at the very least, two people, the qualities of the client also come into the picture.

From interaction to repairs

We could thus consider the relation of service as, first, an *interaction* between people, and resort to the concepts of Goffman[7] to analyse it further. According to Joseph and Gadrey,[8] the relation of service should be seen as a repair – much like the verbal relation between doctors and patients – and has three dimensions:

- a *technical* dimension, which allows a doctor to obtain the information required for the diagnosis and treatment of a patient, or a technician for an object to be repaired;
- a *contractual* dimension, which defines the working area and, most importantly, the cost. Depending on the nature of the service, the payment terms are either more-or-less fixed, or are to be settled between the two parties. This negotiation can sometimes be a lengthy process, because the user or buyer often does not have the means to evaluate the quality of the service; and
- a social or *civil* dimension – that is, the interactions between the concerned parties, which include the usual rituals of politeness and shows of respect. Though, as pointed out by Joseph, the service technician should not confuse his/her work with the nature of these exchanges, as these (such as a show of good faith or, conversely, of suspicion) have a great influence on the two other dimensions, especially the technical dimension, once the contract has been defined.

Such a concept should now help in differentiating clearly between a service and the sale of a physical product: in a service, nothing is given away or alienated, as in the sale of a product. The service relationship is a process that brings two people together (in more-or-less direct contact), and they work jointly to 'repair' the product or 'remedy' the situation. As soon as the repairer comes into contact with the customer, they work together to formulate the contract and devise a solution (exchange of technical information) by the means of more civil exchanges. Such is the theoretical basis of the *co-production of service*, which consists essentially of an exchange of information and the attendant communication between two people. All three dimensions (technical, contractual and civil) depend on communication, and the success of the service relies heavily on the quality of the latter.

Information, communication and co-production of service

To analyse a service is to study the qualified time placed at the disposal of the user by the service provider. This could very well be the definition of an employee, except that in a service there is no idea of subordination, of someone being under the control of another. To say that some qualified time is put at the disposal of the customer is to talk about some active time. For example, a client who wants a loan from a bank has to make an appointment and go to the branch office. There, s/he has to give reasons why the loan is needed, prove his or her earning power (income) and declare any liabilities. For his/her part, the bank official has to set out to the customer the various terms and conditions of the loan (duration, interest, insurance and the monthly instalments). After this oral exchange and the reaching of a mutually acceptable agreement, both parties sign a document with the usual clauses detailing the handing over of the money. This is, in this case, the 'repairs' – an interaction, a co-production, a *connection* between two carriers of information that makes the service provider use his/her time (expensive) alongside that of the client. We could thus speak of a *'chronnection'*, to designate an exchange or a communication between two people in which one of the partners puts his/her time (of work) at the disposal of the other. Almost the whole exchange is a trading of information, including the result – in this case the loan contract – the signed document being only a paper support.

Services and information

One can show that practically all service relations are based on an exchange of information taking place within a specific time frame. By simple extrapolation, we can include within this definition the vast majority of all personal services (barber, dry cleaner, spa and so on) and the various repairs undertaken at home. Apart from the physical action itself, all these services comprise the temporary placement of a qualification at the disposal of the user. It is not only the contract or the civilities of the service relationship that are informative in nature, but the technical exchanges (what is the problem? when? how?) also depend largely on the exchange of information. On the other hand, the qualification (which determines a correct and speedy diagnosis and repair) is more a crystallization of knowledge, know-how and experience – that is, of information embodied by the technician (hairdresser, repairman, cleaner or doctor).

The service relationship can thus be defined as:

- the availability of a substantial amount of information crystallized in the form of the qualifications of the service providers (which shows the importance of their training), or in notices, user manuals, databases, for example. This information is useful only when activated – that is, when selected and arranged in a manner that would lead to the attainment of the objective (which could include the expected working of a product, its repair or any anticipated outcome);

- an (intense) exchange of information between the service provider and the user (including the exchange between service providers themselves, if there happens to be more than one present); and
- the shifting of people and materials as directed by the information specified above and linked to the stated objectives. Thus, except in rare instances, the dematerialization of service activities did not signify the complete elimination of all material infrastructure – there still remained the physical supports of the information.

The question boils down to: What is information? In our context, we could define it as *a signal that has the potential to change the state of the receiver.* In the absence of a receiver, the information becomes a lost or wasted signal. For example, the sun's rays can modify the mood of a holidaymaker or quicken a lizard, but it has no effect on a stone or a derelict building. The concept of a signal is very generic as it refers not only to something significant for a thinking being, but also to the purely mechanical signal that a machine can transmit to another in order to stop it, start it or change its course without there being any question of thinking or any significance attached to its functioning.

We term as *successful communication* any communication that brings about the required change in the state of the receiver, whether it depends on an understanding of a significance and requires thinking or not. A successful communication differs from a simple communication by the fact that it results in a change in the state of the receiver in accordance with what was expected by the sender when communication began. Such a definition of communication is central to an understanding of Gadrey's definition of the service relationship and of the nature of services in general – the informational interactions between two actors with a view to transforming the state of an object in the possession of the user-actor.

Two types of communication

Service can thus be defined as a successful communication between the service provider and the user – that is, as *user B's willingness to see a reality, C, in which s/he is interested, being modified by A, who had been asked to provide the service.* The quality of the service, (that is, B's satisfaction by the change wrought in C) depends on the quality of the service relationship and therefore on the quality of the communication between A and B. We can make a distinction between two types of successful communication:

- the *instrumental communication*, which depends on an exchange of signals without reference to any significance or thought regarding the signals or the language. It characterizes inter- or intra-machine communications, those between people and machines, as in the case of starting a mechanized process, and those between machine and people in which they react purely by reflex. Instrumental communication can also characterize person-to-person relations when one obeys the other without thinking (for example, the automatic response to 'switch off the light', 'could you get me a glass of water?');
- the *comprehensive communication*, which takes into account the significance, and thereby the contextualization and thought in the process of change to be wrought in the state of the recipient. Such are the relations between a machine and person in which the individual has to interpret some signs and refer to a manual or his/her know-how in order to repair a household appliance, a car or a machine tool, for example. Obviously, these comprehensive communications also encompass most person-to-person relations as well as social exchanges.[9]

To succeed, the service relationship must be based on a comprehensive communication – a simple instrumental exchange will not do, except perhaps just barely in the case of a 'service rendered'. As it involves two human beings, the service relationship, just like comprehensive communication, needs to be based on some kind of significance and contextualization. The recipient also takes on the role of an emitter, and the communication becomes reactive and interactive. A successful comprehensive communication would thus result in a reciprocal change in the status of both parties – the user and the service provider – who come together to build the service relationship. Hence the double idea of the *co-construction of the service relationship* and the *co-production of the service*, which we came across regarding the 'repairworker effect' of service taken from the concepts of Joseph, who borrowed them from the analyses of interactions by Goffman.

The idea of co-production of service also includes the uncertain nature of this relationship, which *unites* as well as *opposes* the two parties. It unites because the two must come together and produce a result; and it opposes in the sense that there always exists some uncertainty regarding the contract, with or without any financial consideration. The first cause of uncertainty is obviously the imbalance in the relationship between the 'expert' service provider and the 'amateur' user. But there is also, closely linked to the question of its formulation, uncertainty regarding the process itself, with shades of a symbolic domination and fears regarding the monetary or symbolic cost. A co-production of the service entails active participation by the user – s/he has to keep the service provider informed and detail his/her requirements as and when the 'repair' progresses. Even the end of the repair work is never completely defined in the contract because the contract itself is constantly being readjusted. The service provider's capacity to react while having his/her status constantly changed depends on resourcefulness – the level of expertise being judged by the amount and quality of the information at one's disposal.

Services in an information society

If the co-production of service depends on communication, and thus on an exchange of information, we must take a closer look at the nature of information and in particular its value. It is common knowledge that information can be given and retained at the same time – in fact, that is one of its essential characteristics. At the same time, all information of any user value quickly becomes outdated. This rapid obsolescence makes information the king of all commodities in the capitalist system. Every day sees new editions of newspapers; though TV and radio news bulletins are aired many times in the day, each one is different, with an updated and up-to-the-minute account. Similarly, software needs constantly to be kept up to date, and customer files and surveys have also to be renewed incessantly, replacing the previous, outdated versions. Similarly, repair technicians also have to keep pace with the relentlessly evolving products on the market, products that have become so sophisticated and evolved so fast that the user is all too often left hopelessly out of date and helpless.

There was a time when this characteristic of information – that it could be kept and given away at the same time – led people to dream of a time when information would upend the capitalist system itself. The fact that information could be replicated and distributed indefinitely while still keeping it was thought to cut at the very roots of present-day commerce, which is based on the rarity of an object (its user value). The internet was seen as its herald and first knight (the information within it being often free). But reality quickly caught up and information began to bear the burden of a commercial value based on this very characteristic of transience. This is why it is indispensable that this ephemerality be put at the very heart of any definition of information, because it is this tendency towards a rapid obsolescence that will lie behind all future commercial relations. And, as they spread and their influence turns out to be at least as important to a theoretical construct, it will not do to remain wedded to the production of goods and capital alone.

The service relationship – a double triangle

Thus, while it is true that the seller of any information has the advantage of also retaining it (as opposed to a commercial product), we must also take into account its temporal nature in order to study the information network, and more specifically the nature of its links to the user, because, frequently, the owner of the information network does not normally meet the end users themselves.

Other actors

While in the past the physical separation of the product also severed the link between the seller and the buyer, today things are different: not only is the link maintained through the means of service, but there is also the entry of a third person, the service provider. He or she is an employee who embodies the link between the service network and the client. In other words, instead of a definitive break there is now a lasting triangulation, which associates or separates:

- the user and the expert employee in a service relationship that is to be co-produced through more-or-less direct face-to-face contact;
- the expert-employee and their employer-cum-proprietor of the service network (made of more-or-less dense information) in a wage relationship; and
- the user-customer and the employer-service provider, who is both the owner of the network and the employer of the expert in a commercial relation.

This triangulation between the employer, employee-expert and user can be combined with Gadrey's service triangle. We could thus represent the complex service relationship, which includes the commercial relation between the user and employer and the wage relationship between the employer and expert in the manner shown in Figure 6.3.

The service relationship and the wage relationship

It is possible that A and A' come together in the same person as in the case of craftspeople (hairdressers, mechanics, taxi drivers, teachers of a particular course, for example). In such cases the negotiation of two contracts – the

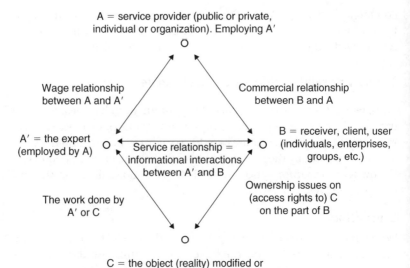

A = service provider (public or private,
individual or organization). Employing A′

Wage relationship
between A and A′

Commercial relationship
between B and A

A′ = the expert
(employed by A)

Service relationship =
informational interactions
between A′ and B

B = receiver, client, user
(individuals, enterprises,
groups, etc.)

The work done by
A′ or C

Ownership issues on
(access rights to) C
on the part of B

C = the object (reality) modified or
worked on by the expert A′ for the benefit of B

Figure 6.3   The double triangle of the service relationship
Source: J. Gadrey, *L'économie des services* (1992).

commercial contract and the contract of the service relationship itself – will reduce to only one. But in a society dominated by wage-earners, the service relationship is most often channelled through an employee of an enterprise (or of any other organization, including the public sector) with whom the user signs a 'service contract'.

This bi-triangular relationship is essential to an understanding of the evolution of work since the mid-1980s. While yesterday a growth in industrial productivity depended on streamlining labour, especially in the manufacturing process, today, an improvement in the service industries depends on streamlining the service relationship – that is, by streamlining the relationship between expert and user (or client). This service relationship depends mainly on a co-production of the service, based in turn on comprehensive communication. The latter is necessarily time-consuming, with the required exchange of civilities, contextualization, reciprocal adjustments and laying out the contract to be settled before going to the heart of the matter and starting any technical dialogue. The technical dialogue is an interaction that helps to develop a mutual understanding between the two parties until the needs of the user have been satisfied.

The whole thing then comes down to this: can we streamline comprehensive communication? If so, how? Should it be reduced to instrumental communication? Do we have other options? And as for ourselves, observers and analysts, where do we stand on this issue?

Introducing tight flow in the service industry

The general effort to improve the competitiveness of services is directed not so much towards improving quality – notwithstanding all the talk and propaganda – as on reducing their cost. This tendency is as true for the public services as for those given by private enterprises to individual or to other companies. The main method of reducing costs usually means increasing the number of service relations established (successfully) per unit of employee-time, by using two or more of the following devices:

- Establishing a procedure in the service relationship to dispense quickly with the civilities and accelerate the laying out of the contract in order to get to the heart of the technicalities as soon as possible.
- To place the waiting users in a tight flow or to make use of this system in the organization of the service production itself.
- The consequent reduction in the small bits of downtime and the systematization of work in 'hidden time' (simultaneously working at frontline activities such as carrying on a dialogue with the client while looking for technical answers in a database).
- Taking recourse to information and communication technology to control precisely the progress of the service relationship as well as the production of service, to reduce the gaps in work time and to implement tight flow or the work in 'hidden time'.

There are a number of studies and research reports that attest to these efforts at reducing the costs by reorganizing work and making extensive use of ICT in almost all sectors – banks and insurance companies, hospitals (including medicine and surgery), social work, the management of human resources (by using e-HRM), in project management using groupware, in the fast food business, in retail business and by sales reps,[10] for example. Obviously, we cannot hope to take examples from and analyse every sector, so we shall content ourselves by giving some examples culled from call centres and retail stores.

From the tele-operators to the cashiers in hypermarkets

Telephone calls are a major distraction and disturbance to service enterprises, be they targeted at individuals or the public sector. Employees and executives are obliged to drop everything and attend immediately to a task that is, more often than not, far removed from the job in hand. After attending to the telephone call they then have to return to their original job, very probably to be disturbed once again after a short time. Moreover, in most cases, problems could have been solved by someone less qualified than these employees, who are busy with other, more specialized, services. It was for this reason that a special job position was created, manned by people who could answer questions with the help of a client file and a knowledge base that could be accessed through a computer terminal. It did not take long for this 'client service' to be externalized and sub-contracted. At the same time, the telephone was being rediscovered as a major commercial tool: telephone enquiries, telemarketing, calls linked to TV broadcasts such as teleshopping, and sales by correspondence.

The variety of the tasks handled by call centres makes it difficult to give a single comprehensive idea. On the one hand we have the internal call centres requiring a high level of expertise, which attend to and repair sophisticated equipment (with long call durations), while on the other hand, we have externalized call centres with employees in insecure jobs handling marketing calls that are often of short duration and highly codified. In the latter category, the high employment turnover (up to 40 per cent per year) is proof enough of the difficult work conditions that prevail. Here, tight flow is manifested by the queue of waiting calls (sometimes displayed on the screen). One call is followed immediately by another, either appended automatically (with a delay of between 0 and 20 seconds depending on the call centre), or taken manually after a maximum of two to three rings. The tele-operators can log themselves out for a breather once in a while, if they do this too often or without a valid reason they will need to answer to the in supervisor.

In these call centres, the employees have to follow a very strict communication protocol, not only to save time and money, but especially to reduce call duration and thereby increase the number of calls attended to per hour. Here too, the operators find themselves under the eye, or rather the ear, of their supervisors, who listen in to make sure that things are proceeding according to script. In most of these call centres, tele-operators are always on the lookout for, and use all their ingenuity to find, ways of escaping this surveillance, or to try to negotiate some sort of autonomy for themselves.

The pressures of tight flow understandably have an adverse effect on service quality. Ergonomists and occupational health specialists talk of the ethical conflict between the quick and the good: can we speed up the call process and satisfy the client at the same time? The Confédération Générale du Travail conducted a survey on workload in a telemarketing call centre where the telephone numbers are dialled automatically (30 per cent of respondents out of 100 employees): 33 per cent of the tele-operators (who were all female) thought that they never had enough time to complete their job satisfactorily; 47 per cent thought this happened occasionally; while 17 per cent felt they had sufficient time. As regards pressure, 33 per cent of respondents felt that they were under constant stress; 36 per cent thought it to was an occasional problem; and 31 per cent found they were never stressed. As for the work itself, 70 per cent thought it repetitive as against 28 per cent who found it of interest them.

These results clearly show the essential characteristics of work in such call centres, which do not deal in any great value addition to the information. Theirs is work that is under constant pressure from the line of waiting calls, impoverished by a routine and a communication that must subscribe to a rigid protocol. Understandably, it needs a high ratio of supervisors (one supervisor for eight to ten tele-operators on average) to push and monitor as closely as possible employees who otherwise would immediately relax or even give up. They must provide both psychological and moral support while retaining to their traditional task of control and discipline. Such an impoverished and scripted service relationship loses its essence and is reduced to the status of instrumental communication, devoid of any significance. But this is to be expected: if the call centres have industrialized and serialized the service relationship, this would naturally eliminate any personal touch or significance from the exchange between user and provider. But that does not bother the service enterprise, which would much rather concentrate on short-term economic efficiency than on the satisfaction of the client. As we shall soon see, this is not too far from recent developments in retail, in which cashiers find themselves placed under similar constraints.

In supermarkets, cost reduction is achieved mainly by judicious management of the pressure of clients and their shopping trolleys. Faced with this pressure, cashiers put themselves on automatic pilot:

> Just as the worker, the cashier is not master of her work. She has no autonomy. She has to follow the rhythm set by the clients and her machine. In a rush of clients, she herself feels as though she were no more than a cork, being swept along with the flood. At the same time, Linhart points out in *L'établi* that it is difficult for the worker to really become an automaton because all kinds of external elements will come to disturb the pure repetitiveness of a perfect automatism. These external elements can be of different kinds: the foreman, a delay in the flow, a machine breakdown, and so on. It is the same for

these cashiers. A complete automatism is difficult to come by because every client interaction is different. Each customer has his or her own peculiarity.[11]

In spite of these difficulties, taking on the attitude of an automaton remained the best way of dealing with pressure. But that was exactly what the management did not want. Against such a 'locking oneself in the state of an automaton', management wanted the employee to develop a real relationship with the clients. In France this took the form of the famous SBAM (see Chapter 4), which the cashiers were required to implement in their dealings with clients. But a closer look reveals the absurdity of this, and one cannot but smile at the neat manner in which a necessarily complex, comprehensive communication has been instrumentalized by codifying it in 'SBAM'. By codifying social interactions in this way, management has once again sided with productivity in the ethical conflict between the speed of dealing with a client and the quality of the relationship. In fact, in some cases, nothing more than SBAM was permitted, and the supervisor could at any moment demand that the cashier justify any ongoing discussion with a customer. The minimizing of the service relationship can also be seen in the set of gestures adopted by staff who used their hand or a finger to indicate what the client was supposed to do: bring a product closer, turn a heavy object so that the barcode can be read, place the credit card in the reader or take it out and so on. Physical fatigue, the retreat into the role of an automaton, part-time work contracts, a lack of interest in the work, stress caused by dealing with too many clients – all of these contribute to a deterioration of the service relationship and the disappearance of its very essence (that of a significant interaction, it being between humans) in the face of streamlining and productivity gains.

The co-production of service and the degradation of the services

Another way of looking at the co-production of services is to see how, slowly but surely, workload gets transferred from service provider to client. As we have already seen, this co-production of service prolongs the social interaction between the two partners, while at the same time there is a slight difference because it consists of work outside the interaction itself. It is work that requires expenditure of energy, or rather, the spending of working time whose burden has slowly shifted from service provider to client, with his or her agreement. But can s/he escape it?

In retail business, clients fill their own trolleys, lug their purchases to the cashier, unload them on to the conveyor belt, pack them into plastic bags,[12] and then have to return the trolley (to get their coin back). In return, clients get to choose their products (especially fruit and vegetables) and do not have to face sales staff (though they also lose their support and advice) – they have the freedom to move around, look and compare without obligation. This transfer of workload helps greatly in streamlining activities within a store: there is no more idle time spent waiting for clients, then having to explain and guide, and having to smilingly witness their unending hesitations. Almost everything can be foreseen in broad outline, from the behaviour of customers to their purchases, and there is a constant process of streamlining, from shelf-stacking to the arrival of the goods at the checkout. The whole setup is geared to improving on the previous year's sales figures. The Auchan Group of hypermarkets has succeeded in creating a veritable cult of sales figures in all its branches, right down to their sales people in the Decathlon sporting goods chain. The entire setup is mobilized by a system of bonuses and shares, and has undoubtedly been a great employee motivating factor.

While retailing has managed to make clients do a lot of the work without minding terribly much or finding it beneath their dignity, a number of other services had to resort to different means and replaced face-to-face interaction with call centres. Air and rail tickets are being purchased increasingly over the telephone, with the company and travel agencies avoiding as far as possible over-the-counter ticket sales. Obviously, call centres were a powerful means of avoiding the porosity of working time enjoyed by personnel who were paid on a monthly basis and who often found themselves with little to do during off-peak times. Call centres maintain pressure on their employees via the queue of waiting customer calls, and peak hours always find too few employees. Customers are therefore obliged to find for themselves time slots when the lines are less busy. They thus organize and regulate tight flow within the enterprise by broadening working time. In other words, the service provider obliged the clients to adapt themselves to certain constraints if they wished to be satisfied. Even better, such a co-production of service meant that the client paid the service provider – through the high cost of the telephone interaction – for buying their ticket, a service that previously had been cost-free! Such a co-production of service seems highly unfair on the client, who not only co-organizes the work of the provider by spreading calls over the day, but even pays for the call centre staff via the surcharge on the telephone calls.

Gradually, the relationship between clients and their banks has also begun to take a similar turn. Gone are the days when clients could drop by for an informal chat with their account manager regarding some discovery or reply to a request for a loan. Banks have now placed a filter between the client and the agent in the form of the call centre and the agent is thus free to attend to other, more 'productive' jobs such as debt recovery, writing out loan forms, other banking services (by appointment), and managing share market orders. The streamlining of bank work meant the pushing of the client out towards the periphery where s/he would be looked after by an external service provider (the call centre). This, of course, meant that the service relationship with the bank itself has begun to deteriorate.

There is no end to the number of examples that could illustrate this gradual shift in the co-production of service where clients have begun to take upon themselves at least a part of the workload: the self-stamping of train tickets, self-service petrol pumps, cheaper hotels with no receptionist in sight (clients have to pay remotely and prepare their own breakfast), holiday clubs where clients have to make their own beds, and fill their own plates from the buffet spread. All this without counting the number of claims arising from the automatic billing systems used by the telephone companies or car rentals. In these cases, the co-production of the service revolves around a complete imbalance, in which the service provider enjoys a monopoly and/or that once the service has been rendered, they have complete control over tariffs and billing, either via pre-payment or automatic money transfer from the client's account.

We must then conclude that the slogan 'the customer is king' is nothing but a myth, told not so much to please the client (who is no longer as gullible) but directed repeatedly at employees to try to motivate and encourage them into taking a more active part in streamlining the service. The service itself has begun to externalize the more easily standardized jobs (call centres, of course, but also different sorts of sub-contracts such as cleaning, maintenance, even the development of standardized products and sub-assemblies), and, in certain sectors, by gradually eliminating comprehensive communication from the service relationship. We can perhaps now draw up a table to illustrate the different ways in which service work, and employment in general, has grown.

Mapping the functions of employees

Figure 6.4 includes the functions and jobs from the industrial sector because it would complete the picture and also because the services aimed at the enterprises can no longer be separated from the production of goods. For example, the maintenance of any installation comes under the heading 'industrial' when it is performed by workers and technicians employed by the mother company, but the very same job is called a service when it is sub-contracted.

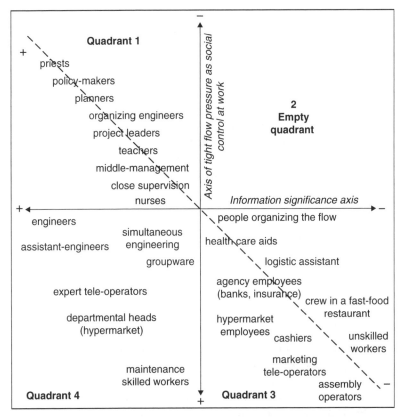

Figure 6.4 Functions according to the treatment of information and the pressure of tight flow

Based on what has been said in this chapter and in Chapter 1, where we showed the importance of tight flow in the *combinatoire productive*, we can now arrange functions and jobs along two principal axes: one that represents the pressure of the tight flow on the employee, and the other representing the degree to which the significance of the information exchanged is used.

As a controlling agent, tight flow does not weigh equally on all company personnel. Close to the heart of the flow are those who have even their gestures regulated by it, while alongside them are those who belong more to the supervisory or managerial ranks, such as project leaders, doctors and teachers. Time-units also differ widely: at one extreme we have a single second as the unit of time (assembly workers and tele-operators at call centres), which may go up to a minute in the case of waiters in fast food restaurants, cashiers, surveillance personnel, and 30 minutes in the case of departmental heads, personnel who organize the flow, and logistics process planners. At the other extreme, it can average a month (even a year for some policy-makers) and go down to the week or a day for engineers and technicians who form part of groupware or are involved in parallel or simultaneous engineering.[13] While in the latter case time exerts a less of a direct pressure, the intellectual problems and diversity of factors to be considered can become just as stressful when the objectives seem to be receding just beyond what is achievable.

From relational work to the codification of significance

The second axis represents a similar hierarchy. At one extremity we have the policy-makers, engineers, project leaders, management and workers or technicians given the task of surveillance. They make extensive use of ICT and need to interpret the signals they receive – that is, they work on the signals' significance and put them in the right context in order to initiate an action: the design of a product or a process, the decision to buy or sell, to invest or not, and so on, or to draw up directives for a group or an individual, for the loading of a tool before its use after a breakdown. These employees use a computer screen (or any ICT terminal) to combine, relate, co-ordinate and place in the correct context all information, as well as to relate to others – this is work that is really about the meaning of information.

This is also the definition of *relational work* as it has been seen since the mid-1980s, and has characterized the new production paradigm.[14] All the employees mentioned above have to put their objectives in relation to their environment or their colleagues in order to achieve the fixed objectives. Obviously, these relations depend on the interpretation and an understanding of the various signals; that is, there must be a free exchange or contextual significance of objects between them. Management is very much a part of this relational work: even if its objectives are different, by definition it is a placing into a relationship, through understanding and interpretation, of management and its human environment.

At the other end of this second axis lie all those jobs that do not deal with interpretation or any thinking that determines the next action. They include not only assembly work, luggage and goods handling, waiting on at fast food restaurants and hotels, but also data entry (typing, data input) which does not necessarily entail working with contextualizing or data analysis. On the contrary, in fact – any time spent thinking might be detrimental to efficiency. For example, motor vehicle assembly workers sometimes have to consult the progress card to ascertain the precise part to be installed – if they start to think about the shelf number and where to find it, or to wonder about the function of the part and how to install it, they will be wasting time and might slow up the whole line. To avoid any such eventuality and to discourage any thinking or the possibility of error, engineers have incorporated foolproof devices, called *poka-yoke*,[15] wherever possible. The signal – which increasingly takes the form of pictograms stuck to the machine tools – is far more important than the object being signified. The same thing can be said by showing that the act of data entry, without giving any thought to the significance of the contents, means that what we are witnessing is a process of instrumentalization.

When we talk of *instrumentalizing the significance* or of *codifying the significance*, what we would like to emphasize is that the information taken in by the worker (or employee) is just a code or a set of signs that correspond to a procedure s/he has previously learnt by heart. Though this code has an object – the thing signified – it does not require any thinking or contextualizing, and the oft-repeated procedure itself is a means of saving time (by a judicious pruning and streamlining of movements), and is automatic and reflexive. In other words, many jobs that deal with or make use of ICT do not entail any growth in qualification apart from being able to read and write.[16] There is therefore no clear link between the widespread use of ICT in the industrial and tertiary sectors and any increase in qualifications, because many of these jobs deal precisely with this process of instrumentalism.

Obviously, there exists a wide variety of jobs between these two extremes of work. There are a number of high-level managerial posts that require repetitive and procedural activities, while codified work in a fast food restaurant might need some form of interpretation under special circumstances (evidently within the limits of what is possible, especially within the bounds of hygiene and profitability).

The monitoring of the manufacturing process, the distribution and the processing of information comes somewhere between these two extremes. In essence, any interruption produces a slew of data (on the surveillance monitor as well as on the machine itself), then comes the diagnosis, and finally the repair and the return to work. Of all these steps, the diagnosis is the most interesting because, in spite of all their efforts, neither knowledge engineers nor psychologists have been able to come up with a general system capable of meeting all eventualities – that is, to eliminate the importance of a contextual interpretation[17] and the necessity for thought. Nevertheless, management has always sought to codify the diagnostic process in any given situation[18] either by delineating a procedure or, as we have already shown, by the use of preventive measures. Most preventive maintenance is itself largely codified and 'procedurized'. Similarly, we could show that the purchase of goods or services within the company and its relations with its clients (and suppliers) depend on extremely refined procedures. And while the reason given is quality of service, its traceability and consequent repeatability, we would rather think that the main justification and dominating factor is an effort at cost reduction by making use of automatic, fixed, tried and tested procedures.

Resistance to the industrialization of services

Thus there is a close link between cost reduction, standardizing procedures (including through the use of ICTs) and the reduction of significance: clearly the aim is to raise employee productivity by avoiding, whenever and wherever possible, thinking and interpretation. The effort to escape meaning and significance in order to transform all input into an immediate, value-adding, productive activity, either by reflex or by having been 'automatized', remains the essential point in the economizing of time, which is the dominant social paradigm of the present time.

While a growing number of people agree with this view, the resistance to this industrialization – that is, to the process of a radical streamlining that was first evolved in the industrial sector – in some services (education, health and engineering consulting bureaux, for example) must be looked at with care. Basing his work on other studies, Gadrey has emphasized the

> difficulty in standardizing the problems to be resolved and the solutions to be implemented. In effect, the methods used by professionals are intellectual methods (based on personal knowledge) of identifying and solving problems under uncertain and often unstable situations. They provide, for specific, 'typified' cases, the steps to follow, the information gathered, the intellectual 'routines' to set in motion. They often contain prefabricated modules which need to be combined with other, tailor-made modules. But at the same time, they leave a wide margin of freedom and their improvement does not seem to curtail this freedom in any way. It is of course possible that these professionals make sure that these exercises do not start encroaching on this margin by, for example, constantly creating more incertitude by coming up with further innovations and thus continually pushing the frontiers of streamlining.[19]

As shown by Gadrey, resistance to the industrialization of some services does not stem from a scientific impossibility inherent in the nature of the activities themselves, but from institutional factors. The well-entrenched and influential professionals in these services and institutions did not allow new entrants into their domain, newcomers who might break the rules of engagement. At the same time, they also prevented any sponsoring authorities or clients from imposing new ones. At most, these professionals give the simpler and easily standardized jobs to less qualified employees (back-office staff). On the other hand, they sometimes take to using standardized methods and routines in a bid to gain time for themselves. This is not at all the same as following the standardized procedure and applying it mechanically, keeping to the prescribed rules without any autonomy or freedom of judgement.

Apart from these professional services, other activities, such as maintenance departments, engineering and banking also put up some resistance, though with a varying degrees of success. Employee functions thus divide into a two dimensional space (see Figure 6.4).

Autonomy and working on the significance

The 'empty quadrant' (panel 2) in Figure 6.4, which represents the intersection between the lower end of tight flow (in other words, longer time spans) and the non-use of information (codification of the significance, with automatized answers) is in fact quite logical. This is because, in the absence of stringent time constraints, all activities necessarily involve the gathering and control of information (knowledge in general). At the other end, the pressures of tight flow prevent employees – especially those who deal directly with physical goods – from having anything to do with the significance of the information. This is, in other words, what we mean by instrumentalized communication.

Thus, over and above the two principal axes shown, there is a third, virtual axis that passes diagonally through quadrants 1 and 3. The axis represents the autonomy in work (control over one's own time and the freedom to organize it) and the interest shown in their work by the different categories of employees in relation to their work conditions (whether subjected to the pressures of the flow, or not). At one end stand the policy-makers, the planners and the engineer-organizers, while at the other end are the assembly workers, labourers, cashiers and employees in the retail stores and fast food restaurants. It follows that, on this virtual axis, the functions that depend more on significance also help to motivate employees and hold their interest while giving them some measure of autonomy because their work is not subjected to the time pressures of the flow.

It is not the same matter at all for those functions and posts that appear in quadrant 4. Here, though work does involve taking into account the sense of the information, it relies too heavily on fixed procedures and is subjected to the temporal pressures of the flow. Such is the plight of engineers and technicians who are charged with the execution of a project, including those certified personnel who are responsible for the supervision of the flow. These functions and posts do not figure on the axis of autonomy. In fact, they have given rise to heated debate, and their status as well as their work has remained ambivalent since the 1980s. They clearly show the difficulties inherent in any scientific analysis of the changes wrought in work in different sectors by the two main paradigms that have transformed the entire concept of work today – the massive use of information and computer technologies, and the generalization of tight flow. Both these tools help in streamlining work by increasing its efficiency per unit of time. Chapter 7 will consider the nature and sense of these transformations in relation to the autonomy, or the constraints, that present working conditions might bring about.

7
More Difficult but More Interesting Work? Intensification and Autonomy

Sociologists of work and employment, managers, trade unionists, managers of human resources, corporate executives all have a different interpretation of the transformations that have so shaken our concept of work since the 1980s. But before going into these various interpretations, it might be better to step back a little and question the status of the researchers themselves, or rather, question the reasons that made them take up their investigations. We must also remind ourselves that a social reality, in this case the enterprise, can never be understood completely, and that its every fold, far from being a metaphor and revealing some aspect of reality, is in fact a screen that hides empirical reality.

No wonder, then, that every investigator has his or her own interpretation of the dramatic changes that have taken place in the post-Fordian productive system, the massive utilization of ICT and the significant rise in the educational level of employees. Moreover, these debates and disputes are not confined to the no-man's-land between different categories of scholars or researchers, but can also be found bubbling up within and between the members of every group. As regards the scholars and observers who are more or less external to the enterprise, the differences between them revolve around three main points: focusing on any particular category of employees, the principal reason for entering the enterprise, and finally, the depth of their study – that is, at what point they stop their investigation because they feel that they have now pierced the opaque veil surrounding the 'social object' known as the enterprise.

Can we see through the veil?

We can take for granted the reality that no researcher, let alone research team, is able to study absolutely every facet of an organization of any respectable size, including the different categories of employee. Each one therefore embarks on their study with a specific set of questions dealing with a certain category of worker. They must limit themselves to addressing either the employees, the technicians, the engineers, the management, or the newer employees in the fast-emerging sectors such as cashiers, the crew at a McDonald's outlet or tele-operators in call centres. Moreover, these studies can each focus on only one of a range of subjects: qualifications or competencies, the nature of employment, autonomy in work, evaluating work efficiency (or the productive apparatus as a whole), management methods, or the means of employee motivation. While some concentrate on analysing work in the context of time constraints, others would rather study relational work and the role played by mediators. Though all these choices are made ostensibly in order to satisfy a 'social need', they are in fact influenced in large part by the personal interests of the researcher, by political and emotional predilections, and their current status within this or that research institute.

Apart from these obvious biases, analysts also differ from each other on another important criterion – the objective. Some come not only with their own research in mind (these are also the ones who have the most difficulty in accessing the enterprise), others arrive on the scene and at the behest of national or European institutions for similar work, but within clearly defined guidelines. They often find themselves hampered by difficulties in accessing data or approaching some personnel. Still others come as participant-researchers – that is, at the request of management, and deal primarily only with those issues of interest to managers – obviously at the cost of others that might be more systemic to the enterprise but that management would rather see swept under the carpet. Finally, it is always possible that experts are called in by some sort of labour union, either the Works Council or the Industrial Health and Safety Committee. Obviously, one's starting point and approach have a considerable influence on the results of any analysis. But the issue here is not to accuse any person or team naïvely of being a victim of their affiliation or position within an institution: all of us are more or less subject to this. The point is simply to highlight some of the possible reasons on offer for the variety of interpretations of the same phenomenon.

On the other hand, the corporation also happens to be a particularly difficult nut to crack. While the enterprise and its wage relations are at the heart of western society's social relations, it is also a critical factor in the constitution of the individual (work relations that determine a person's personality and their position in society). In other words, the enterprise is a particularly dense web, rife with dissimulation and the unspoken, more difficult to untangle than one would have at first thought. In fact, we can even say that what we call an enterprise in fact comprises three distinct, though linked, enterprises:

- The *normative enterprise*, which represents what the enterprise should be. It comes closest to the ideal of the incorporated company because it sets the objectives and draws up functions and services. It embodies the institutional enterprise, the enterprise born of company rights and neat flow charts. Born of a model enterprise project, it exudes corporate culture. It is thus the ideal enterprise, with standards to be aspired to, and the concept of operating reports and quality drives.

- The *standard enterprise* is the one that attempts to implement the standards listed above. It constitutes the visible part of the 'enterprise', the part we visit and study. Grounded more firmly in reality, it evaluates the situation in relation to objectives and explains why and how they could not be achieved. It is the enterprise of completed operational reports, of suggestions and of the monitoring of quality and productivity.

  It is also the enterprise of executives who say what they do – their slogan for quality management could be: 'I write what I do and I do what is written.' It is the enterprise that shows itself, the one that is analysed and debated. It is the actualization, the materialization of the objectives and expectations of management and thus it also showcases the differences between these aims and actual achievements while also helping to unravel the causes.

- The *feigned enterprise* is the one that remains invisible behind the formal and standard enterprise. It is the one that shrinks from being seen, which puts on a mask to seem other than it is. It could also be called the informal enterprise, an entity without any fixed reference points and thereby difficult to describe and analyse. At best, some casual visitors can claim to know a little more, but that is only on the horizontal, never the vertical, plane.

  This enterprise hides behind a veil of 'lies' or behind a mask of one of the other two kinds of enterprise (especially the standard enterprise), or behind simulated practices.

  It is the enterprise of:

  - the diversion of material (thefts) and services (as, for example, using computers for private purposes during working hours);
  - 'dealings' (diversion or embezzlement of funds, keeping double or hidden accounts, various commissions);

- in accurately completed operating reports (regarding quantity and for quality) to compensate for some unaccomplished work and to hide the results;
- wastage: in this case it is no more a 'ghost' enterprise, but quite the reverse – a real one;
- concealment of facts by the management (in the case of production reserves or an undeclared surplus of posts);
- corporate control that spills over into personal life (with workers being required to mow their boss's lawn or other similar tasks);
- sexual harassment; or
- fear at work (fear of losing one's job, fear of losing one's position, fear of making mistakes, fear of machines or industrial accidents and so on).

In this feigned enterprise, everyone plays the role required by the situation or their status, but always following *their own interpretation* while claiming loudly that they are doing what is expected, especially by superiors (the standard enterprise). We thus feel that, despite the verbal paradox, the feigned enterprise is in fact a real enterprise – real, but unknowable precisely because it is feigned. It is only to the extent that analysts begin to look beyond managerial jobs alone (generally those which add value) and the categories below managerial level, and begin to take note of and consider the actual execution of jobs and functions, that they begin to approach the *real* enterprise. As it is, because of time constraints and mutual trust – today, where does the intellectual stand regarding relations between capital and labour? – access to the deeper recesses of the enterprise remains closed and the researcher must, willy-nilly, remain satisfied with a study of the standard enterprise, the one that shows itself and lends itself to analysis.

The difficulty of accessing the hidden reality, compounded by the differences in the stance and the points of view adopted explain the wide divergence of interpretations regarding the recent transformations that have shaken the whole concept of work and labour. To say, for example, that Taylorism is not dead, as is now recognized by many company directors, means two things in fact: on the one hand, by making a systematic division of labour between the work designers and the labourers, Taylorism represented the most efficient manner of organizing work, and especially of retaining some form of control in a society torn between capital and labour, which continue to pull in opposite directions. In fact, Marx had foreseen such a division of labour as a precursor to rationalizing production and managing labour.[1] On the other hand, Taylorism's efficiency stems from the effectiveness of mass production. And as the whole trend is now towards producing a growing diversity of goods, it becomes a question of delaying the process of differentiation of the common base elements until the very end of the assembly process or the service delivery (in restaurants, for example). The idea of using common base elements, or *commonizing*,[2] stems from the need to reduce costs by mass-producing the basic components via the traditional Taylorian and Fordian methods, modernized only by the introduction of tight flow and its companion, teamwork. From the point of view of labour organization, this delayed differentiation or flexible mass-production is based on what has been called 'flexible Taylorism' – something we have already defined in a previous publication.[3]

In this chapter we propose to investigate the transformations of work that have made it at the same time both harder and more interesting. In the first place, we shall see how the new *combinatoire productive*, which has been in force since the 1980s, has led to an intensification of work and a certain lengthening of working hours for some categories of employee – and this in spite of the introduction of the 35-hour week in France in the last decade of the twentieth century. Following this, we shall try to understand how the fear of unemployment itself is insufficient to explain the acceptance of new labour conditions. 'Acceptance' also depends on a number of social adjustments and games to allow an increase in work satisfaction. This will also allow us the opportunity to take a second look at the status of the collectivity and its massive use of ICT.

Innovative ways to intensify work

While a single process can explain both the intensification of work and the lengthening of the working day, we can also see it as a series of steps along the way: on the one hand we can see it as beginning with the moving out of the productivity crisis of the 1980s, and on the other, the implementation of the 35-hour week in France.

A wide diversity of activities, but nevertheless a convergence in the intensification of labour

As we saw in Chapters 2 and 4, the implementation of tight flow led to the 'natural' reduction in the porosity of working time. The need to maintain a 'tight' workflow meant that all those involved had to remain constantly on their toes, and be ready to intervene at a moment's notice. From just-in-time production in industries to shelf-stacking in supermarkets, whether it be as part of groupware or parallel engineering, everyone was required to meet demands and especially the schedules of the collectivity. Time pressures were so much at the very heart of all work that some authors even talked of *'urgent work'*. But of all employees, it was assembly workers in the automobile, household appliance, furniture and electronic industries, together with those in logistics departments (for example, chauffeurs, forklift operators) who lived directly under the constraints of tight flow and were the most affected by time pressures.[4]

For white-collar workers, efforts towards increasing productivity were targeted more at reducing the support cast. The 1980s witnessed the growing use of computer technology, with the micro-computer and the personal computer (PC) replacing human typists. Secretaries too were minimized and put to 'better' use in the classification, monitoring and following-up files and communication. In Schlumberger (a large enterprise making precision tools for oil-drilling companies), the gradual reduction in the number of typists and secretaries resulted in the departmental heads having to put in 50–55 hour weeks, while the 'chargés d'affaires' limited them to some 45–50 hours.

Mid-level managers and engineers themselves were handed down practically non-negotiable objectives. In fact, their knowledge of these objectives was delivered in increasingly impersonal ways (the press, in-house journals and executive gatherings) and which had to then be translated, transmitted, shared and, most importantly, achieved with their teams. In a certain sense, team members could in fact offer greater resistance and had more freedom than the executives themselves – a major source of job dissatisfaction among the managerial ranks. It is true, however, that mobile telephones and laptop computers with integral faxes/ modems has helped them to cope with pressures set by objectives and time constraints.[5]

In universities, the number of students has increased at a much faster rate than the number of teachers (on average an increase of 10 per cent per year between 1980 and 1995, compared to only 3 per cent for teachers from 1986). During the same period, the number of secretaries helping these teacher-researchers has in fact reduced. The combination of these two trends has resulted in a significant drop in the time spent on research, and the participation of French academics in international conferences has seen a parallel decline. At the same time, the demands of teaching have increased to such an extent that these teacher-researchers are obliged to take their work home and to toil over it in the evenings, on Saturdays and even during vacations.

Thirty-five hours and the intensification of the work

In France, the laws which ushered in the 35-hour week in 1998 also brought about a further intensification of work and, paradoxically, a lengthening of the working day for contract executives who 'benefited' from the extra holidays. The law was based on the premise that work reorganization would increase productivity and compensate for the reduction in working time. In other words, a better organization of work, set to a steady pace and rhythm, would immediately result in significant productivity gains. While this reasoning was completely justified, it had its blind spots, especially in those situations where work was linked directly to workflow, that is to say, where work had already been subjected to the pressures of intensification and with little scope for further productivity gains.

In short, we can say that the two Aubry laws pertaining to the reduction of working time ('RTT' in French) were passed on 13 June 1998 and 19 January 2000, under rather peculiar circumstances. They were proposed and voted in by a left majority but without attempting to mobilize labour unions, and the MEDEF rose against the government and the RTT. The result was an industry-wide agreement between the Employers' Federation of Metal Industries and three reformist unions, signed on 28 July 1998, which the employers' association would have liked to use as model for other sectors. The idea was to develop more flexible working hours through the annualization of work time, increasing overtime and extending time-independent contract jobs to non-executives. To give one example, everything was arranged (and sponsored by the Ministry of Employment), so that the first major signatory would be in the motor vehicle industry. It was thus Peugeot which, after a few hiccups, signed an accord with all the labour unions except the CGT. The agreement opened up possibilities for resorting to more flexible working time, excluding breaks (which had already reduced the 38.5 hours per week to 36 hours and 40 minutes)[6] and removed Saturday working. It also included a clause reducing the average age of the employees by retiring the older ones (who would be supported financially by the state) and hiring younger recruits while at the same pursuing a general policy of reducing the labour force.

On the whole, the very existence of this law forced labour unions to restructure their negotiations along new lines: with the advent of the RTT, it was no longer just a question of the pay, but also of adjusting working hours and reorganizing the production of goods and services. For their part, some managers used the occasion to introduce what they regarded as modernization and work reorganization. In SMEs, where labour unions were absent, the law provided for a union to empower any employee to sign an RTT agreement, and four out of ten were in fact signed in this way. Some of the larger trade unions mistakenly thought that such a measure of empowerment would allow them to gain a toehold in the SMEs.

In effect, the implementation of the 35-hour week played no small part in the electoral defeat of the Socialist Party on 21 April 2002. Apart from the inevitable problems for the Left as a result of too many candidates, the reduction of working hours did not go down well with a section of manual workers, who found that their buying power was stagnating, if not actually decreasing, while overtime was abolished almost completely.

Apart from workers who found that their purchasing power was stagnating (or declining), most other beneficiaries of the RTT found something positive to say. They now had much more time for their families, and especially their children. Many employees took up newer leisure activities – but without changing in any way domestic gender roles,[7] or that new social associations developed in the manner predicted by some commentators. But, more than anyone else, it was the executives who benefited the most from the 35-hour week, with a windfall of some eleven to fourteen days of additional annual paid leave.

As for working conditions, many employees indicated a particularly negative response to the accords signed (some saw them as having been imposed[8]), with 45.6 per cent of those interviewed saying that they found no difference in their working conditions, 28 per cent felt these had worsened, and only 26.4 per cent thought that their working conditions had improved (see Table 7.1).[9]

The number of new jobs created by the RTT remained relatively limited – according to the Department of Labour, the RTT was instrumental in the creation or preservation of some 357,000 jobs in the 73,419 enterprises that signed the accord. If we consider that about 6.8 million employees benefited from the 35-hour week, this signifies an enormous leap forward as regards production efficiency. Or, seen from the other side, it suggested a significant intensification of work (or a lengthening of the working day in the case of executives). We could even say that, from the point of view of actual work efficiency, the RTT had a similar impact on the French economy as the rise of the yen had in Japan in 1985. Corporate managers pushed their employees by repeatedly telling them not to endanger competitive advantage gained over the previous years. This was a feeling shared by a number of employees, engineers, technicians and executives.

Most employees found they had to complete in thirty-five hours the same amount of work they had previously done in thirty-nine, but in the absence of additional jobs: 'The intensification of work was closely tied to its reorganization in keeping with the RTT. Its effects took a milder form wherever there was an increase in manpower, while it came down more harshly wherever the number of employees stagnated or decreased.'[10]

Table 7.1 Changes in working conditions related to the RTT (percentages)

	Percentage of employees	Change in the work conditions		
		Better	No change	Worse
Total	100.0	26.4	45.6	28.0
Flexibility and intensification of work tends to worsen working conditions ...				
Required flexibility	48.4	27.1	37.4	35.5
Has more time for the same job	41.9	20.7	34.9	44.4
Work is more stressful	31.7	11.8	24.5	63.7
Additional tasks in the same job station	22.5	20.9	32.2	46.9
Work carried out with less care	10.1	10.5	21.6	67.9
... but could also be taken positively by some employees				
Find themselves better organized in work	25.6	42.4	35.0	22.6
Has greater autonomy in work	15.8	39.8	33.2	27.0
The assessment is more positive when the RTT is associated with an increase in the workforce				
Increased workforce per work unit	50.4	33.0	43.4	23.6

Interpretation: overall, 48.4 per cent of employees claim to have become more flexible in their work. Of these the 27.1 per cent feel that there has been an improvement while 35.5 per cent think that their working conditions have deteriorated.

Source: *Premières Synthèses*, DARES, Department of Labour and Manpower, May 2001, no. 21.1, p. 3.

Many executives carried out the same amount of work as in the previous year, but with eleven to fourteen extra days – which was no simple matter considering deadlines had to be met in spite of paid leave and RTT days. Obviously, it often meant either a lengthening of the working day or doing office work at home during holidays.

Then, with the return of the Conservatives to power in 2002 and the constant pressure exerted on the government by the MEDEF to annul the 35-hour law, what employees had feared most occured: a return to 39- and 40-hour weeks, with poorly paid additional hours and in particular, the intensification of the work, that had been the price paid a couple of years before for the 35-hour week! In industries as well as in services, labour in

France became one of the most productive in the world, leading to a rush of foreign investment.

We thus come back to the problem of the intensification of work that has been challenged so often by employees, the press and special agencies, who talk about its stressful nature, the moral harassment that goes with it and the suffering caused.

Work-related suffering

As a result a of a slack labour market for qualified and highly qualified personnel at the start of the twenty-first century, work-related suffering surfaced as an issue and became the subject of heated debate in France. The lack of employment pressure meant that these employees could express themselves more freely, giving voice to their discontent. At the same time, labour unions were finding it difficult to come up with any unifying themes of protest, but quickly expressed their solidarity with those employees suffering from the impact of work intensification. But it seems to us that we need to interpret these things more carefully in order to clarify them and give them their due importance. There is no gainsaying the fact that there was an intensification of work caused by the implementation of tight flow or the 35-hour week, notably while keeping the same (if not reducing) worker numbers. But should these new work conditions not be seen in the light of workers' own ambivalent reactions? Are we not talking of admittedly more difficult, but at the same time more interesting, work?

We have to remember that the intensification of work has been taking place for several decades, as, for example, in the case of the motor vehicle industry and its sub-contractors, and that workers are finding it more difficult to 'survive' in the way they might have in the past. In the case of ageing workers, having to hold up the entire assembly line because of their physical ailments (lower back pains and other musculoskeletal problems) is itself a cause of suffering. And apart from purely physical issues, the worker's inability to meet the requirements of the job because of a lack of proper training, badly organized work, or the snubs of colleagues and superiors, also adds to this distress. But does this mean that work necessarily leads to suffering, and that 'normality does not mean the absence of suffering, but on the contrary, we could posit a concept of "suffering normality" '?[11]

Perhaps we could describe this suffering as arising from a form of 'moral harassment'. Yet what is so often proclaimed as moral harassment turns out to be only a form of stress or distress felt by an individual working under difficult work conditions: perhaps the inability to meet objectives, peer pressure, conflicts with colleagues or the hierarchy, contradictory orders, ethical issues (having to do something which goes against one's moral values) is at the root of this. Stress is thus the psychological and sometimes even the physiological consequence of living (consciously or not) in an impossible situation, impossible to bear because the individual does not have the wherewithal to come up with any adequate solution. While in the case of moral harassment there exists an aggressor (whom the management can transfer, unless of course, s/he mobilizes it to meet his/her own aims!), stress and distress at work arise from the manner in which work is organized according to particular requirements based on social or economic considerations. There is thus a clear distinction between them: stress or distress at work is not caused by an individual – even though an individual could embody the institution and be the conduit for its reprimands – but rather a social organization.

All this leads us to turn the whole analysis on its head. It is no longer a matter of knowing how repressive forces maintain order at work, or how an enterprise rules by fear (fear of another worker, fear of the boss, fear of unemployment), or even how everyone is busy creating a defensive shell. On the contrary, we need to question why there is no sustained revolt against the established order, why there is no loud protest against the stringent rules, and in particular the oppressive work tempo, why there is no murmuring against repetitive and monotonous work.

In other words, how is it being sustained? Why has the wage relationship, which was never quite fair, been so easily accepted? How is it that with *constrained involvement*, not only is the constraint borne happily, but there is also very often sustained involvement? Perhaps we need to take a closer look at all these micro-social situations while remembering not to neglect the macro-social forces which shape them.

Constraints, autonomy and social games

The notion of all-powerful and univocal constraints must be tempered by the well-documented autonomy of the individual, together with those collective drives that broaden the margins of autonomy. Some of the social ramifications of this autonomy, besides being crucial to production, are inevitably of interest to the sociologist. Could it not be that in order to be able to interpret rules and to make new ones it is necessary to push back social constraints to open up some breathing space. In this way, work can be made more interesting because it achieves some kind of micro-significance.

The growing interest in work and the development of autonomy form the necessary and coherent adjuncts to all the concepts addressed in the previous chapters, including the notions of constrained involvement, tight flow, the mobilization of manpower caused by labour market changes, and the evaluation of actor behaviour, among others. To be able to create an interest in (and give meaning to) work in the face of, on the one hand, macroeconomic requirements for greater profitability and market share value, and on the other, the micro-social constraints of the work process, is to affect employees where it matters most – their day-to-day and immediate work experience. Constraints, as well as autonomy, vary greatly in different work situations, especially between those jobs that form part of tight flow and deal directly with material or information, and those that deal with surveillance or which simply run parallel to them (indirect work). Obviously, therefore, the results of any investigation depend greatly on the situation studied, and obviously conclusions differ from one investigator to another. For example, a study focusing on process industries, planning departments or the commercial or publishing sectors might conclude that constraints were on the decline, while autonomy was growing apace, especially with the development of relational work. On the other hand, a focus on industrial activities such as assembly work (or machining by sub-contractors), the retail or fast food business, or call centres, for example, would find a growing multitude of ever more precise and strict procedures, with very little scope for autonomy. Between these two poles lies a whole continuum of activities that takes something from both, finishing with a mixture of activities that is often difficult to untangle.

Rather than dealing with this continuum, we shall focus our attention on those situations which span autonomy *conceded* by management to autonomy *captured* by employees. We shall then see how autonomy is utilized by the employees themselves, and management or the organizers who might find there something to their advantage.

Conceded autonomy and captured autonomy

Since the mid-1970s, ergonomists have shown how much difference there is between tasks prescribed and the actual work performed, and how illusory is the notion that a scientific management of work would be able to include and control everything related to work. In fact, we now know that the smartest and most efficient way of going on strike or stopping production is to become an 'ideal' worker who follows every prescribed procedure to the letter. In other words, all organizers leave some leeway in interpretation and implementation so that the smaller, day-to-day problems can be resolved by the workers themselves. Generally speaking, social control in these simple work situations is manifested by a check on working time, and here the margins for autonomy are quite slim.

The advent of teamwork did help to widen this autonomy somewhat with its concepts of versatility and a relatively greater integration of diverse functions (see Chapter 2). This autonomy prepared the ground for the formation of a collectivity that would subsequently make its own unwritten rules.[12]

Wherever the work group is able to create its own unwritten rules – a symbol of its autonomy as well as of the necessity and obligation to produce – we can talk of a *captured* autonomy. We describe it as captured because employees have proved to management that they can function more efficiently on a daily basis without being overly burdened by formal rules and regulations. Even if the function of this autonomy may be similar to that *conceded*, the fact that it is captured increases its scope and field of activity, giving it more options for self-organization (via the unwritten rules) and in particular greater control over time. At the same time, management tolerates this autonomy because it helps to motivate and mobilize employees, while the all-important implicit obligations (regarding volume and production quality) still hold good.

It must be remembered that this exchange is unequal, because it takes place within the wage relationship, with its inherent obligation of worker production. Workers exchange their respect for management and their involvement in work (the obligation to produce including formal rules) for a heightened autonomy (the unwritten rules) and the possibility of developing their competencies, which in turn helps them to get a better hold on the production process and further widens their margin of autonomy. But this widening of autonomy necessarily has limits – otherwise, in the long run, the result would be the workers having complete control over the production of goods and services, and in particular over delivery schedules. It is hardly surprising, then, that management keeps a wary eye on the growth of this autonomy.

De Terssac (1992) shows how the process of rationalizing work maintains the margins of autonomy by obtaining the shortest route to achieving production. But this autonomy is neatly enclosed within clear bounds. For example, it may amount to an autonomous management of authorized solutions (that is, choosing from among a range of 'expert' solutions), or building and restructuring the competencies required to meet any eventuality, or in the best case, giving free reign to worker creativity within pre-decided limits. In other words, management needs this autonomy, not only so that there is some room to interpret the formal rules, as in the case of ceded autonomy, but also so that employees have the freedom (within this captured autonomy) to come up with the unwritten rules so necessary for the production process.

From the concept of joint regulation to productive compromise

This dialectic between worker autonomy and management control brings us to the ideas of J.-D. Reynaud. While the constant push to widen their autonomy pits workers against management rules, they must both meet and agree when it comes to the question of production. According to Reynaud, they must come together in a *joint regulation* indispensable for meeting common objectives.[13] We would rather replace the term 'joint regulation' – which gives the impression of social harmony between employee and employer, and between labour and capital – with 'productive compromise' which denotes the existence of contradictions and conflicts within the wage relationship. It provides a clearer idea of the more-or-less latent violence which always lurks behind the double accord between the two parties:

- the accord on the captured autonomy. On its being recognized by management, which then is constantly looking to either circumvent or reduce it (the social control over labour); and
- the accord on the necessity of producing (the wage relation and the labour contract), and the need to come together and to create a minimum number of rules.

At the same time, this productive compromise is always a provisional solution, constantly tested by market constraints (including financial considerations), the organization of production and labour, the conditions of production (including technological issues), and obviously the nature and personalities of the people involved. We thus have the concept of the dynamic productive compromise which designates the double nature of the work relationship: the conflicts and contradictions of continually shifting agreements.

In fact, the very mention of the word 'margin' in this bargain between margins of autonomy and the obligation to produce, signifies the heavy presence of social control. It can be exerted *directly* through the system by which workers can choose only one from among a range of solutions given by experts, or *indirectly*, by the development of competencies – which was dealt with in detail in Chapter 6. Wherever the margins of autonomy are widest (found generally – but not necessarily – in work requiring highly qualified personnel), and wherever the instructions for any job are inadequate, instructions are given upstream. Management assures itself of its behaviour by keeping tabs on employee loyalty *vis-à-vis* the employer. Thus we see that the question of behaviour as a component of competency does not stem from any 'ideological' view of the nature of competencies, but is a deductive process taking into account changes in the conditions of production: the 'complexification', 'fragilization' and the greater place occupied by communication, with its unpredictable nature in the usage of ICT. The control and guarantee of behaviour is coherent with the ideas of de Terssac regarding labour rationalization through the implementation of new production rules. Individual employee evaluation, together with its behavioural component, is a means of controlling not only work results, but also the manner in which the employee uses the autonomy ceded by management: an autonomy that is ceded precisely because management no longer provides the rules and regulations required to handle the increasingly complex situations in uncertain conditions. But in fully controlled situations such as 'hands-on' work subjected to the constraints of tight flow, and where the margins of autonomy are greatly reduced, there is also hardly any behavioural control. The reason for this is that work is controlled directly by the process itself, because of unavoidable formal rules.

Yet there is one question that has been hovering around the edges for the past few pages and still remains unanswered: why are workers, and in fact, employees in general (everyone, other than the top bosses, is a worker who has to follow a superior's directions) looking for, or in need of, some sort of autonomy in work?

Autonomy, games and social accommodation

One possible answer to this question of autonomy may be found, as we have just shown, in the functional requirements of the enterprise. However, in itself this is insufficient, and any satisfactory explanation must also take into account the individuals themselves, and their pursuit of liberty, together with their need for self-assertion.

Employees react to constraints imposed by the production process[14] by creating for themselves various forms of autonomy, including paradoxical ones. For example, in the extreme case of assembly-line work carried out under time constraints, all employees who have acquired some seniority prefer to adopt an attitude that might seem like some kind of resignation, as though they prefer routine and repetitiveness to job rotation. Between the two solutions offered, and since the heart of assembly work remains the same, they choose the path along which their acquired skill has given them most free time and, more importantly, a degree of psychological escape.[15] The autonomy thus acquired within such harsh constraints would hardly satisfy any humanist observer. Elsewhere, motor vehicle assembly workers add some sort of preparatory work to their main job – for example by threading washers on a rod, or arranging parts in order of their assembly. Often, however, practice undermines the theory as a result of changes required by the reality of the production needs of the wide range of manufactured goods. This pointless work would seem to be a kind of revenge taken by the worker – the time freed by speeding up the tempo of work was occupied with small chores (of little functional use), which helped the workers to feel that s/he had some control over him/herself and the job.

As we have already seen, in some other situations such as call centres, the expert tele-operators forged some autonomy for themselves by either being smart and reducing conversation time or by resorting to repeated calls for 'rebooting' the customer's system in order to give themselves some free time – which was spent either chatting on the net or listening to music. Though this stolen time constitutes the heart of the fight for autonomy in a job tightly hemmed in by time constraints, it also has other objectives, such as asserting oneself in front of one's work group peers, in view of neighbouring colleagues or *vis-à-vis* management.

The conquest and creation of this autonomy, this 'making up of regulations', is achieved with or against other people in the workplace. They usually all belong to the same level and are subjected to the same regulations and constraints, or the same symbolic violence perpetuated by management. We shall use the term *social game* to designate these social relations, for important reasons. Functionally, a game gives everyone some margin of freedom and autonomy – which is why we have used this metaphor to designate labour relations. The notion of a game also offers several possibilities and probable 'moves' allowed by the rules of the game. At the same time, this freedom is limited by formal rules that are independent of the players. In both play and work, the people who are made responsible for making sure the rules are followed have a larger share of the pie than the simple players. Moreover, whatever the function of the regulation may be, it is never completely fixed or acquired – in fact, it is in itself an issue and opens the way to constant negotiations that are fundamental to social transformation. To give a concrete example: Tarot players generally follow rules that have been established for a long time, but every time a new player joins them, they have to adjust the price of every point and redefine the number of points accorded for every successful contract. Moreover, with unwritten rules they can even influence the functioning of the formal regulations themselves.

Second, the concept of a social game is intrinsic to the social life of human beings, whose objective is this relationship itself, with no other function as such than to exist. This is sufficient in itself. At the same time, having no fixed objectives, and even though it may be serious, it gives the players pleasure. But the game is not cost-free; it brings with it issues and challenges, and in this sense it *is* serious. The issues and challenges may be symbolic or strategic, so long as they hold the players' interest. But just as we have little choice regarding participation in social life (except in pathological cases), we have also no alternative but to live with its innumerable games and challenges.

The concept of equating social relations with a game has been contested by Appay:

> It seems to me that the term 'game' is a complete misnomer, it carries a sense of entertainment instead of giving the impression of the struggle for survival which characterize these social and psychological phenomena. Fundamentally, they are a form of violence, of obedience, of imposition, domination, conflict and suffering. It is true that games are also a sort of struggle and include competition, domination, bending of rules and even violence. But on the whole, a game is localized in time and space and subject to the voluntary participation of the players.[16]

But far from removing any idea of domination, conflict and social contradictions, the concept of playing a social game within social and economic constraints (with formal rules governing work) turns the whole issue on its head in seeking to explain how *such impossible situations become acceptable by the introduction of the concept of a game* in which the vast majority of the workers take part.[17]

The fact that the social game played by workers takes place within the spaces allowed by the formal regulations – that is, within the margins of autonomy created by them while respecting wage relations, means that the rules and objectives of the game are compatible (while retaining their autonomy) with those of the formal regulations. For that matter, this social game can even influence formal work rules, bend some of them or force management to modify them. We shall call this reciprocal adaptation and constant mutual change *social adjustment*.[18] Adjustment denotes shaping to the right size – that is, regulating the play between the two parts or controlling the freedom of movement – in mechanics we talk of a 'tight' or a 'loose' fit.

We have used the label *adjustment* to denote the social relationship between labourers and management while differentiating it from the interactions between colleagues, which we define as a *game*. By this we hope to show that though the two spheres function in close proximity, overlap and mutually influence one other, they each have their own logic, with distinct issues, and are guided by laws that are sometimes contradictory and do not have the same effect on day-to-day work. In this sense, our concept of social adjustment corresponds roughly to Reynaud's idea of joint regulation (see above). We could also say that the concept of social adjustment forms part of, or is the micro-social sub-set of, the dynamic productive compromise regulating the wage relationship at the level of the enterprise or installation, office or workshop.

Social functions of the workspace game

An analysis of these social games may shed some light on what makes wage relations actually work, on how a labourer is impelled to sell labour power day after day, acceptable and accepted even under trying and difficult conditions. These social games play a mediating role between the structural constraints of employment and the actual work conditions, while providing the required 'play' to satisfy the need for participation and recognition by the community. The presence of this social play among peers (which, by the way, may also include lower management and secondary actors such as fork-lift truck drivers, technical officers and storekeepers), renders formal regulations acceptable and work conditions, even deplorable ones, bearable.

Social games and labour acceptability

Practically every work situation has within its folds some form of social game. This is particularly true of the lowest type of labour, where the constraints of time and the monotony and repetitiveness compel a sort of restructuring of work in order to make it acceptable, if not obviously attractive.[19] In call centres, the tele-operators reinvent their work through individual or collective rearrangements. In retail stores, cashiers cushion their information input and cash collection by choosing their working hours or some forms of work practice over others, or by engaging in extra-curricular and voluntary interactions with clients.

In our study of Peugeot, one of the most popular, though never admitted, social games was the well-known one of working up the line. In fact, the existence of this game was doubly denied: first by the workers themselves, who were concerned to guard their autonomy jealously, and second by their supervisors, who had to prove to themselves that everything was under their control. In fact, workers moved up the assembly line before every break, so as to lengthen it, or at the end of their shift to enable them to leave their post before the appointed time.[20] The time saved by working up the line was enough to take a short break. In every case, playing this game signified a certain control by the workers over their time, and added a certain aura to those workers who could thus demonstrate their dexterity or virtuosity[21] and their capacity to hold a 'good position'. An entire implicit hierarchy was thus established – from the person who could leave a workstation after working seven or eight cars up the line, to the one who had to be helped by the team leader to finish their quota before the bell. However, as with all other challenges in the workplace, this working up the line was double-edged. On the one hand, workers could not refuse to play, as they would risk social marginalization if they refused, but on the other hand, this competition clearly proclaimed the capacities of the champions, who could finish their work well within the allotted time. This introduced yet another rule of the game: to display one's free time and to win the respect of others (supervisors, technical agents) for oneself and of one's job, so as to avoid any changes to it. The winner thus gained a double advantage: by earning some symbolic capital and retaining the status quo. Rare were those who dared to attack anyone with significant symbolic capital (and guaranteed income), for fear of reprisals.

Similarly, balancing operations between different jobs involved playing a complex social game that went hand-in-hand with the social adjustments taking place between management and workers. This rebalancing, which occurred on a monthly basis, involved a more-or-less drastic change in every workstation. The changes were made in response to three principal objectives: to eliminate 1 per cent of manpower from the manufacturing process each month, to implement product improvements, and to adapt production to demand. For every worker, the objective was to give him/ herself a 'good position' on the line, or to make one with the others involved in balancing (team leader, foreman, assembly line boss and time-monitoring agent). As far as the assemblers were concerned, the 'good position' was the one that did not entail too many diverse tasks, that granted a maximum of autonomy, and that allowed some freedom to go up the assembly line. There were also a number of other subtle advantages to a good position: not being posted directly under a mechanical assist, not having to handle an electric screwdriver, not having to use a pneumatic screwdriver for different operations (the changing of bits being a tedious process), and not having to contend with only manual jobs (which are always very diversified and often difficult to complete).

To ensure a good position, or workstation, every month became every one's prime preoccupation two weeks before the next scheduled shake up – that is, before the implementation of the new monthly arrangement. Every assembler tried through their network – here, material resources were of primary importance – to be knowledgeable of the changes planned for their post, and to eliminate the more negative ones such as additional operations, replacements of some, an increase in the number of physical displacements or added security-related functions. Each one tried to pull as many strings as possible, such as providing that medical excuses or attempting to show the incompatibility of the different functions assigned to them.[22]

Apart from the obvious advantage of holding an 'easy' position, the social game that accompanies this rebalancing has the added strategic function of giving a direction to individual initiative in work besides the immediate objective of increasing/improving production. This also explains why rebalancing sometimes leads to what might be construed as irrational outcomes. If it happens that the 'good positions' are given to compliant assemblers, in fact the 'grumblers' close to the unions (assuming that they proved themselves to be efficient), then the 'bad jobs' go to the poor assemblers with few social resources or networks to fall back on. The first to be given such posts are the young new arrivals, but in the main they go to the really senior assemblers who could never quite build any lasting relationships because of their 'personality', or their ethnic minority status, or because of their difficulty in expressing themselves. They may have been alone and outcast throughout their professional life and now, always being given the most difficult jobs, found themselves the first to be worn out. Games and adjustments combined closely to form what we have already described: the disheartened, the embittered, and in particular the excluded, no longer have the resources to play. Excluded from playing around rebalancing, of working up the line, or other 'games' and challenges, they remain marginalized in these social adjustments and can easily find themselves driven out of the enterprise at any time without even the comfort of the benefit of early retirement.

As for the others, that is, the majority of workers, their participation in social games gives them a wider and less negative view of their jobs and employment. Outside the factory, at home and with neighbours, these workers do not talk of their actual jobs, but rather of the environment that is constituted, socialized and learnt largely through these social games. In day-to-day work on the line, workers' thoughts are not only diverted by domestic or extra-professional themes – these multiple social games (several games going on simultaneously and overlapping) also serve to hold their attention. These social games clothe repetitive and sometimes difficult jobs in a way that renders them acceptable by masking some of their deeper characteristics.

Moreover, these social games do not have any intangible, fixed or formalized rules, essentially because the formal rules that encompassed them and their environment are changing constantly. For example, the reduction of tubes in pneumatic screwdrivers or their replacement by electrical tools limits worker autonomy and thus the playing field, including the number of participants. There was talk of doing away with this monthly rebalancing (Japanese manufacturers have already reduced these to only two or three such adjustments a year), which could well result in an increase of these plays and counter-plays regarding the allotment of positions.

On the other hand, if there are too many winners, or if the game itself becomes overly repetitive, it is imperative that the rules are changed. We saw that changes take place in gradual steps, with the players' personalities taking the major role in deciding whether to choose greater individual risk or, on the contrary, a more cohesive collectivity. As regards working up the line, the rules determining the allotment of posts or their content are quite subtle and volatile, and vary considerably from one team to the next depending on the personality of the team leader or the decisions of the balancing agent. Thus the adaptation, elaboration and production of the rules is at least as important as the game itself, because as soon as they are established, the margin of autonomy and initiative is reduced considerably. By the time the post is created and allotted, it is already too late – the possibility of working up the line depends more on the position itself than on any worker skill *per se*.

Moreover, while the games themselves cannot be dissociated from the social adjustments undertaken *vis-à-vis* management, the construction of their rules combines and supports those rules that govern the latter. By establishing rules within the team or work group, the act of working up the line brings together all workers participating in the game. These include team leaders, technical agents and the person in charge of the balancing process. The same rules can thus apply to more than just workers, provided they all subscribe to the same objective: the continued production of quality goods and services. Work in such a community is felt to be acceptable because, on the one hand, it includes (partially) some lighter activities, while on the other, workers have opportunities to participate (also partially) in its elaboration as a result of their influence on job composition. To say that the act of rule-making fascinates the players as much as the game itself is to concur with Reynaud, for whom 'the social rule is truly a social fact par excellence, but with the addition that the regulatory act is itself a social challenge'.[23] The production of rules in social games and even more so in social adjustments (where the challenges are greater because they have a direct impact on the wage relationship) add to the meaningfulness of work – not in some general or ontological sense, but directly in immediate work relations. Over and above these constraints focused on streamlining the entire process, there is always some place for social relations that can only be built through constant rearrangements and readjustments of rules, which in turn to have to be invented or modified continually.

At the same time, these social games and adjustments, and the construction of the rules that govern them, are shored up on one side by the compulsion of having to produce and the formal rules that go with this compulsion, and on the other hand, by having to respect rules regarding work within a collectivity. For example, as Durand and Stewart (1998) demonstrated, the game of social transparency played in the assembly workshops of a Japanese factory making outboard motors, was not, truly speaking, completely open. Workers supervised each other, making sure that others respected certain rules that kept the group functioning collectively. To display one's aptitude for neatness and discipline also meant that the competition was public – neither private (between the individual and the boss) nor merely discursive. In this case, the public face of the game entailed the retention of a certain *opacity*. Workers told the management only what they could reveal to their peers: the path of transparency was edged by borders of opacity. The pendulum swung from transparency to opacity, depending on the changes made to the rules of the game by the players. They themselves were subject to the relationship of power within the work group and its relationship with management. On the one hand, the construction of these rules turned into an activity that was as important as the game itself, while on the other hand, it took place within the framework of the pre-existing meta-rules which, though partly established by the group itself, was for the most part conditioned by the constraints of the wage relationship. In fact, these meta-rules – that is, the range of autonomy enjoyed by these employees, depended first on the method of work organization (formal rules and instructions) and management methods, coupled with the reactive capacity of employees. Moreover, these meta-rules were thus much less mobile and volatile than the preceding ones and gave rise in turn to a large number of 'games' and adjustments (including the constitution of their own rules).

Autonomy and rationalization of subjectivity

The first major effect of autonomy and the resulting social games and social adjustments was to induce the workers to change their perception of work, turning even the worst jobs into acceptable occupations. This aspect seems to us to be of paramount importance for an understanding of a persistent social phenomenon which, by all appearances, should have been discarded long ago. In effect, this 'rule work', so to speak, plays a critical role in taking rigid, formal instructions and transforming them, by a sort of social alchemy, into acceptable (if not necessarily satisfying) conditions. We can ask ourselves whether the work of creating these rules, which ameliorate so magically cold, hard instructions, belongs to the workload itself as we defined it at the beginning of this chapter. In fact, the workload itself, as a given thing, imposed and prescribed by management, cannot be handled immediately. At least two conditions have to be fulfilled (obviously, apart from having the necessary means): to have the required training, the tacit know-how or skill, and the establishment of social rules that would allow them to be learnt from others and to organize collective life in and around the workplace.

One could always claim that the acquisition of a tacit qualification is part of the work itself and that it could well be – provided that the load is not too heavy or the training too arduous (the changing of a position on an assembly line could prove costly from this point of view) – the most interesting moment, it being the most creative. But what of the construction of the rules of social games and adjustments, which are necessarily associated with accomplishing assigned work? Does it represent the workload by creating the conditions that make it acceptable and help in accomplishing it? Does it not, on the contrary, form part and parcel of the autonomy that employees carry with them, and by which they take the initiative to build social relations and participate in the elaboration of the rules of functioning within the work group?

According to one interpretation of ergonomic studies, we could conclude that the implementation of psycho-physiological functions which regulate work belong to work itself.[24] While the physiological and psychological effort needed to adapt individuals to their working conditions may be separated from the work itself, it cannot be isolated from the *social work of translation*, which must be taken into account in understanding how the job, even if difficult, becomes acceptable. This work of translation can also take on the nature of protest when the instructions seem unacceptable to the collectivity, with the objective being to modify the instructions themselves when they cannot be adjusted internally. Apart from what ergonomists specify as individual effort to attain the norm, it seems to us that the adaptation and regulation, in the sense of rule construction, does not belong to work itself. On the contrary, the subjective involvement of every individual in the establishment of these social rules of functioning within a work group – that is, the emergence of local behavioural norms helps in the conquest of a margin of autonomy, is what makes the work itself acceptable. This is because it is very much this social game played around rule construction that gives work some meaning, and in a way, makes it more pleasurable – not because of any intrinsic quality, but because of the (social) activity that it engenders. Such is the paradox of captured autonomy, the main task of which is to render even the worst tasks acceptable.

At this point we could ask ourselves another question regarding management's capacity to recuperate, or recycle, the beneficial effects of employees' captured autonomy for its own ends. That is exactly what de Terssac sees in the construction of new production rules by which formal instructions are replaced by the freedom to choose from among a set of preselected solutions to the competencies required for these functions.[25] The creativity evinced by workers for the recovery of their autonomy is recycled and used to mobilize and motivate them – and of course, always within the framework of this autonomy.[26] This does not, of course, in any way deny worker creativity and dynamism at the heart of the work itself.

On the one hand, widening the margins of autonomy has shifted the rules in workers' favour, while on the other, their involvement in work, and in the construction of rules, has been used to increase productivity and improve quality. This recycling[27] – that is, the systematic utilization of involvement for production gains – has been called, by Sebag, the *streamlining of subjectivity*.[28] The same can be seen in the competency model whenever individual evaluation includes an assessment of employee behaviour. The mobilization of employee subjectivity for the capturing of autonomy is recycled in the pursuit of management objectives.

The development of these social games and adjustments and of their rules depends on the existence of a workplace collectivity, a sort of collective life, or the existence of a group formed by the workers themselves. As a matter of fact, and notably with the development of teamwork which goes hand-in-hand with tight flow, the construction of these rules comes up against a number of difficulties requiring investigation. The development of worker mobility blocks work group stability (part-time employees gathering around a small, stable nucleus) while the deliberate breaking up of old collectivities (too fertile a ground for labour demands) is compounded by the pressures necessary for the maintenance of tight flow in the context of a steadily decreasing workforce. This is the origin of disorientation that has been so much discussed: employees at the same level have neither the time nor the possibility of creating the necessary rule for micro-social cohesion.

The concept of 'working together separately' described in Chapter 6 is a way of taking charge of worker autonomy and of minimizing, if not completely eliminating, the formation of their groups. But if such a new organization were to remain in force without employees resorting to a reciprocal change in strategy through the construction of new rules and other areas of autonomy, it is very probable that their involvement and creativity would also suffer as far as the work was concerned. They would probably find other places to manifest themselves where there would be more freedom and symbolic value. What remains is to make sense of the extent to which behaviour offers the scope for an infinite number of games, especially those feigning the expected behavioural traits, which obviously open other possibilities for the creation of new rules for social games and adjustments.

In fact, however the organization of work might change, we cannot imagine that, to the extent that some forms of autonomy are squeezed out, others will not emerge elsewhere. Which does not mean that we can ignore the enormous gulf separating the margins of autonomy enjoyed by tele-operators and assemblers on the one hand, and teachers and engineers on the other. Evidently, there is a marked difference between the resources wielded by each to widen their autonomy and construct rules that may be more favourable to them. Moreover, there is also a clear inequality between the resources held by management and workers, with one of the functions of the former being to limit the resources of the latter, including increasing the workload, as we have already seen.

But the crux of this chapter lies in the analysis of the functions of the social game and the construction of its rules which accompany the manufacture of goods and services. Even in the most trying situations, workers create for themselves resources that help them to widen their margins of autonomy. This autonomy allows them a degree of auto-organization within the framework of formal rules and instructions, and creates the social games that an outside observer might find hard to identify and apprehend. Such is the 'third enterprise', which we defined at the beginning of this chapter. It is the actual enterprise, the one that concerns the employees and gives sense to their work, the one wherein social relations are lived from within, with all the feelings that they carry, whether of tension or cohesion. This third enterprise, the playground of these social games and the creation of their rules, is the one within which we can bear workplace conditions and the most tedious jobs which otherwise would be rejected outright. This is exactly what happens in the second, official, enterprise. The social game and the development of its rules to a large extent help in this acceptance because they distract attention from the contents and conditions of work. Instead, the game draws workers to the game itself, with its fun, its challenges, and its emotional and intellectual content. The social game brings a satisfaction to work which thus becomes acceptable. According to Burawoy, 'two consequences of this game must be distinguished: in the first place, the game masks the production relations for which the game had been invented originally; secondly, the game makes the social relations of production acceptable – relations which had defined the rules of the game in the first place'.[29] The author goes further and likens the enterprise to a pacified (battle)field, thanks to social games that are simultaneously part of the fight to capture greater autonomy.

At the heart of the contradictions between labour and capital, the enterprise is 'pacified' by social games devised by the employees (often the ones who are on the lowest rung of the corporate ladder) within the margins of autonomy, which were themselves captured through conflict. Within these complex social relations, trade unionism played (and still plays) a role in creating these conflicts even while sustaining macro-social regulations. However, its strategic functions are no longer what they were. In part, this is because employees have for the most part opted out of unions, but also because capitalism itself has undergone major transformations, in terms of financialization and globalization.

8
Unionism and Globalization

With the advent of the new 'productive combination' (see the Introduction), there has been a complete change in the way in which goods are produced and services are rendered (see Chapters 1, 2 and 4). Qualifications have been replaced by competencies (Chapter 3) and the very structure of employment has changed labour statutes and contracts (Chapter 5). The implementation of certain micro-social arrangements has made the increasing intensity of work acceptable and easier to bear (Chapter 7). Although unionism has been present throughout the course of this study, especially as an essential component of the wage relationship, it seems to have lost much of its weight and does not wield the clout it used so effectively in the previous Fordian system.

After analysing this weakening of the labour unions and changes in the wage relationship that have practically eliminated all unionism, we shall look at some of the major hurdles faced by these unions (which have also been faced by some other social movements) – such as globalization and long-term underemployment in most parts of the world. Though weakened, unions can still put up a fight, particularly when co-ordinated with some political agenda, if they consent to reform some of their traditions and give a worldwide view its rightful place in their organizations.

The causes of the weakening of labour unions

We shall not provide a detailed description of the 'crisis of unionism' or delve too deeply in reconstructing the recent history of how unionism in general, and particularly in France, has lost both ground and adherents. As a number of specialists have already discussed these fundamental questions in great detail,[1] we shall limit ourselves to sketching the broad outlines of the transformations of the wage relationship (organization of labour, wage system, management methods, ways of mobilizing employees) and how they gradually 'cut the grass from beneath the feet' of the unions and eventually removed their very *raison d'être*. But before that, we shall need to take a small detour to have a quick look at some of the salient features of unionism.

In the nineteenth century, workers' associations (which later became unions) were created to defend worker interests at the micro-social level. They were formed to help fight against poor working conditions in the workshops, increase wages by staging protests in the presence of an employer, and reduce the number of working hours by mobilizing the workforce within similar enterprises in the same district. We hypothesize that the power of the unions was first formed around the work process, and that it has continued to exist only because of the strong and deep-rooted support of the unions and their members for the work process itself.

It has always been easier to mobilize the employees by linking discontent and protests to the process of the work itself (the hectic pace, unhealthy conditions in the workplace, discomfort, relations with the hierarchy) rather than relying on any slogan or rallying cry of a confederation. The US union system was based mainly on complaints and grievances addressed to the union delegates, who would bring to a halt the whole production if the demands (even if they had no connection with the grievances) were not met. The grievances by themselves justified the existence of the union delegate within the American automobile industry. An institution of more than 100 types of speciality among an unqualified workforce facilitated the system of grievances: a worker of a specific category would refuse to do a certain job because it did not belong to his speciality: s/he would do it only if s/he were adequately compensated (most often financially).

Thus the demands arising from the work process justified and founded the establishment of the unions. On their side, the unions, like all social institutions, paid for themselves in several ways: materially, through increased income or improved work conditions, and symbolically, by the dignity bestowed on the workers or, for example, by giving workers a sense of identity. Collecting union membership dues through the monthly sale of stamps shows how close the union needed to be to the work process in order to remain alive. Similarly, the revival of the union's activities just prior to the elections, including a rush of meetings and a flood of pamphlets, illustrates how close the ties were between local politics and the work process itself.

What roles did the branch federations ('trade federations' in the UK) and the confederation of the national trade unions play in France? Although they did help in defending the employees, organizing and centralizing them, giving substance and volume to the demands of the weaker voices (from the small enterprises), the principal function of the national unions was to *represent* the employees. The Fordian system gave them an honourable status and the right to negotiate salaries and working hours; and it also gave them a pre-eminent position in the government (in France, the Scandinavian countries, Belgium and Switzerland). However, the main function of these federations and confederations during the 'Golden age' was recruiting new members and increasing active participation in the various elections to establish their legitimacy (in legal terms, representativeness). To that aim, the unions based their actions on the realities of the work process and the negative, or positive, perceptions the workers had of it.

But how is this today? Are there as many complaints regarding the work itself? Do these complaints always need to be channelled through the unions? What are the functions of the representatives chosen by the personnel themselves, and those elected by the unions? What of the unions themselves and their relationship with the work process, which had been its very *raison d'être*?

The general improvement in physical work conditions

Globally speaking, the development of the service sector or, in other words, the tertiarization of the economy, meant that there was a major shift from manual labour towards office or commercial work, which was by its nature more comfortable and physically less taxing, and naturally resulted in a reduction in complaints regarding the physical aspects of work.

Moreover, even within the industrial sector itself, the rising use of information and computer technologies has meant that workers often do not need to engage directly in physical labour; there are machines to do that instead (exceptions include assembly work, handling of finished products, and some activities within the industrial services). This evolution has led to a major improvement in physical working conditions: fewer heavy loads to shift, the ability to remain at a distance from heat or toxic chemicals and fumes, and so on. At the same time, ergonomics have been used to improve and further humanize the work (though, admittedly, also aiming to increase productivity at the same time). For example, a reduction in the distance between the parts bins and the assembly line saved time and energy that, as Henry Ford so astutely remarked, were not productive in themselves!

These changes and improvements in the physical work conditions deflated the role of the representatives elected by the Comités Hygiène, Sécurité et Conditions de Travail (CHSCT; Committee of Health, Safety and Work Conditions, CHSWC) and consequently also weakened indirectly the function of the union itself, which was in charge of these CHSCT delegates. The number of complaints went down to such an extent that the role of the CHSCT delegates changed – from merely receiving to encouraging complaints.

In the USA, and to a lesser extent in Europe, the extreme fragmentation of jobs and work specialization (with workers often occupying the same post for decades) prevented any mobility – which was just as well for the workers and their unions, who were also against this mobility, which demanded more involvement, training and a new dexterity. Thus there arose a complex and subtle labour structure that gave rise to many more complaints and grievances (see Chapter 7 regarding social games/play and adjustments). The birth and spread of versatility through the concept of 'group work' (or the Japanese concept of teamwork) put an end to all these complaints because, by its very nature, the acceptance of versatility entailed the possibility of occupying more than one post. If versatility could be accepted by the unions as a way of improving a worker's qualifications (which were not always recognized or compensated), it should come as no surprise that the unions also accepted a system of teamwork (the US labour unions being the exception), which, by admitting the concept of collective responsibility, practically eliminated the possibility of making demands. Every team was held responsible for its methods and its results, and the moment this responsibility was accepted, even the idea of a protest, let alone any sort of unionism, lost any meaning.

The improvement in the physical conditions of the work environment, and the fact that the group had taken over much of the responsibility, did not mean that other aspects of working conditions had not deteriorated. First, shift work continued to increase, as has been proved by all the statistics. This kind of work not only broke natural work rhythms and isolated shift workers from their environment (family and friends, and even their accustomed leisure time when they worked weekends) but alternating between morning and night shifts also produced an adverse physiological effect on workers' health. And though the unions did fret and voice their grievances about this problem once in a while, nobody dared go against a structural trend (because it was presented as an inevitable consequence of competition). Second, the system of 'continuous operation' (a consequence of the generalization of tight flow) resulted in an almost complete elimination of official breaks,[2] and even of the micro-breaks that the employees had managed gradually to insert into their working day. Here, too, unions could not do much more than denounce the 'infernal pace' and show that it was getting worse all the time. But even this soon lost the little weight it carried, because tight flow was presented as the logical outcome of growing international competition, and the unions themselves had not given enough thought to the possible results of tight flow.

To top it all, stress began to appear in almost all workplaces and under all work conditions, including among manual workers, something that had previously been unthinkable – so well protected were manual workers behind their walls of unionism. But at the time of writing, teamwork, the concept of an individual as well as a collective responsibility, and the fact that enough resources are not always available to meet the objectives set, have led to a net increase in psychological problems and a mad rush for pharmacological solutions. More than any fear of the boss, it is peer pressure that weighs most heavily – the fear of losing the respect and esteem of colleagues in the face of newer constraints add greatly to the stress factor. And because this deterioration of working conditions is less visible, and in particular less quantifiable than the situation the representatives and unions are used to, they find themselves quite helpless. This has resulted in a slew of militant articles (sometimes from universities) dealing with the suffering of workers. These pessimistic views have largely overlooked the joys and satisfactions, the social standing and status that come from work, and that explain, among other things (such as fear), why work, in spite of its bad press, is both acceptable and accepted.

Managerial methods as substitutes for unionism

The increase in the educational level of the employees, coupled with the changed nature of the work – which now requires a greater subjective involvement on the employees' part – means that workers cannot be subjected to the kind of managerial dictatorship that was prevalent in previous industries and the larger service sectors (data entry, for example). The older generation of authoritarian bosses had to give way to a new breed of managers who, though no less exacting, used a softer, lighter touch. Apart from in some well-known enterprises, personnel and union representatives had less and less to do regarding the relationship between workers and their hierarchy, which led to a reduction in the power of their role and the necessity of their presence in the workshop or the office.

The disappearance of bossy heavy-handedness was accompanied by an increase in communication, which short-circuited unions and personnel representatives. In the UK, the USA and to a lesser extent in some other countries, workers followed an unwritten rule that they would go to a personnel representative only when it concerned a demand regarding promotions or transfers. Today, with the 'open door policy' maintained by managers, and more important, by the team leader, who is part peer and part boss, another channel of communication has opened that is parallel to and in competition with one of the main functions of the unions. In fact, the employees' claims are even felt to have a greater chance of success. This phenomenon in fact strikes more deeply at the heart of the unions than is immediately apparent because, on the one hand, it deprives the unions of their monopoly, and on the other, it further marginalizes them by proving to be a more effective system.[3] The union representative is relegated to being used as a last resort, only when all other ways have failed to produce the desired result. It is also quite clear now that the unions do not enjoy the same respect and trust as do the other ways of making labour demands.

In France, the Auroux Laws, partially implemented at the beginning of the 1980s, institutionalized this parallel outlet and channel for employee grievances. They were soon replaced by 'quality circles' and 'progress groups', which were themselves eventually supplanted by more powerful tools such as *total productive maintenance* (TPM), the move towards total quality (TQM – with ISO 9000), *kaizen* and the *single minute exchange die* SMED. These laws generated the idea and practice of a unanimous social integration that no one could escape: who would declare him/herself to be against quality? Who can afford to be against a growth in production that would maintain the viability of the enterprise, and consequently the retention of his/her own employment?

These socio-technological tools also turned out to be excellent managerial devices: they brought in freedom of speech (as in ISO 9000: 'write what you do') and transformed workers into a force for suggestions – or at least that is what they thought for a time. In fact, freedom of speech gave rise to a better dialogue between workers and management regarding technical matters and on other issues of mutual concern. In doing so, the whole debate was sidetracked and moved away from the question of hierarchies and demands. Moreover, being close to and sharing the same preoccupations meant that the blue-collar workers identified themselves with the white-collar workers (technicians, engineers, auditors). The same thing happened in retail business and large-scale service sectors. By mobilizing their subjectivity and motivating them in this way, these practices diverted workers' attention away from other, more delicate, issues, such as the rhythm of work, stress and so on. Complaints, problems and distress at work were hardly mentioned, and the unions found themselves completely out of place within the working process.

Moreover, the manner in which the employers arranged their employees' work time was itself a major problem as far as these workers were concerned. In fact, during the 1970s and 1980s, the unions protested loudly against the institution of variable work hours, as they would not allow the formation of labour collectives – the ridge pole of the union movement itself. As far as the workers were concerned, they felt that variable hours would give them the flexibility to co-ordinate their jobs better with their private lives (particularly with regard to shuttling their children to and from school). Thus, gradually, and in spite of the unions, variable hours were accepted by the employees. Even better, in many cases it led to the disappearance of the time clock, the devil's own device that stole human freedom and the employees' dignity.[4]

To summarize, the profound transformations that have taken place in the production process and its techniques, and the new modes of managing and mobilizing employees have resulted in a slow whittling down of the functions and power of the unions, in their original construction. There is less and less reason to complain:[5] on the one hand, certain types of distress – such as stress – have no way of expressing themselves, and on the other, management has built a number of alternative routes for employees so they can express their concerns directly to the management. The unions have thus lost out on all counts: the number of adherents (except at election times, when it still retained its function of judging the expressions of discontent), its financing ability and its representativeness.[6]

The pursuit of anti-union policies

There was no doubt a policy of repression continuing to target union activists (*militants* in French).[7] Despite being protected by the law, unionists were the first to feel the chill of any upcoming economic layoffs, early retirements and so on. On the one hand, the new production paradigm was reducing its functions at the very heart of the work process, and on the other, the steady reduction of its membership almost brought the curtain down on Fordian unionism as a whole!

There were also other types of *union discrimination*; that is, ways of discouraging people from joining unions: when it was found (sooner rather than later) that the assumption of union responsibilities resulted in a reduction (if not an elimination) of the prospects for promotion, why would anyone choose this option? This sort of discrimination had long been denied by the company before it was finally recognized and acknowledged when the labour unions at Peugeot-Sochaux, the CGT and CFDT, forced management to compensate 169 factory workers at its Sochaux plant in 1998.[8]

There was also *positive discrimination vis-à-vis* unionists: the smarter managers promoted the more active and able union members. This not only enriched the higher levels, but also reduced by the same amount, the power of the unions. This practice was quite common in the 1980s and 1990s, when the older, hardened unionists were giving way to a younger, better-educated and better-qualified generation. A number of them, especially in small and medium-sized enterprises, were seduced by their management and chose to climb the corporate ladder rather than to remain with the uncertain future and long working hours that are the lot of a unionist. A variation on this method allowed workers (unionists) to neglect their working hours in order to join their local or departmental unions and engage in their activities: their absence from the workplace could not but benefit management.

Though not organized with such an objective in mind, the growth in the number of unions or para-unions in and around an enterprise began to take the elected representatives (a diminishing number, as we have already seen) away more and more frequently and for longer durations. This institutionalization of unionism and proof of a growing democracy (though lacking the numbers required for a true democracy) had the effect of cutting off the unionists from their area of influence (workshops, offices). As this took place at a time when they were not needed as much by their colleagues, their absence was practically unnoticed.[9] These two elements together did much to marginalize labour unions.

The institutionalization of unions meant that their elected representatives often rubbed shoulders with senior-level managers (during wage negotiations, enterprise committees, various ad hoc meetings). This, in fact, helped to bring them closer together, to the extent that the representatives began to dress like managers, to speak like them and even to go as far as to admit that the *principle of reality* of international competition applied to them as much as to the managers. Obviously, the degree to which this reality was recognized differed depending on the nature of the union and the strength of the conviction of its people. In every case, the gulf between them and the other members, or even more, with the employees in general, yawned widely enough to destroy the union's legitimacy.

Ray Marshall has called these ways of battling the unions – whether it was through building 'positive relations with the manpower' or through 'bitter and relentless legal campaigns' fought against them[10] – *forms of employers' opposition*. Taken together, they show just how much the balance has tilted against employees in the post-Fordian world. To top it off, the labour movement was threatened by yet another danger when employees were promised a second source of income – the part-owner's profit through ownership of company stock. This, in fact, dealt a double blow to any continuing wage demands: on the one hand, if these demands succeeded, they would reduce the profit, the dividend and finally the value of the company's shares. On the other hand, if the stocks remained high and strong, the increase in income would no longer justify an increase in wages. In this sense, the promise of preferred stocks put a large spoke in the wheel of unions' work, especially because it also affected other employees (technicians, executives, engineers, service employees), who could start taking an interest the moment they found that their salaries were stagnating or that their jobs were threatened, or even when their work began to lose its appeal and interest.

Full-time employment: the 35-hour-week mirage

Since the mid-1970s, the story of most enterprises has been a story of massive layoffs. The 1980s finally managed to come to terms with the malfunctioning Fordian 'virtuous circle', and profits made a comeback. Faced with the market's actual needs, the overcapacity of the productive apparatus caused many enterprises to close. At the same time, a return to healthy functioning often came about as the result of mergers and acquisitions that eliminated the 'doubling' of manpower. Subsequently, the logic of the share market further accelerated this process of pruning the labour force. New socio-productive tools such as tight flow could highlight stagnating reserves of productivity and thus eliminate pockets of redundant manpower. Newer waves of capital concentration and enterprise restructuring wiped out millions of jobs in the USA, Europe and Japan – though some of these were absorbed by new jobs being created in the service sector.

These compensatory forms of employment failed on two major counts. On the one hand, rejected employees were often older and with few qualifications, and the new job openings required much higher qualifications. Moreover, although lost jobs had often been 'stable' (long-term and full-time contracts in France), a large proportion of the new jobs, especially in the service sector, were unstable and poorly paid. In the USA and the UK, many employees were forced to work more than 70-hour weeks (that is, do multiple jobs) to earn the minimum required for a decent lifestyle.

There are two major causes for this change in the nature of employment. The first is a natural consequence of a reduction in the consumption of industrial goods from the peak they attained during the Fordian era;[11] and at the same time, these industries had also markedly improved their production capacity by the 1990s. The second cause stems from the nature and manner in which informational goods and services are consumed. A number of analysts thought, and some of them still do, that the coming decades would see ICT play a role similar to the part electricity and the internal combustion engine had played in the Golden Age: that is, although they helped and accelerated the production process, they themselves were also consumer goods – which set off a new virtuous circle, similar to the Fordian one. An extrapolation of the long Kondratieff cycles seems to support this view: we are at the time of writing at the lower point of the sinusoidal cycle, with an upward trend ahead of us. This places us right at the beginning of the virtuous phase of the cycle, whose apex would come some time during the years 2025–2030 with a return to full employment (the probability of which would rise to the extent that this period will see a very small number of young entrants to the labour market!).

Can ICT really create large-scale employment opportunities?

Is it really that mechanical? Can the discoveries of Kondratieff be extrapolated so easily and can we assign to ICT the role played by technologies in the previous revolution? Is ICT of the same nature? The same optimistic analysts very quickly realized that the material base of ICT – that is, electronics in general – could not play the role that industrialized goods did for the previous generation. This is because they are manufactured mainly in one region of the world, namely Asia, and especially because of the rapid pace of technological innovation; the value addition they represent is continually falling. In fact, over the past several decades, the cost of manipulating a unit of information has decreased a hundredfold every five years. In other words, only the software industry – items such as computer software, video games, television serials, telefilms, internet services, CDs, DVDs and so on – has the capacity to drive consumerism and create the large number of jobs that were required by the demand for industrialized goods during the Fordian virtuous circle.

Nevertheless, this analysis is worth further consideration. On the one hand, these software industries cost very little to set up, and the production of software is rather expensive, with doubtful profits. On the other hand, it would seem that programming industries have an intrinsic limit to their consumption: can one consume more information than the amount that can be used within the length of a day? And can one stack several sources of information – that is, can one receive simultaneously several types of information? It does not seem very likely. In contrast to the simultaneous consumption of a car and a household appliance (the repayment of the loans can go on at the same time), the consumption of information by people is limited by their physical and mental capacity for absorption. It seems that this limit of the amount of information that an individual can receive also limits the possibilities of expanding the spread of paid information – that is, of being able to form part of an ascending economic spiral. These physical and mental limits of individual consumption of information explain the limited success of the large enterprises specializing in the software industries. Microsoft is, of course, an exception – but how many Microsofts are there in the world?

In short, the theory propounded so far can be expressed thus: the return of consumerism through ICT has not led to any boom in the demand for value-added goods and services. This in turn means that the new norms of consumption have not resulted in any significant rise in the creation of new jobs, as we might have thought from an analysis based solely on the Kondratieff cycles or from the compensatory theory of employment over successive technological revolutions. Therefore, if we take into account the massive layoffs described previously and the paucity of new jobs in this new form of consumerism, we are faced with a *long-term imbalance of employment* – that is, a situation of *long-term unemployment*.[12]

Officially, the rate of unemployment in France stands at more than 10 per cent. If we also take into account those who are looking for part-time jobs and/or are on fixed-term contracts despite themselves, the subsidized jobs that will never become permanent, the financial aid recipients, older workers or the young who are excluded from unemployment statistics, the number would add up to some 5 million unemployed people in search of a job, out of an active population of 27 million – which in fact computes to an unemployment rate of 18 per cent. In an effort to contain this unemployment and remove job subsidization, the Jospin Government introduced the Aubry laws, which sought to reduce the weekly working hours from 39 to 35 over four years – 1998 to 2002.

The 35-hour law and the creation of jobs

In November 1997, one of the economic advisers to the Minister of Employment announced that decreasing the working week by four hours had been done primarily to create employment. According to him, the reduction in working hours would result in the creation of between 1.2 and 1.4 million jobs! In fact, the experts had used a simple rule of three weighted by a coefficient of 0.6 to take into account the flexibility of economic situations in general, and of employment in particular. Everyone agreed that, for example, if 100 hours-worth of work was left undone because of a reduction in working hours, it did not mean that those hours would be translated directly into x jobs, which would add up exactly to the 100 extra hours. In fact, only about 60 per cent of the hours would be used in the creation of new jobs, the rest would be taken by the employers in the form of increasing the *efficiency* of the work, a concept that is somewhat 'elastic' and difficult to quantify.

In fact, going by the official figure of some 35,000 to 400,000 new jobs created or preserved by the Aubry laws, the assumed coefficient of 0.6 in fact turned out to be no more than something between 0.15 and 0.2. In other words, as far as creating jobs was concerned, the reduction in the work time was something of a failure, though it must be admitted that it did improve the lot of the majority of workers, as long as the pace of their work during the remaining 35 hours did not increase (by too much). Unfortunately, even that did not seem to be the case too often, judging from the changes in the workload in recent years.[13]

The failure of the expected boom in the creation of new jobs was due to a number of clearly foreseeable reasons: in the first place, in response to employer pressure, a succession of statutes helped to increase the flexibility of working hours by annualizing it. This allowed employers to allocate and use their labour force in accordance with their seasonal or weekly requirements, and thus eliminate the need for new jobs. Second, these same statutes greatly reduced the cost of overtime, which on the contrary, should have been discouraged by increasing this cost. Obviously, employers took full advantage and resorted systematically to overtime work and did not have to resort to hiring new personnel. In the third place, a 10 per cent reduction in working hours over four to five years corresponds almost exactly to the growth in productivity (about 2 per cent at the national level, and much more in the trade sector). In other words, the productivity gains realized during the implementation of the 35-hour week have more or less compensated for the reduction in working hours. We have to say 'more or less', because there is obviously a big difference between medium- and large-sized enterprises on the one hand, and the small and in particular very small (micro) enterprises on the other. Similarly, situations were also very different between the trade and public sectors, with the latter giving rise to very few new jobs.

Sharing jobs and wealth

For all the reasons given previously, the dream of creating large numbers of new jobs by reducing the duration of working time remained just that – a dream. Moreover, the robust and sustained economic growth required for the creation of new employment did not materialize, and at the same time, increasing numbers of jobs were being axed by the continuing process of mergers and acquisitions. Economists have calculated that, while in the past a growth rate of between 5 per cent and 6 per cent was required to create new jobs, at the time of writing, something between 2.5 per cent and 3 per cent would be enough to create tens of thousands of new salaried employees in a country such as France. But there is no economic model that can tell us whether the trend in the creation of new jobs is following the curve of the economy. At the same time, the global economic situation is such that there is not much likelihood of any sustained economic growth in Europe that might guarantee full-time or even quasi-full-time employment. In other words, unemployment in Europe is here to stay, and it has hardly been affected by the reduction in working hours.

Employment for all seems to us a basic anthropological need in our capitalist society, because it is salaried work that situates and classifies individuals in their immediate and global surroundings. Employment thus helps to create an order and forge consequent relationships, not only in the workplace but also beyond it. It helps to establish social hierarchies and to prop up the social ladders that everyone tries to climb in order to be seen, recognized and appreciated.

The manner in which each one enters and participates in this social game no doubt depends to some extent on the individual's social heritage, but much rests on the his/her personal effort to retain or build personal resources in order to improve his/her position in the game. It is no wonder, then, that work at school and later in employment are so important, and why 'universal allowance' schemes such as the RMI (financial aid) proved to be useless. Employment for all is a necessary condition for weaving the social fabric of a town, a community or a nation. Necessary, but not sufficient – there is also a need for proper education and training at home and at school that would instil the moral values that are so essential for life in any civilized society. We believe employment for all – that is, salaried work in general – is one of the essential conditions that needs to be created by the government in order to avoid the social disintegration that would result from the disorientation and sense of loss among those deprived of jobs, because it is gainful employment that gives some meaning and support to life in today's world.[14]

At the same time, it is no use creating non-viable jobs sustained artificially and of little social use, such as was done in the French national workshops in 1848. From this point of view at least, the majority of present-day new jobs do have some social utility because to some extent they replace older jobs that have disappeared: invigilators in schools and colleges, personnel on metro platforms, bus conductors, and so on. The whole problem then boils down to creating enough jobs for everyone (not necessarily full-time, as long as the pay is adequate) without using artificial means and creating useless posts that are impossible to sustain financially. The only radical solution would seem to consist in *sharing out the existing jobs* (that is, with a socially equal volume of work) *while retaining the income and without increasing the labour cost to the employers.*

In European countries with a strong social tradition, the only way of squaring this circle is by taking into account the enormous amount of money locked up in the form of social aid, unemployment benefit funds and various employment support, which in themselves have proved so often to be ineffective. In France, the cost of unemployment has been estimated at some €60 billion – approximately equal to the budget of the national education board, or more than a fifth of the entire national budget. Employment-sharing must be based first and foremost on a real-location and redistribution of those jobs that are physically demanding. Hundreds of thousands of people could find work if working time were to be reduced by 50 per cent to 80 per cent of the present level[15] without salaries being affected in any way. Part of the income would come from the employers, proportionate to the work, and the rest from a 'compensation fund' created with the €60 billion already mentioned. It could very well happen that senior employees approaching the end of their careers could choose to work for no more than 80 per cent of the legal amount, with their salaries reduced by only a few percentage points, and thus open the way for younger job-seekers. At the same time, there could be others who could choose to continue working beyond the legal retirement age, especially on a part-time basis, on a salary that would be supplemented by retirement funds.

Such a job-sharing programme avoids, by its very principle, the pitfalls of a simple reduction in working time, including having little or no effect on unemployment. In this case, because the objective is to give employment to every eligible individual, the sharing of jobs – which, at a constant volume of demand for goods and services would undoubtedly result in a decrease in working hours – would necessarily lead to a significant reduction in unemployment. The only thing left is to question the conditions and manner of implementing such a scheme. Because it is very important to avoid any disaffiliation within the 'social network', the sharing of employment seems to be the most acceptable solution – though requiring great political courage to initiate and implement. In fact, it calls for a complete paradigm shift in the management of the workforce, because it is not the duration of working time that is paid for any more, but the workforce itself, even when it is not working full-time. This solution to the social ills caused by unemployment might well subvert the economic logic of those enterprises that depend on the existence of a fragmented 'army of reservists' (see Chapter 5), which not only maintains pressure on the employees, but also pushes them into accepting the principles of the 'Competency Model' (loyalty, implementation of a tight flow). Apart from the political agitation initiated by every leftist government within its own country, other social forces such as unionism, the reformist polit-ical parties and public opinion should come together to demand the inclu-sion of a fourth clause to the Maastricht Treaty (something that goes beyond meeting certain financial conditions such as limiting the public debt, the budget deficit and inflation): to limit unemployment (whose method of calculation could be refined) to no more than 4–5 per cent. For this, the governments could design policies that would encourage enter-prises to create part-time jobs while paying them full wages. One of the first incentives, particularly for the more painful, repetitive or boring jobs, would be a reduction in the working hours: if the employees were less tired, they would perform better and become more efficient and productive. Moreover, part-time work would also have the legal advantage that it would not need the same number of breaks – a fact that a number of employers have already taken full advantage of, especially in retail business.

One of the criticisms levelled against the sharing of employment is that it would perpetuate the unemployment umbrella (as we saw earlier, costing some €60 billion). In fact, it is liberalism itself that perpetuates it, by holding it up to shelter the unemployed and predicting that there would be none left jobless by the end of the 1970s. That never happened. In fact, numerous experts now see unemployment as a chronic illness that is here to stay. However, the demographic changes will result, by 2020/2025, in fewer young entrants to the labour market (particu-larly in France) – thus the majority of employees would be assured full-time jobs.

The sharing of employment and income[16] is also often criticized, on the grounds that it would completely disorganize enterprises and adminis-trations. We have two distinct answers to this. In the first place, employees at every level and of all levels of qualification have seen a tremendous growth in their mobility since the 1980s. The development of multiple competencies, versatility, multi-functionality and working in groups has led to a greatly increased interchangeability among employees. At the same time, the increase in part-time work has multiplied the number of people who can do similar tasks or attain specified objectives. Thus the sharing of employment and the growing number of employees working for shorter periods fits in well with this mobility of personnel within the enterprise. Second, working for 80 per cent of the time does not neces-sarily mean having the time spread over four days. On the contrary, that would confuse the enterprise as much as it would the employee. Other forms of scheduling working time, such as a sabbatical year, or an increase in the amount of paid leave, could be investigated and solutions found that would suit all the parties concerned.

Thus the sharing of employment and money carries some political risk – it might be easier to apply a simple mathematical formula and neatly reduce the working week to 35 hours than to encourage job-sharing and advocate a completely different manner of reallocating funds raised at the national or international (European Union) levels.

The main reason for not implementing job-sharing is that the unions do not (or rarely) meet the unemployed who, by the very fact of their situation, remain dispersed and isolated. Throughout history, nothing has succeeded in bringing them together – on the one hand, employees and their unions are perennially occupied by their struggle to retain threatened jobs, and on the other, the unemployed are physically scattered.

Time to transform the unions

Thus, even in this post-Fordian era, capitalism, with its sharp dichotomy between capital and labour, has remained very much the dominant principle behind the acquisition of wealth. At the same time, the class struggle is no longer as physically violent as before and has assumed other forms. In fact, living conditions (as well as working conditions) have seen a vast improvement. Bosses have become less authoritarian, and hard physical labour is largely a thing of the past. Although the crisis of accumulation, or rather the post-Fordian ways of resolving it, involved a reduction in the workforce (often peremptory lay-offs in a number of countries) and increased pressure on employees (demanding faster work rhythms, and longer, more flexible working hours), it also helped, more than ever before, to motivate employees and keep them focused on the objectives set by the management. On the one hand is the need to motivate and involve the employees, while on the other, rising international competition and globalization have made sure that employees, managers and part-time workers were all together 'In the same boat' and working collectively for the survival of the enterprise. Meanwhile, the social structure of capitalism has also become more complex. Apart from the fragmentation among the workers, enterprises have also seen the disintegration or formation of subdivisions among its employees, executives, engineers and technicians. The whole aspect of unionism was forced to undergo a radical change: the lack of social identity and especially the work itself (the basis of all union activity) was no larger the problem it had been for the previous two centuries.

During the course of this turmoil, the dichotomy between revolutionary and reformist unionisms reincarnated itself as the opposition between protesting and co-operative unions, which only goes to prove that the nature of unionism is very much alive. In France, a number of unionists and scientists were troubled by this division between confederations, which set these two great tendencies of the unionist movement against each other. But they were forgetting that it was the same within the large unions themselves, as well as the large confederations in the USA, Germany, the UK, and the Scandinavian countries.

As long as the opposition between capital and labour remained, the two parties had no other option but to have their interests represented by institutions – unless they preferred a blind struggle and violence. This was exactly what was felt by some managers, such as those at AXA, Casino and FNAC in France, who went as far as to partially finance some of the unions (obviously with the hope of seeing them co-operate rather than protest).[17] Although the necessity of having unions was recognized in all industrialized countries, it did not mean that there was no effort to weaken them or to see their influence wane.

If unionism is to continue to exist and even to grow, the central questions are: why, and how? Though its function as an agent for solidarity and the construction of a group identity has been greatly curtailed, unionism still retains its role of representing the labour group(s) and defending their interests. Already, we find it increasingly more active in the defence and management of social work (leisure activity for employees, holidays, educational trips, for example) and at the same time becoming more and more efficient and using increasingly sophisticated techniques. But more important, unionists must apply themselves more strongly in their role as representatives of employee interests.

Towards an expert unionism?

Unionists were compelled by the force of circumstances to develop their expertise and gain the necessary knowledge to be able to stand up to management or government representatives. This level of expertise was required by those unionists or specialists who were engaged specifically by unions and confederations to negotiate with employers on behalf of employees, or, in general, between management and workers. This, of course, ran the risk of turning into a certain 'bureaucratization' of the body of unionists and experts – with an even bigger rift developing between them and the majority of the employees. However, the danger of weakening the union by an inability to address deeper questions and get to the root of a problem seems to be even greater.

Unions could develop their expertise in at least three different ways:

- by increasing the number of permanent unionists; this would ensure that they would be working either full-time or part-time;

- by training the permanent or elected members, who would then no longer be only 'politicians' but also be technicians and experts in management, communication, negotiation, company strategy, and so on; and
- by increasing the number of high-level professional experts (either as full-time workers or as consultants) who would help the unionists to do their various jobs.

These three ways are in no way exclusive, and certainly other avenues are possible – at least in France. But, as always, this proposition too has its share of critics, who have advanced two major counter-arguments: first, that it might turn the union into some sort of pressure group cut off from its base and its primary objectives. As such, it would not have the support of employees, and neither would it be able to meet their demands because any successful campaign would require a power base organized by and favourable to the employees. Second, they say that it would be almost impossible to finance these experts, especially in Latin Europe and among white-collar employees, because of the weak financial status of the unions.

If it comes down to a choice between an unavoidable weakening of traditional unionism and the risks – they are nothing more than that – of the possible negative effects of institutionalizing the unions, would it not be better to take those risks? After all, the trend towards reducing the labour force and watering down the effects of the post-Fordian regulations are already well under way. Moreover, these risks could always be minimized by periodically holding elections and choosing new union representatives. Nobody contests the limits of a representative democracy, but in the absence of a participative democracy, the former ensures a better democratic functioning! The financial question could also find itself gradually resolved if experts were recruited in stages and to the extent that the employees begin to feel the necessity of having on their side expert negotiators[18] or people who could influence the strategic orientation of the company, the nature of the work, or professional relations.

The various options, such as developing the required expertise among permanent workers and in those elected by the unions, or taking recourse to other experts, are not mutually exclusive; in fact, they complement each other. Expertise can be developed in at least five different fields: *social work*; the *technology* behind the production of goods and services (particularly around ITC); the *communicative skills* used to address the employees, anyone outside the enterprise or the administration; the *management of human resources;* and *company strategy* (products and processes).

As far as social activities are concerned (leisure and cultural activities, holiday resorts, tourism and so on), it is unfortunate that they, and sometimes even societies, do not interest employees any longer, because the workers can now get much better deals from the commercial market, which offers them better service and at a lower cost. If we consider that the social activities taken up by the committees within the enterprises are in fact subsidized by them – at least in France – it just underlines how mismanaged they are. Nevertheless, there do exist ways by which the activities taken up by the company committees could regain their former lustre, but for that the elected representatives must develop some real expertise, and more experts need to be recruited.

The technology behind the production process, whether it involves the use of ICT or the institution of organizational reforms, must always be discussed between the two parties involved before being implemented. Only then would it be universally accepted and result in the expected gains, be it in production, quality or flexibility. The reorganization of work, the need for further training, changes in the classification of the professional status or its future prospects must be mutually agreed. Unfortunately, at the present time unions seem to be skirting some of the major issues (such as the sharing of any gains in productivity, the pace of the work, mutual transparency), which cannot but result in a *simulated involvement* and ultimately be counter to the expected results. The unions could very well take advice from a number of experts (sociologists, ergonomists, psychologists, trainers and so on), as was done for a time by the German union IG Metall with the computer integrated manufacturing (CIM) centres in the mid-1980s. It is interesting to note how the French unions persistently under-utilized 'technological expertise' (which had been provided for by the Auroux laws of 1982). Similarly, the management of human resources (general strategy, development of the age pyramid, classification, mobility, planning work schedules, and so on), which should usually go hand-in-hand with any changes made to the work process, was neglected in most union negotiations; these were concerned solely with wage increases or an early retirement scheme for older employees. A similar situation arose regarding the implementation of the 35-hour week – nothing was said about the actual conditions or the hectic pace of work, particularly in the tertiary sector.

Strategic and financial expertise of unionists

The almost complete absence of any expertise regarding financial and economic management is a glaring omission from the negotiating table. And yet, if we consider the extent to which the unions were involved in the economic and industrial strategy of the enterprise, it should have been easy for them to go right to the top of the administrative hierarchy, which dealt with the management of work and human resources, and to identify a number of structural bottlenecks.

If we accept the hypothesis that the modern enterprise is organized into several power levels (strategic, tactical and operational) and that each power level corresponds to a specific level of economic management (financial management of profitability, management of trade competitiveness, and the physical management of productivity), it is easy to understand why, at the time of the great debates on the efficiency and performance of enterprises, it was difficult to apprehend anything more than work and human resources at the operational level, and the micro-regulations or the games played within the narrow confines of the workshop.

The role of the unions should not just be some sort of damage control trying to contain the social consequences of a restructuring process; instead, they should act proactively and intervene during the decision-making process itself. Therefore, union negotiators should never neglect the dynamics of the relations between the evaluation of work, management criteria and market strategies. These negotiators could also study and be greatly helped from an economic point of view by the work done on 'production combinations' by highly qualified professionals. Basically, the unions and personnel representatives should gain a wider perspective and enlarge their understanding of the various happenings. The methods for organizing work would then be seen in their entirety, with the causes (choice of technology, forms of production) and their consequences (level of employment, work conditions, and so on).

Unions would then be in a position to be more innovative, to suggest alternatives and pit logic against logic. There is never a single, uniquely correct economic or managerial solution; there are always multiple answers, each logical and valid from its own perspective of the work, the market and the enterprise. Therefore, the question of economic or social efficiency in the context of an overall transformation of social relations cannot be the sole prerogative of either the financial or managerial experts. In fact, an abstract definition of economic efficiency does not even exist, because there is no specific and unequivocal unit for measuring performance. The apparent productivity of work, the global productivity, economic profitability, financial profitability, social efficiency, and so on, are all factors that can be considered and given their due place only by a combined effort of all the partners.

Today, for example, it is evident that the hierarchy of the managerial system and the predominance of financial considerations can have a number of adverse effects on the 'human resources' variable: though the enterprise enriches itself in terms of personnel who are competent and versatile, this labour force is counted as an expense that depletes the enterprise financially, and lay-offs are seen to be beneficial because they improve company results and improve the balance sheet.

Brodier has shown how the majority of the traditional tools of management lead to a decline in the entity called *company* (in the legal sense of being the property of shareholders) instead of the entity called *enterprise* in the sense of a system of production that results in the creation of wealth (goods or services).[19] Labour belongs to the enterprise and not to the incorporated company because it is the source of all value addition and development. However, because the employees do not have the status of being partners – that is, they are neither shareholders nor proprietors, they do not form a part of the incorporated company and their work is seen here only in terms of an expense that constantly needs to be checked and minimized. The enterprise itself has no legal reality, and as such, effort will be required to find the most appropriate legal forms and the most pertinent managerial tools required for it to create wealth, which is not being reflected in any value addition for the shareholders.

Thus it is extremely important for the unions themselves to question the managerial tools, as all too often the decision-makers make a stand not as a function of objective reality, which is too complex and contradictory to be apprehended with any certitude, but based on their individual and collective representations of it. As a number of authors have pointed out,[20] management tools are not really there to state an absolute economic reality, but as the base of certain collective representations of performance, and consequently as the base for evolving languages for describing performance. This implies that these tools will always remain objects of study, discussion and conflict. In fact, 'competitiveness' and 'productivity' are constructs invented by economists and managers – that is, concepts created by social actors. For example, management indicators and ratios that measure productivity contribute to the co-ordinating of the work and govern the relationships between the different actors within the enterprise. At the same time, one must also know how to deconstruct and/or reconstruct them in order to be able to break out of obsolete and wrong constructs.

Obviously, strategy remains the most difficult aspect to tackle. But as long as the unions do not surround themselves with experts who are at the same level as those fielded by the management, they will never be able to change anything, be it the refocusing of the acquisition of interest, mergers, delocalization of activities, and so on. The exclusion of unionists from the board of directors is part of the very fabric of capitalism, but it is always possible, by constant agitation and harassment, to gain access to strategic information, force management to come to the negotiating table, and try to influence their decisions.

Thus we see that co-operative unionism could not exist without debate and participation, without some sort of confrontation and the mobilization of as many employees as possible. Co-operation and confrontation, participation and conflict are not mutually exclusive; on the contrary, they help each other and belong to a single unionist policy. Even more, they constitute a nature of unionism that can never be exclusively confrontational or completely co-operational, except at the cost of its soul. That is why it is of paramount importance that the unions surround themselves with communications specialists who can convey, justify and convince the other party of the validity of the reasons behind the demands or the strike. It is all right as long as unionists have a physical presence within the enterprise, but in two-thirds of the cases where it is not so, almost everything still has to be done. Unions must use every medium available within (especially in the case of enterprises with subsidiaries and sub-contractors) and outside the enterprise, particularly now that leisure time has begun to grow so much in importance in public opinion.

Communication and mobilization

It is not enough simply for expert unionists to gather information or know-how in order to come up with counter strategies or alternative ways of reorganizing labour – these plans must be communicated to all the employees and, more importantly, be understood, accepted and adopted by the majority of them. That is why it is so necessary to have communications experts and specialists in the handling of language and other symbolic tools – people who can stand up to management and who can try to convince workers of the merits and genuineness of their proposals. As long as the contradiction between capital and labour persists, employees have no other means except that of collective agitation to put across their point of view to management or the shareholders (or managers of large administrations). We see here all the difficulties that need to be faced in order to transform unionism into a force of suggestion without having the capacity of rallying workers. To choose the German form of unionism does not mean only to please enough of the workers (and consequently be easier to implement), it also entails, on the one hand, the demarcation of a line beyond which any proposal would be unacceptable, and on the other, the mobilization of employees against managerial abuses or for pushing through important reforms.

French unionism used to be riddled with contradictions. First, they had a confederation that thought of following the German example without a complete knowledge of German unionism. Second, their newly-founded organization refused to make any compromises while remaining confined to the protected sectors. Finally, they had a central parent body that refused to sign most of the major national agreements while taking part in their implementation. But, though the different unions did not boast a large number of adherents (around 9 per cent of the active population – meagre compared to other North European countries, Italy and Japan), it did have a sizeable impact. Compared to some of the larger union movements of the world since the 1980s the French unions seem to have shaken their employers quite a bit – either compelling them to reverse certain unfriendly decisions, or to instigate vociferous demands. Although analysts have divergent views regarding the union movement of December 1995 against the Juppe Government, it does not deny the fact that it shook the entire government and led to the dissolution of the French parliament in 1997.[21] Despite the low union membership, French employees effectively demonstrated their agitation – proof that the general mobilization depended as much on symbolism as on the structure of the union. Indeed, the French were rather sensitive in this regard, as can be seen by their solid participation in the anti-globalization movement (if we look at the role played by ATTAC[22] and the peasant confederation). At the same time, apart from the interiors of big international institutions, the internationalization of unionism remains largely unexplored.

The internationalization of unionism

The organization of unions at the multinational level or in a large enterprise with subsidiaries and sub-contractors came some ten to twenty years after the organization of capital itself. In contrast to the nineteenth century, when the 'Internationale ouvrière' presided over the labour movement, unionism at the time of writing is neither efficient nor effective at the international level. All too often the regional confederations acted as UN bureaucracies and the works councils had only just been created and were as yet too immature.

To become organized internationally, unionism had to negotiate a number of pitfalls: the historic traditions that were often sectarian and vindictive, the diversity in union structures (by job, by sector), the difference in culture (revolutionary/protest unions versus the reformist/ co-operative unions) and the differences in the degree of unionization – not to mention language problems.[23] Although growing liberalism brought about some cohesion among the methods of handling socio-economic problems all over the world, it did not seem to have any such effect on unionism. More important, national heritage seems to discourage the creation of organizations that would be able to represent the employees efficiently and effectively and at the same time be in step with the organization of capital.

The greatest disparity in the nature and functioning of capital and labour lies in the fact that capital has no nationality – it is in fact completely fluid and can and does circulate at the speed of light through globe-spanning computerized networks. However, labour is bound, to a large extent, to the country, to its very soil ('working the fields'), to a culture, a house, a family, to groups and social relations. Though we could try to freeze this fluidity of capital by insisting on the *physical* aspect that is fundamental to any organization in the production of goods and services, we also know how easy it is for capital to break camp at a moment's notice and move to another site, and especially how quickly the production of services can be teleported to another country. Try as we might, we cannot escape the fact that although labour remains firmly anchored and bound to the territory, capital is characterized by extreme mobility and has no such restraints.

National roots and international needs

Not only did the management drive different establishments within the same consortium to compete against each other[24] – generally more in terms of profit margins[25] rather than any actual competitiveness – but the unions also, as a reflection of this competition, fought among themselves within their European Works Councils:

> often, the [EWC] meetings turned out to be nothing more than occasions for sly and underhand confrontations between the delegates of different countries. It was as though the main issue was the adoption of the social model of a country to the detriment of another. In such situations, if a union happened to be clearly dominant (perhaps because it represented a large section of employees and/or the headquarters of the parent company), the other unions would withdraw themselves in a bid to regain their autonomy and solve their problems at the national level, without taking any more active part in the committee.[26]

Moreover, within Europe's Fifteen member states, the differences in the prevailing labour laws of each country made it very difficult to co-ordinate unions and to implement any general regulations regarding the duration of working hours, temporary work and so on: '[T]he harmonization [meeting points] tended toward the common minimum, especially because of the restrictions applied by the principle of "subsidies" within the institutions which formulated the European regulations.'[27] Although Europe as a whole improved its labour laws, this did not benefit the well-placed employees who had fought hard to attain their comfortable status. And while workers in the poorer countries (in southern Europe, Ireland and Eastern European) were helped, which resulted in a certain reduction in the disparity between them and their more fortunate counterparts, it did not lead to any significant convergence of unions, because the employees of northern European countries found that they had in fact lost some ground, while it was mainly those from the south of Europe (and the east) who had benefited the most.

Consequently, unionism in Europe found itself pulled in different directions and sometimes even torn between its work at the national level and its pan-European activities. Even today, the European Union gives precedence to its individual national governments:

> It's as simple as it is stupid. Who decides at the European level? It is the Council of Ministers, or eventually, the European Council. Thus, the labour union (which remains national) which has some political clout and which would like to influence the decisions taken at the European level, has to try and move its own government ... There are massive forces which hold the unions and prevent any Europeanization. And even though we might feel otherwise, unions have many sound reasons to limit themselves to their country.[28]

Thus, even though the confederations of trade unions understand the strategic issues regarding the internationalization of capital and the necessity of dealing with the main questions at the European level, the community structures send them back to their countries, and for greater effect, to Brussels. These international institutions prevent the internationalization of European trade unions, and the capital continues merrily towards further concentration and internationalization.

At the heart of these tensions between the national activities and the inter-European organizations, unionism ensconced itself in Brussels because 'globalization and regionalization undermined the very pertinence of national institutes and procedures in matters regarding the management of employment and professional relations'.[29] Established in 1973, the European Trade Union Confederation (ETUC) includes today most of the national confederations. According to the left front, the ETUC is much too subservient to the European Commission, 'which is the same as saying that its manner of working is too European'.[30] In other words, because the employers set their standards too low in the European Works Councils (EWCs), legislation has now replaced negotiation, and the major portion of the articles adopted, such as parental leave, seem pretty meagre compared to the proactive social situation in the Scandinavian countries, Germany or France. The laws regarding non-standard employment do not in any way change the actual conditions of its implementation, and those on consultation/information of workers lead only to some drastic consequences because the management is in no way obliged to listen to the employees' side of the story.

The EWCs deal with the 600 enterprises that employ more than 1,000 people and that are present in at least two member countries of the European Union, with establishments of at least 150 employees. Though mandatory since 1997, only about half of the eligible enterprises have such committees. Those that were most open created them before the cut-off date of 1 January 1997, as did the shrewder ones, who were afraid that forthcoming directives might be more stringent. In answer to the information and consultation needs of employees, these EWCs concerned themselves with the future developments of the company without taking the place of any existing national bodies – the financial situation of the group, the restructuring, the establishment or relocation of units, the employment status, mass lay-offs, and so on.

In every country, the role of these European Works Councils was similar to the functions of the local personnel consultation forums (wherever they existed). In other words, though not exact duplicates, they were coloured by the experiences and values accumulated by the unions in each of these countries.[31] Similarly, the various stands taken by the management were derived from their heritage: some of them saw in this a great opportunity to integrate personnel and have them share the company's objectives, and others fought against it tooth and nail because they felt that strategic information should never be shared, let alone discussed in public. In any case, the EWCs were not places where decisions were made, or even places where any industrial policies or economic or financial strategies were discussed. At best, they provided an opportunity for the management:

> to prepare the ground for future developments, test the initial reactions to the planned changes and establish relations with unionists. The whole idea being to create a climate of confidence, to test the positions taken by the social partners and to predefine the modalities and

the rhythm for implementing the changes. Rare were the occasions when union delegates made any counter-proposals.[32]

In fact, all agree that these EWCs – at least at their present level of development – are a hotbed of experiments conducted to co-ordinate the different unions present in the group. In addition, issues that were closest to the unionists' hearts are reopened: union rights, work and social security, employment and training policies wage policies and so on. Labour conditions were improved significantly through the efforts made by these committees towards co-ordinating (though it was not its prime objective) and later toward standardizing them. Thus, from the point of view of the employees, these EWCs played a much larger role than the European directives co-produced by the European Trade Union Confederation and the European Commission.

Having said that, it must also be noted that the results fell a long way short of expectations because the EWCs were far removed from the field. On the one hand, the employees were not informed about the debates and the orientations taken up by consortiums – which also explains the weak employee participation in the issues raised by the unionists who were elected to the EWCs, except when it concerned lay-offs, and even then it was often too late. On the other hand, the enterprises that were not represented directly in EWCs (those of the periphery) found themselves left out of the debates or simply not informed. Also, as far as the consortium itself was concerned, there was practically never any question of the other components that make up the large or networked enterprise, such as the suppliers and sub-contractors, who nevertheless form an essential part of the daily life of the group. In a certain sense, this new system also favoured (because it is in the very nature of capitalism) the social and economic reincarnation of the core of the production process while maintaining the periphery as a necessary adjunct.

There have already been other attempts at internationalizing unionism, such as in the US motor vehicle industry and in the agri-food industries of the International Union of Food and Allied Workers Associations.[33] They involved the creation of 'Worldwide Works Councils' that would bring together union representatives from the parent companies as well as from the subsidiaries of large conglomerates. This long and exacting task met numerous obstacles, such as the friction between enterprises that had differing labour norms, the misunderstandings created by contrasting social and political histories and, of course, the great mismatch at the level of union organization. All these problems were of a much more complex nature than those encountered by the European Works

Councils, which dealt with union representatives from corporations that had reached more or less similar technological and capitalistic standards. Although enterprises from the developing nations formed part of the 'Group-level Works Councils', they also belonged to all that made up the periphery of the large enterprises in Europe. Often they were companies with a large workforce having few or no qualifications (or even illiterate). This made for widely divergent labour demands, especially if we consider that some of these enterprises were created with the express aim of completely undermining the competitiveness of employees working in the industrialized countries.

Nevertheless, it was this internationalization of unionism – very much in a close relationship with the local sentiments in the workplace and in direct touch with realities on the ground – that held the keys to the resurgence of unionism. Creating a worldwide and/or regional co-ordination of a group of unions in order to deal simultaneously with the economic and financial strategies of the group and its consequences on labour itself has now assumed a high priority, though without it being implemented concretely. Some associations, such as the International Labour Organization (ILO) attempted to enforce the minimum social recommendations in countries where certain companies were exploiting the population. It tried to push the governments to pass laws that would regulate, if not ban, child and female labour, limit working hours and so on. Occasionally, ethical considerations prompt a public denouncement of companies that do not implement these recommendations. But, in spite of it all, the imbalances among different regions of the world persist: according to the data provided by the United Nations (UN) and the OECD, the 'development of under-development' goes on, and neither unionism nor the ILO nor the many NGOs have done anything to bridge the gap between these regions and the industrialized countries. This is the reason behind the growing discontent and worldwide protests against the injustice of a situation where a small percentage of the population consumes more than three-quarters of the energy produced and almost as much steel, and entire regions continue to be ravaged by hunger, epidemics and malnutrition.

From class-conflicts to 'anti-globalization' wars?

All these movements came together in Seattle in 1999 to protest the implementation of a new round by the World Trade Organization (WTO). Later, they also set up camp in Nice and Prague to protest against certain political decisions taken by the European Union, and finally they converged on Geneva to condemn the hegemony exercised by the G7 countries over the rest of the world. In fact, these protest movements were not really against the *internationalization* of the economy, but against the effects of the *globalization*[34] of production, trade and, in particular, of capital. In fact, most of the movements lived and moved in harmony with globalization, using its best technologies to move its own members rapidly from one place to another, or to communicate instantly with anyone anywhere in the world. What these movements fought against as a group, while retaining their own focus (branch of activity, status regarding labour, level of income, age, gender) was the nature of the ongoing developments and the consequent increase in the imbalances between regions, social inequalities within each country, and the destruction of the entire ecosystem.

For the most part, these movements integrated themselves into the social trends from previous decades and centuries, though they often assumed other forms and had somewhat different objectives. These social movements perpetuated, in a certain sense, the class struggles initiated by Marx's proletariat in their effort against the most obvious results (such as the misery in the world) and against the mechanisms that underlie them (financial speculation, for example). It was always, and remains, a case of social struggle against the domination of capital, and against its economic and social effects. Thus these internationalist social movements – international in the sense that they gathered together and publicly on the international scene after Seattle – followed similar objectives to the labour movement, after its own failure to construct an aggressive alternative to capitalism. Except that they did not propose an alternative, but rather a different manner of working with capitalism – that is, to implement one or more worldwide regulations to eliminate the present confusion. This idea of a worldwide regulation is nothing new – it was discussed at length after the Second World War, but the more powerful partners were not in favour of it, and the others could not agree among themselves as to who would really benefit from such a regulation.

The idea of a worldwide regulation gave rise to yet another conflict: the USA[35] wanted it to be formulated by and within the ambit of the WTO, and the majority of the other countries, especially the anti-globalization movements, felt that any new regulations should be made by new institutions, well away from the imbalances of region and political power that characterize all UN organizations. These movements were initiated and animated by the younger generation, which did not accept the inequalities that govern most social relations. Disillusioned with the humanitarian movement and the NGOs that did not reach the root of the problem, these young firebrands hoped to take the fight to the very spot where these decisions were made – at the major world summits – with the annual Davos summit finding itself besieged ever more earnestly year after year.

Looked at more closely, a number of these internationalist social movements turned out to have direct links with labour – they functioned as mediating agencies between labour and nature, and among different people. ATTAC came up with the suggestion of recycling a minute part of the financial speculations – that is, a value produced by labour and taken by share markets. According to this movement, the Tobin tax[36] would help in the economic and cultural development of the poorer nations by initiating programmes to fight against inequalities. Environmentalist movements such Greenpeace made their presence felt all over the world and turned into household issues the problems associated with the use of fossil fuels, the production of non-biodegradable waste (especially nuclear waste), which would continue to contaminate the planet when it was inherited by the grandchildren of our great-grandchildren, and the dangers of further disturbing the fragile balance of nature. Taken together, these protests, condemnations and warnings raised fundamental questions about our way of life, our processes of production and our relation with the planet.

The farming movements also demanded other ways of producing – first, to put an end to their poverty, and next, because they hoped to pass on to the next generation a better world. The Via Campesina (established in 1993 when farm managers in Central America joined hands with those of Europe; later spread all over the world) brought together some 50 million farmers from Sixty-five nations and included the MST (the movement launched by the landless rural workers of Brazil) and the Assembly of the Poor (created in Asia in 1995). They fought against the WTO in a bid to regain control of their development – for example, by preventing the Monsanto Consortium from manipulating seeds that would result in a sterile second generation (the famous 'Terminator' seeds). They also fought for the future of different species, against the patenting of living organisms and to prevent the growth of 'junk food', which would lead to the development of species or varieties with no taste or flavour.[37] These were reinforced by other movements led by the unemployed and the women, who protested against the economic effects of globalization and the consequent segregations and widening of social inequalities.[38]

Having all these groups, *anti-globalization-as-it-is* movements are undeniably a novel form of social protest that take into account simultaneously the deteriorating living conditions of tens of millions of people all over the world and the uncertainties regarding the survival of people. Seen in this way, this movement would seem to have a solid and long-lasting hold on people, as it combines a radical critique of a tangible and hard reality with the hope for a different and better future. Can we then say that it has a better chance of success than its predecessors, especially the labour movement? No one knows for sure. By attacking the growing inequalities and the increasing imbalances created between people and nature by capitalism, these movements go to the other extreme and become counterproductive. In fact, they begin to act like memory-springs. These springs are no doubt indispensable for the survival of humanity, but they cannot stop the proliferation of capital.[39]

However, we could also read in these social movements an alternative to a *laisser-faire* attitude at the global level. By their very differences, these movements are carried by political values and programs (ATTAC being a case in point[40]). They prevailed upon the others to give a greater priority to economic policies that would avoid creating social and environmental imbalances. Broadly speaking, it meant the reconfiguration of the present power structures by relocating people and placing them at the heart of the economy while suppressing the financial aspects. The economy is made for people, and not people for the economy. This also presupposes giving priority to the majority over the few. Moreover, the new criteria of socio-economic choices cannot be based solely on the production of goods, but rather on the individuals who make them.

Economic, and especially financial, growth, which is based on an individual striving for material profit in the short term, cannot provide a stable principle of political or social organization. Any development must have other aims, especially if the project would like to remain environmentally friendly. Therefore, globalization that stems from another, more permanent, form of development would imply that policy should be given priority over economics. Obviously, governments would play a decisive role by keeping an eye and a heavy hand on the economic monopolies formed by private interests through mergers, acquisitions and other ways of gathering economic power. But recent years have not seen governments taking the required steps to meet the challenges posed by globalization (failure of the Multilateral Investment Agreement in 1998, failure by the negotiators in Seattle to launch a new cycle of trade liberalization in 1999, failure of the conference in La Haye on climate change in 2000, the refusal by the USA to sign the Kyoto protocol on the protection of the environment, and so on).

The more liberal of the anti-globalization movements would like to see the setting up of a global political framework that would permit the formulation, on a concerted and democratic basis, of public policies on an international scale. The developed countries must come together with the developing ones to define new policies that would replace those set down by the group of G7 nations, a group whose legitimacy is increasingly suspect. These protest movements have also called for the restructuring of international bodies such as the International Monetary Fund (IMF), the World Bank and the World Trade Organization (WTO), which they feel should reform themselves and not continue to be the instruments of certain powerful interests, be they private or public. Their internal functioning must become more democratized and transparent. Moreover, they should not be dominated by the rich G7 countries; instead, all nations should participate in their management and have a say in proportion to their demographic weight.

The IMF would then be in a position to widen its portfolio and would therefore go on to other, broader objectives rather than being preoccupied exclusively with the stability of financial markets and the fight against inflation – objectives such as sustained growth and employment. At present, international bodies aim only at regulating the world economy through means of finance, which is also their way of exerting political power and hegemony. It could well be that the USA would not be too keen to give up its prerogatives so long as it continues to benefit from its economic and financial clout, and so long as nothing happens to disturb its political advantage. But the USA now finds itself less and less able to have its own way, because it not longer has the required economic strength. The world has thus become semi-anarchist, which has given rise to the US tendency to flex its military muscle in order to impose what it fails to secure through economic means.[41] These social movements attempt to show that capitalism in its neo-liberal avatar is destroying the traditional order of social relations, and that at present it is incapable of replacing it with any better and lasting arrangement.

At the time of writing, these reforms and reorientations of the international institutions are only in their infancy, as is the emergence of an 'international civil society'. Newer forms of regulations and mobilizations are constantly taking shape. We could presume that they are, and will be, the product of ideologies and policies far removed from those that have dominated the capitalist system since the 1980s. But will governments be able to co-operate with each other and create new institutional mechanisms so that the citizens can regain their rights and their liberty? Would the social movements be able to come up with new ways of controlling international organizations?

The coming changes will most probably be derived from compromises made among governments and international institutions in order to solve the conflicts created by the spread of financial globalization.

Conclusion

The speed and extent of the changes brought about by capitalism in its utilization of labour pushed capitalism into the next phase of its development, characterized by the search for solutions to the crisis of accumulation between 1975 and 1985; by the globalization of the economy; and by the advent of non-material technologies.

The conditions of work itself were changed considerably by the new organizational paradigms that, coupled with the persistent high rate of unemployment, shook the entire social structure of Europe via a change in the capital-to-labour relationship that swung in favour of the former. In fact, the strangest part is the quasi-silence that greeted these transformations. There have hardly been any protests at all, apart from a few French grumblings – or were they simply a death rattle? – and some anti-globalization protests.

From globalization to tight flow

This globalization of the economy and of the financial system was initiated by and benefited most the multinational corporations – that is, their principal directors and institutional shareholders. It developed as a reply to the crisis of accumulation of capital because, by extending its vision, market and strategy, a group could increase volume and thus reduce unit costs, and in particular, could have the freedom to transplant entire production and R&D units to any place in the world to take maximum advantage of emerging markets, salary levels or intellectual resources. To admit that globalization has contributed – for the time being – towards resolving the crisis of accumulation of capital by a rapid transfer of commercial activities from one place to another is also to admit that the crises of capitalism continue to control and orientate the activities of the vast majority of the people on our planet. The actual forms taken by the financialization of the economy, though of little importance, should not mask the durable nature of the driving force behind the global economy: at the other end of the production chain – that is, at the level of labour organization and actual work activity – was the same concern with profitability that had in the past been behind the solutions proposed for the labour crisis. All the various means of making labour more efficient come under this heading, whether by increasing the flexibility of labour, which makes it convenient *to pay only for the time spent productively*, or by the invention of new *ways of motivating the employees* or by *rearranging the entire production process into a tight flow*.

The concept of tight flow revolutionized the production of both goods and services from the point of view of a general reorganization of the production process into segments and a reorganization of labour. Though the revolution in the organization of labour brought in by tight flow was more subtle (and therefore, less studied by specialists and unionists), in no way was it any less important and far-reaching as it weighed heavily on the work and profoundly influenced dealings and relations with colleagues. As we showed in Chapters 1 and 2, tight flow is a solution – necessarily provisional – to the financial exigencies of capital seen in the most transparent manner by US pension funds. In effect, tight flow put matter, which is just another form of capital and the labour that gives it its value, in perpetual motion. More powerful than Taylorism, which concerned itself mainly with eliminating idle hands, tight flow made matter move continuously (thereby increasing the turnover of the capital) and established a system that, without resorting to an over-vigilant or strict environment (thus reducing costs), elicited a certain auto-engagement and auto-motivation on the part of the workers, who appropriated he company's objectives as their own and thus eliminated human downtime.

The power of tight flow lies in its ability to be generalized far beyond its traditional strongholds, such as slaughterhouses, the motor vehicle and agri-food industries, and generally all process industries. The principle of tight flow has spread through the entire industrial world (including designing), as well as in most of the services (see Chapters 2, 4 and 6). To maintain a tight flow is to eliminate all breakdowns and at the same time 'fragilize' the whole process by removing all buffer stocks. When applied to the fast food business, to the retail markets, group ware or the air transportation sector, and so on, the principle of tight flow requires that every individual commits totally in order to avoid any rupture that would have negative consequences on the whole team.

Critics who do not quite believe in the strength of tight flow try to show that its principle applies only to the simpler work situations because it enriches the dreary nature of labour by increasing the number of complications. Labour managers used this new paradigm to bring in radical reforms in every activity they could think of, especially in intellectual work, where Taylorism had largely failed. In this subtler field, it led to significant gains in efficiency and productivity, as evidenced by the effectiveness of parallel engineering and the concept of group ware, which keeps a tight check on every participant's time. *Management by project* would thus seem to be the first result because, by its very nature, tight flow compels the policy-makers and the intellectual workers to organize themselves into a network, but to retain interdependence by providing results in the short term, knowing that any breakdown of group discipline would penalize all the members of the group.

From the dynamic point of view, it is very difficult to establish the links between complex work and tight flow. The entire history of capitalism has been, and remains, a story of how to divide and simplify labour – even though, globally, production processes have continued to become more complex – so that it could be done by less-qualified and lower-paid workers. Though we can always talk of an enrichment of the job or the humanization of labour, we must not forget that the strong tendency toward the simplification of labour was checked only at very specific moments (generally of very short duration) that coincided neatly with the times when employers lacked qualified and/or motivated personnel. Instances of such 'coincidences' include the installation of 'new factories' in Sweden and the 'humanization of labour' in Germany towards the end of the 1970s. Historically speaking, the simplification of jobs has always led to their being automated and the elimination of the lower-qualified jobs. At the same time, the supervision of these new, automated procedures required a smaller number of more qualified personnel. But this is not the end of the story – it was followed by a new phase: the simplification of the work of surveillance. This was done either by integrating certain intellectual functions into the 'intelligence' of the machine, or by breaking down and simplifying the surveillance work itself. At the same time, this new simplification of jobs needed slightly higher qualifications than had been required for the labour that dealt directly with the material (or in the services), but less qualified than those required at the beginning of the surveillance. This brought in the possibility of externalizing these jobs and functions, and directing them toward enterprises with lower pay scales and more flexible working hours. Thus, though we do witness a slow and steady rise in qualifications, it should not be confused with a reduction in the size of the division of labour between those who design and plan the work and those who execute it (including services and intellectual activities). In other words, *the heightened demand for qualification and competency was not accompanied by an equal sharing and growth of strategic responsibility and autonomy in the work, that would encourage and give room to individual creativity.*

In fact, tight flow was accompanied for the most part by a widening range of jobs, because the work group shouldered the collective responsibility for an entire segment of the production process, be it of goods or services (see Chapter 2). The versatility that was thus required meant that each had the capacity to occupy several posts while simultaneously keeping track of what was happening upstream and downstream, and keeping an eye on the entire segment. Some observers have described this as a 'complexification' of production and labour. Although the increasing dependence on ICT, the quickened pace of production (with the consequent fragilization of the tight flow) and the need for better quality has led in general to a complexification of the production process, these same technologies have also helped to simplify the work by 'objectivizing' the knowledge based in both machines and programs. Meanwhile, the organizers were busy trying to simplify jobs so that the labour involved would be less onerous. Again, we see that *although the variety of jobs and the required versatility expanded, the delegation of responsibility, so highly vaunted by the 'new organizers', was confined only to those procedures and was retained only by those executives who were chosen unilaterally by the managers and organizers.* At the same time, the growing range of jobs and group work stimulated the employees because they found themselves faced constantly by newer objectives and greater challenges.

Thus tight flow, which guaranteed an involved and motivated workforce, was highly dependent on a suitably organized labour force. Just as a fluid dynamism and perpetual movement had come to replace the dead weight of stocks and loans, the mercurial work group supplanted the more static individual post. In fact, the work group, which is in fact a kind of network, matched the requirements of tight flow in more ways than one: specialization by some within the group led to an improved collective efficiency, the so-called co-operative effect that touched every individual within the work group. Although it remained unpaid (as Marx has so clearly pointed out), it raised the standard of the entire group. Moreover, it would also mean that leaves of absence would no longer pose as great a problem as they had done previously – the widespread versatility (interchangeability of personnel) and peer pressure would keep everyone on track (and eliminate the 'little bosses' who poison the collective life). In such a system, everyone would keep an eye on everyone else as well as on the clearly charted company objectives – there is no way that a work group could stray from these objectives without being caught, sooner rather than later. To complete the picture, the ambivalence of the status of the team leader (instructor, animator, group leader), a colleague and peer without any real hierarchical power but obviously on the way up the corporate ladder, obliged the worker to establish and maintain a clear channel of communication between the hierarchy and his/her group, while at the same time encourage group members to apply themselves to the ever-increasing demands of corporate objectives.

For all these reasons, tight flow seems to us today to be the most advanced form for streamlining labour. It integrates the principles both of Fordism (the flow) and Taylorism (the renewal of labour division), while solving a problem that Taylorism found hard to crack: how to motivate and involve the employees in the objectives set by the company. In fact, by accepting the principle of tight flow, employees are compelled to organize themselves (within the limits of the fixed and compulsory procedures) to keep the flow of goods and services 'tight'. This explains the concept of *constrained involvement*, which includes the idea of being taken up by the flow and at the same time of being compelled by the dual necessities of having to keep the flow tight and of having to accept the principle behind it (in Japan, it was through the advantages given by a large enterprise, while in Europe and the USA, it was to retain one's job). In such a situation, the competency model assures, *a priori*, the management (recruitment and promotion) that the employees would adopt the principle of tight flow. With monitoring behaviour an essential component of competency (as opposed to qualification, which is based on knowledge and know-how), social control over labour was no longer done simultaneously with or *a posteriori* to the activity; instead, it took place upstream, as the employer could now be ensured of employee loyalty through a battery of tests and constant vigilance over the employee's behaviour.

All these interpretations regarding the recent changes that have so radically transformed the nature of work and labour gives rise to yet another question: why have the employees, as a whole, accepted these changes – changes that do not pass on to them all the advantages brought in by the new technologies or by the new forms of management that claim to give so much importance to dialogue and participation? Some answers may be found at the micro-sociological level in labour interrelations and, in a more general way, in the organization of a large enterprise in an environment of sustained unemployment.

These new conditions of labour were not accepted out of fear and/or the suffering at work – even though there was a constraint that, as we have already said, was closely linked to the labour market. The acceptance of a greater workload was, on the contrary, related to a more positive perception of work. On the one side, there was now a greater freedom of speech than before (on condition that it steered clear of labour demands and company strategy) and on the other, the widening and diversification of jobs made them more palatable. At the same time, an ethnographic study (such as the one we have carried out) of the work process in the workshops, offices and stores, shows just how rich were the games and the social adjustments that rendered the work interesting and even satisfying (see Chapter 7). Too often this micro-social 'knitting' has been largely neglected by analysts, and thus most have missed the important role they played in the acceptance of this new social order. The daily construction and reconstruction of the rules of the game that surround and pervade labour relations (among peers, with the team leader, with the hierarchy, with other teams or services) play a significant part in the immediate work, and act as a screen to shield salaried work in our social system.

At the other end of the sociologist's field of view, the labour market has a central role in accepting new work conditions whose essential characteristics can be summed up as a reduction of idle time for some (the workers), the lengthening of the working day for others (executives and especially the professionals), and a self-motivation that pushes all to apply themselves to the objectives set by others – what we have called *constrained involvement*. But this labour market is no longer what it was in the past, in which the less qualified could threaten only the unqualified employees and the other, more highly qualified categories were only mildly pressurized by those individuals in the lower categories who aspired to a higher status. Today, the labour market is much more fragmented, both in terms of qualification and type of activity. The result, in times of continuing underemployment, is competition at all levels – in enterprises as well as in public ventures and NGOs, a fight for survival that breaks out between the unemployed or with short-term employees (the temporary and part-time workers, fixed-term contract holders and so on) along with the pressure that they themselves exert on full-time, permanent employees.

In fact, the core–periphery model, with its constant tendency to push the lower level and least-protected employees (the fixed term employees, the temporary and part-time workers) towards the SMEs, has spread into every kind of production process, including the corporate headquarters of multinationals. The competition, too, has thus been generalized. On one side there are full-time employees with stable jobs who have constantly to be on their toes, knowing that the less productive ones will soon find themselves at the periphery[1] (by a process that will exclude first the older and less qualified employees) and on the other, there are the workers at the periphery holding on to precarious jobs in a constant struggle to access the core of the enterprise or the service. This fragmentation of the labour market, caused by the spread of the core–periphery model, makes sure that the poor employees are under constant pressure to perform, with no choice in the matter and moreover having to prove themselves time and again. So here we have the real cause behind the rising stress levels recorded in the workplace, and the reason why the French judiciary has woken up to the concept of moral harassment. This neat trick merits a second look: while stress should be defined as a consequence of the lack of adequate human and/or material resources to attain the objectives fixed by management,[2] the problem has been 'individualized' and 'psychologized' to hide its real corporate nature and to screen the company's responsibility. In fact, one of the major changes that came about at the end of the twentieth century in the debates and discussions among management, political parties or union representatives was this shift from the collective to the individual, from the social to the singular. This, in turn, created a greater confusion, further obscuring the issues surrounding the nature of salaried work, and led to it being accepted without too much ado.

The riddle of salaried work today

The concept of constrained involvement captures quite neatly the situation that employees find themselves in nowadays: obliged to adopt, imbibe and adhere to the culture and objectives of the enterprise. It illustrates the inherent ambivalence by the juxtaposition of paradoxical terms (*involvement*, which is always voluntary in nature, and *constraint*, which is quite the reverse of voluntary application). In effect, this paradoxical concept begs the question: why do employees accept to live for any length of time in the tension between involving themselves and being constrained by this involvement? A first reply could be: because they have no choice! But, that is not quite correct, as it only repeats the idea behind *constraint* without saying anything about the reasons why this constraint was accepted in the first place, and especially without giving a clue to the issues underlying this *involvement* that, by its very nature, carries a voluntary element.

The concept of constrained involvement in salaried work encompasses several contradictory ideas that can be summarized as follows:

- Each individual who does not have the means to maintain him/ herself and his/ her family (food, lodging and so on), or the ability to manufacture goods, is obliged to sell his/her labour. It is the same idea that was propounded by Marx, who then developed it further and talked of the alienation of the product from the worker, who, bound by the labour contract, had to continue to present him/herself to his/her employer.

- Compared to the erstwhile Fordian system, the employee of today is constrained to *work well* – that is, to submit to the requirements of tight flow. In order to ensure the quality of work, employers have refashioned the work contract to incorporate a certain *behavioural control over the workforce*.
- The employee has to mobilize his/her entire being to conform to the new norms. We thus have the concepts of know-how-to-be, the mobilization of the subjectivity, involvement and, even more, loyalty to the culture and objectives of the enterprise. Although the enterprise aims to pay only for the time spent working, for someone who is *available in every way*: mentally, emotionally and, obviously, physically.
- The employee is paid for the time spent working and his/her acceptance of the control imposed during this time. Contrary to the claims made by management, this exchange is not a win – win situation (as it was previously with the system of bonuses and wage incentives), as the only thing the employee gets in return for his/her involvement is being retained as an employee.
- Every employee talks him/herself into accepting the constraint that s/he then turns into a voluntary involvement by inventing a system of beliefs and participating in several social games that are interwoven with the formal rules of work, and thus make the labour at least acceptable and interesting, if not truly satisfying. The creation of new rules gives the employee the possibility of giving significance to daily work. The concept of 'work contentment' illustrates this auto-reversal of perspective from the point of view of the employee. We have thus the idea of a *paradoxical satisfaction* in work – a satisfaction stemming from someone else's suggestion. As the involvement is constrained, the paradox emerges in the voluntary acceptance of the work. We could also talk of *submission to an imposed situation*.

According to La Boétie, the regime of constrained involvement is nothing more than a form of *voluntary servitude* borne by the people. Although today there are no genuine tyrants in any of the countries of the Northern Hemisphere, the yoke of capitalism is no less tyrannical than any king in the time of La Boétie. The feverish pursuit of wealth moulds our entire society and subdues to its will all social or political resistance. For La Boétie, the foundations of this voluntary servitude lie in the customs (transmitted by education) and the cowardice or the stupefying effects of the games and beliefs that people invent for themselves. As though the use of games as a mask for social relations was something new! Ultimately, the main cause behind voluntary servitude is the delegation of power. The tyrant gives up some power to a few chiefs who, in their turn, recruit others, and they in their turn recruit still others and so on. Thus, in this way, millions of people can be linked to the big boss: 'who deals with his or her subjects by using some of them to help control the others while in turn he or she is protected by those whom he or she was supposed to protect'.³ This is reminiscent not only of the traditional corporate hierarchy, but also of the manner of working within a group, where peer pressure ensures collective discipline, and the competition to become team leader pushes everyone to serve the company to the best of their abilities.

This willingness to serve better makes the worker blind to his/her own situation – that is, a loss of freedom that gradually ceases even to be questioned:

> Truly speaking, what else is this getting closer to the tyrant than to distance oneself from freedom and, in a manner of speaking, to hold with both hands and to embrace servitude? ... It is not only that they have to do what he says, but also that they think what he wants and often, to satisfy him, that they even anticipate his very thoughts. It is not enough that he be obeyed, he must also be kept pleased. They must bend over backwards, torment themselves, kill themselves in his service, and then, they must learn to be happy in his happiness, renounce their taste to take on his, change their very constitution, their very nature ... But you say that they serve to get something in return? – as though they could call something their own while they do not even possess themselves and as though anyone could ever have any private possession under a tyrant!.⁴

The entire theory of social alienation is contained in this idea of voluntary servitude: on the one hand, these corporate practices matched the demands of a tyrant; moreover, the fact of being shut up within these practices prevented the individuals from appreciating how groundless they were and to what extent they contradicted their very justification in their eyes, including the possession of goods and one's freedom.

Like voluntary servitude, constrained involvement also sets up a double-walled enclosure:

• The first barrier, which also acts as a social bond, keeps a check on the behaviour of every individual and prevents any deviation from work in the face of the requirements imposed by tight flow. Underemployment (and the resulting behavioural control that it permits) and the work in a group combine to turn this constraint or servitude into something 'normal'.

- The second barrier is the one built around every individual by him/herself by the acceptance of his/her condition and the negation of personal liberty (or at best, the restriction of autonomy). This brings us back to the theory of alienation and leaves little space for any protest movements.

Does this mean that we must rely on the actions taken by the elite as long as they themselves have not been compromised and do not contribute to the Boétian form of tyranny? The least that can be done is to dig deeper and extend our critical analyses by eschewing any kind of social fatalism or hiding behind indetermination and the absence of law. The cry for freedom, for creativity and for a return of aesthetics as a social project brings us back to the demonstrations held by the intermittent workers of the entertainment business in the autumn of 2003. This was a result of a demand for the retention of a law that organized the lack of job security for public entertainers that had certain instructive paradoxes that went well beyond the concerned sector. On the one hand, the demonstrators were not the only beneficiaries – a number of employers also took advantage by abusing the system, especially some of the larger television production companies and the big brand names that declared their commercial animators as artists. On the other hand, before MEDEF could embrace this status, they foreshadowed what could happen to an extremely flexible employment system: employees who were paid on a part-time basis learned to cope with the unpredictable nature of their income because it was complemented by subsidies derived from a compensation fund. At the same time, as the work given generally fascinated them, they accepted pay rates that were significantly lower than in other branches. As freedom and creativity formed the core of their activity, the intermittent workers in show business put themselves heart and soul into their work. In this sense, they are emblematic of all salaried personnel today: their consent to voluntary servitude going hand-in-hand with social upheavals that shake the balancing mechanism of history.

Notes

Introduction

1. M. Castells, *La société en réseaux. L'ère de l'information*, Fayard, 1998.
2. Apart from the question of the 35-hour week, which in any case concerned only Germany and France, the number of working hours began to go down from the end of the 1970s, mainly because the economic crises of that decade led to a reduction in overtime. Employees slowly took to the 40-hour week (which, in France, had been established since 1936). In the UK, there is some dispute over the reduction of working time. See K. Doogan (2001), 'Insecurity and Long Term Employment', *Work, Employment and Society*, vol. 15, no. 3, pp. 419–41.
3. Cf. D. Méda, *Le travail. Une valeur en voie de disparition*, Aubier, 1995.
4. We retain the French term *'combinatoire productive'* because a literal translation (combinational) would be heavy and ineffective. By retaining the French version, we would like to lay stress on the dynamic nature of the concept, which integrates the tensions between the elements of the system and the essential contradictions in the production paradigm.
5. The concept of *constrained involvement* does not refer to physical coercion or to any new totalitarianism. On the one hand, it should be compared to previous methods of involvement, through wages or improvements in working conditions; and on the other, it relates to a social form of coercion – that is, to a situation or an order of things in which, if one wishes to attain one's socially determined objectives (to stay in a big company or not to lose one's job, say), then one is forced to submit to the norm.
6. The question regarding the reduction in working hours (the 35-hour week in France or Germany) will be dealt with in the penultimate chapter, as will be the point regarding the increase in work pressure on some and the lengthening of working hours for others (executives on contract, for example).
7. K. Marx, *Early Writings of Marx*, Pelican Marx Library, Penguin, 1975 (1844), p. 60.

1   Reforming Corporate Structures

1. The idea of *delays* often replaces the idea of variety in managerial jargon. This involves shortening design times and increasing product variety (through product differentiation, product or service innovation, technical–commercial response to competition and so on).
2. See, notably, B. Martinet and Y.-M. Marti, *L'intelligence économique. Les yeux et les oreilles de l'entreprise*, Editions d'Organisation, 1995. Note the existence of a French Association for the Promotion of Economic and Competitive Intelligence.
3. See C. Midler, *L'auto qui n'existait pas. Management par projets et transformation du travail*, Inter Editions, 1993; K. Clark and T. Fujimoto, *Product Development*

Performance. Strategy, Organisation and Management in the World Auto Industry, Harvard Business School Press,1991.

4. *Groupware* is any groupwork organization software fulfilling participants' requirements as well as the co-ordinator's. By associating messaging facilities, shared IT memory access and automatic threshold reminders, it can be an efficient tool for management by projects.

5. See J. P. Womack, D. T. Jones and D. Roos, *The Machine that Changed the World*, Rawson, 1990; J.-H. Jacot (ed.), *Du fordisme au toyotisme? Les voies de la modernisation du système automobile en France et au Japon*, La Documentation française, 1990.

6. See R. H. Coase, 'La nature de la firme', *Revue française d' économie*, winter 1987; O. E. Williamson, *The Economic Institutions of Capitalism*, The Free Press, 1985. A clear depiction of the debate pitting market-based versus firm-based advantage, from a transaction cost perspective, can be found in B. Coriat and O. Weinstein, *Les nouvelles théories de l'entreprise*, Le Livre de Poche, 1995.

7. Prime contractors have generally made drastic cuts in the number of first-tier contractors they work with directly. In the motor manufacturing business, these numbers have fallen since the 1980s, from several thousands to 600 or 700 for each carmaker (with some sub-contractors, of course, supplying more than one manufacturer).

8. See the chapter on networked enterprise in the book by M. Castells, *The Rise of the Network Society*, Blackwell, 1996.

9. See J.-P. Durand and N. Hatzfeld, *Living Labour, Life on the Line at Peugeot-France*, Palgrave Macmillan, 2003.

10. L. Boltanski and E. Chiapello, *Le Nouvel Esprit du Capitalisme*, Gallimard, 1999, p. 157.

11. For a more conceptual presentation of this analysis in productive model terms, see our chapter 'The new productive model', in G. Bollier and C. Durand (ed.), *La Nouvelle Division du Travail*, Par's, Editions de l'Atelier, 1999. It would appear that the emerging *combinatoire productive* being discussed in the present book is only one part (that is the extended enterprise constituent) of a productive model characterizing society at a given moment in time. The development and long-term preservation of a productive model such as the Fordian one mainly depends on its *coherence*, meaning the coherent solutions it offers to a society's *social contradictions* – solutions that will clearly always remain temporary in nature.

12. R. Boyer and M. Freyssenet, *The Productive Models*, Palgrave Macmillan, 2002. Their term 'productive models' corresponds to our concept of industrial models. However, since for us the productive model makes sense of strategy and structure at the macro level, we prefer the use of the concept of industrial model to account for firm-level processes.

2   The Tight Flow Rules

1. T. Ohno, 'Introduction', *Toyota Production System: Beyond Large-scale Production*, Productivity Press, 1988.

2. Ibid. For a detailed history of the implementation of just-in-time and the changes in the production methods of Toyota, see also B. Coriat, *'Penser à*

l'envers'. Travail et Organisation dans l'Entreprise japonaise, Christian Bourgois, 1991.

3. P. Cohendet and P. Llerena (eds), *Flexibilité, information et décision*, Economica, 1989.

4. For more studies in French on tight flow, see Y. Clot, J.-Y. Rochex and Y. Schwartz, *Les caprices du flux. Les mutations technologiques du point de vue de ceux qui les vivent*, Editions matrice, 1990; G. Duval, *L'entreprise efficace à l'heure de Swatch et McDonald's. La seconde vie du taylorisme*, Syros, 1998.

5. T. Ohno – as Nt. 1.

6. B. Coriat, *'Penser à l'envers' Travail et organisation dans l'entreprise japonaise*, Christian Bourgois, 1991.

7. See M.-N. Pécout, 'La maintenance productive' in G. Bollier and C. Durand, *La nouvelle division du travail*, Editions de l'Atelier, 1999.

8. See J.-P. Durand and P. Stewart, 'Manufacturing Dissent? Burawoy in a Franco-Japanese Workshop', *Work, Employment and Society*, vol. 12, no. 1, March 1998.

9. See F. Mispelblom, *Au-delà de la qualité*, Syros, 1999.

10. See M. Imai, *Kaizen: La clé de la compétitivité japonaise*, Eyrolles, 1989.

11. For a more living presentation of the TPS, see our video on NUMMI (joint venture Toyota/GM near San Francisco), J. Sebag and J.-P. Durand, *Dreams on the Line*, Production Centre Pierre Naville, Université d'Evry, 2001 (English version).

12. See K. Shimizu, *Le toyotisme*, La Découverte, 1999; C. Berggren and N. Nomura, *The Resilience of Corporate Japan. New Competitive Strategies and Personnel Practices*, Paul Chapman Publishing, 1997.

13. K. Shimizu, as Nt. 12, p. 33.

14. M. J. Piore and C. F. Sabel, *The Second Industrial Divide. Possibilities for Prosperity*, Basic Books, 1984.

15. At the same time, this did not stop some decision-makers, in a different field from the organization of production and work, to continue to evaluate the efficiency of an enterprise or corporation by considering the ratio of the turnover to the number of employees. Without bothering too much about the nature of the enterprise, a turnover of some €150,000 per employee continues to be quoted as an acceptable ratio for an SME. Thus *kaizen* entered the Western system: instead of the Japanese bottom-up approach, which sought to improve productivity by addressing problems and implementing improvements at grass-roots level through kaizen specialists, Western companies went for the top-down approach, by adjusting the number of employees to their profitability figures (the famous *downsizing*). Every service or workshop was then left to adapt itself accordingly; that is, to produce as much as they did before, of the same quality, but with x% fewer employees.

16. See F. Mispelblom, as Nt. 9.

17. Quoted by K. Shimizu, as Nt. 12, p. 37.

18. L. Althusser, *Positions*, Editions sociales, 1976.

19. In a certain sense, these micro-objectives were very close to the functions assigned by Taylor to the principle of work: according to him, workers only have the personal ambition of climbing the corporate ladder by means of a higher salary, and would not be interested in the management of the company. The definition of work as a 'body of specialists' separate from and external to workers themselves, should lead to an increase in their income (through the sharing of the productivity gains stemming from the principle of the task), and make

them accept the new production conditions. Here, by holding the interest of junior employees to certain micro-objectives corresponding to their aspirations, and limited to the perception and knowledge of their immediate technological environment, they were made to deal only with these objectives and with those of the company that included them.

20. See S. Wood, *The Transformation of Work?*, Unwin Hyman, 1989; and 'Le modèle japonais: postfordisme ou japonisation du fordisme?' in J.-P. Durand, *Vers un nouveau modèle productif?*, Syros, 1993.

21. M. Gollac and S. Volkoff, *Les conditions de travail*, La Découverte, 2000. See the references in this book on the deterioration on the work conditions of most of the categories of workers.

22. Womack *et al.* (1990).

23. K. Marx, *Capital*, Book 1, Vol. 2, ch. XIII.

24. Ibid. Marx adds, 'The productive power developed by the labourer when working in co-operation, is the productive power of capital. This power is developed gratuitously, whenever the workmen are placed under given conditions, and it is capital that places them under such conditions. Because this power costs capital nothing, and because, on the other hand, the labourer himself does not develop it before his labour belongs to capital, it appears as a power with which capital is endowed *by Nature* a productive power that is immanent in capital.'

25. See F. Vatin, *La fluidité industrielle*, Par's, Les Méridiens–Klincksieck, 1987.

26. C. E. Larson and F. M. J. Lafasto, *Teamwork: What Must Go Right/What Can Go Wrong*, Sage, 1989.

27. Though, for the most part, variation in the work and the movements involved remained minimal, with the same muscles being used (hands, back, eyes, etc.) at the different stations. Thus the effect of job rotation on musculo-skeletal problems was in fact quite small.

28. See chs 3 and 4 of Durand and Hatzfeld (2003).

29. *La chaîne du silence* (The chain of silence) is a fine and probing documentary on the suicide of an assembly-line worker in a Volkswagen factory in Belgium. The isolation and solitude experienced by the employee (after suffering an injury in the workshop), and the pressure and tension he felt because his colleagues thought he was holding up the work process, combined to drive him into depression and ultimately into committing suicide at his workplace (E. Monani and A. Lejeune, *La chaîne du silence*, RTBF Liège, 2001).

30. In this context, one could read V. de Gaulejac and N. Aubert, *Le coût de l'excellence*, Le Seuil, 1992.

31. J.-P. Durand and P. Stewart, 'Manufacturing Dissent? Burawoy in a Franco-Japanese Workshop', *Work, Employment and Society*, vol. 12, no. 1, March 1998.

32. Our video film already referred to. (See note 11.)

33. Durand (1998).

34. The MEDEF's (French employers' federation) aggressive policy regarding the supervision of competencies transformed the management of human resources in France in a more visible manner than in the other countries, including those in the Anglo-Saxon world. Therefore, the French term '*Competency model*', which is difficult to translate, has been retained.

3 The Competency Model

1. MEDEF, is the acronym for the *Mouvement des Entreprises de France* (formerly the *Confédération nationale des Patrons français*, or CNPF), the principal employers' federation in France.
2. F. Chesnais, *La mondialisation du capital*, Syros, 1995.
3. See F. Lordon, *Fonds de pension, piège à cons? Mirage de la démocratie actionnariale*, Ed. Raisons d'agir, 2000.
4. T. Coutrot, *L'entreprise néo-libérale , nouvelle utopie capitaliste?*, La Découverte, 1998, pp. 219–20.
5. Ibid., p. 224.
6. Discussions regarding competency include thoughts stemming from two major sources (in French): M. Stroobants, *Savoir-faire et compétences au travail. Une sociologie de la fabrication des aptitudes*, Editions de l'Université de Bruxelles, 1993; and G. de Terssac, *L'autonomie dans le travail*, PUF, 1992 (particularly ch. 5).
7. CNPF, *Journées internationales de la Formation. Objectif compétences*, 1998, vol. 9, p. 18.
8. Ibid., vol. 1, p. 5.
9. Alain Dumont, ex-Director of Education and Training, MEDEF, interviewed by M. Anger and B. Roy, *Développement des compétences. La position des partenaires sociaux*. Agence Nationale power l'Amébioration deo Conditions de Travail (Anact), June–July 1999.
10. CNPF, *Journées internationales de la Formation*, vol. 1, p. 17.
11. For a radical criticism of the lack of confidence shown by employers towards their employees, see D. Linhart, *Le torticolis de l'autruche. L'éternelle modernisation des entreprises*, Seuil, 1991; or, by the same author, *La modernisation des entreprises*, La Découverte, 1994.
12. Ibid., vol. 1, p. 11.
13. CNPF, as Nt. 10, vol. 1, p. 27.
14. Ibid., vol. 1, p. 27.
15. CNPF, as Nt. 10, vol. 6, p. 25.
16. CNPF, as Nt. 10, vol. 8, p. 49.
17. P.-J. Rozet, 'Des négociations (provisoirement?) interrompues', *Nouveaux Regards*; a review by the research institute of the Fédération Syndicale Unitaire (FSU, a federation of teachers born of the split in the FEN (Fédération de l'Éducation Nationale) and which at the time of writing constitutes the main union in the educational sector), no. 15, Autumn 2001, p. 20.
18. Ibid., p. 119.
19. *La compétence comme prise de responsabilité*, Séminaire ETMT, Dijon, 1997.
20. CNPF, as Nt. 10, vol. 9, p. 22.
21. P. Zarifian, *Objectif compétence*, Editions Liaisons, 1999.
22. The *Confédération Générale des Cadres*, a national body for executives (managers, engineers and many postgraduates) has remained unique to France.
23. J.-J. Briouze, National Secretary of the CGC, interviewed in M. Anger and B. Roy (see note 9).
24. Ibid., pp. 22–3.

25. In the *Anact* file already cited, a representative of the *Force Ouvrière* (FO) declared: 'It is said that the organism (in the sense of enterprise) should "select" and that the competencies must be "demonstrable". The employee thus has the responsibility of "proving his competence in order to be employed". If that is true, it would be a complete reappraisal of the notion of the work contract ... Therefore, vigilance!'
26. CNPF, see Nt. 10, vol. 9, p. 30.
27. P. Méhaut, 'Cinq questions, autant de defies', *Nouveaux Regards*, as Nt. 17, p. 4.
28. P.-J. Rozet, *Nouveaux Regards* ...

4   The Reshaping of Labour

1. Quoted by Steffen Lehndorff in 'Human Beings as Buffers. Time Constraints and Autonomous Time Management under the Just-in-time Regime', Mimeo, GERPISA, Université d'Evry, 1997.
2. In particular, J.-P. Durand and N. Hatzfeld, *Living Labour. Life on the Line at Peugeot France*, Palgrave, 2003; A. Gorgeu and R. Mathieu, *Recrutement et production au plus juste*, Centre d'Etudes de l'Emploi, 1995; A. Gorgeu, R. Mathieu and M. Pialoux, *Organisation du travail et gestion de la main-d'œuvre dans la filière automobile*, Centre d'Etudes et de l'Emploi, 1998; J. P. Durand, P. Stewart, J. J. Castillo (eds), *Team work in the Automobile Industry – Radical Change or Passing Fashion*, Macmillan, 1999; S. Beaud and M. Pialoux, *Retour sur la condition ouvrière. Enquête aux usines Peugeot de Sochaux-Montbéliard*, Fayard, 1999.
3. For more regarding the organization of work in a 'U' see J.-H. Jacot, *Du fordisme au toyotisme*, La Documentation française, 1990; or Y. Monden, *Toyota Production System*, Institute of Industrial Engineering and Management Press, 1983.
4. In practice, there is never zero stock: there always is a little margin, and by mutual understanding, anyone who wants an advance has simply to inform his/her colleagues upstream – the only obligation being not to penalize in any way people downstream, which would have an adverse effect on the whole line.
5. M.-N. Pécout, 'La maintenance productive', in G. Bollier and C. Durand, *La nouvelle division du travail*, L'Atelier, 1999, p. 65.
6. Ibid., p. 68 et seq.
7. Y. Clot, J.-Y. Rochex and Y. Schwartz, *Les caprices du flux. Les mutations technologiques du point de vue de ceux qui les vivent*, Editions Matrice, 1990.
8. Definition proposed by *l'Association française pour la Cybernétique économique et technique* (AFCET).
9. G. de Terssac and J.-L. Soubie, 'Systèmes à base de connaissances et organisations', *Sociologie du Travail*, vol. 1, 1995.
10. B. Faguet-Picq, 'Le groupware: un travail collectif paradoxal?', *Séminaire du Centre Pierre Naville*, Mimeo, Université d'Evry, February 1999, p. 3.
11. Ibid., p. 8.
12. S. Craipeau, *L'entreprise commutante. Travailler ensemble séparément*, Hermès, 2001, p. 50.
13. Ibid., p. 90 et seq.
14. A. Briole, S. Craipeau, B. Faguet-Picq, *Groupware, contrôle et gestion des activités: le sens des convergences*, Mimeo INT-Evry, roneoted (undated).
15. B. Faguet-Picq, see Nt. 10.

16. The following analysis is based on data taken from the works of N. Fourmont, *Quel modèle de relation salariale pour le transport aérien?*, Centre Pierre Naville, Université d'Evry, 1998.

17. A variant of the hub, the *aerial shuttle* is a link between two cities in which the aircraft remains on the ground for no more than 30–45 minutes. While the commercial principle might differ, the constraints remain the same.

18. Sophisticated software is used to calculate the precise number of counters required, depending on client flow observed in the previous year (including the day of the week, the date, any special event, and so on) weighted for the weather forecast.

19. Quoted by S. Viards, *Des diplômes en caisse*, Centre Pierre Naville, Université d'Evry, 1998, p. 27.

20. C. Magnier, *Leroy-Merlin: pour réussir? De nouveaux services donc de nouveaux métiers*, Centre Pierre Naville, Université d'Evry, 1996, pp. 23–4. (Leroy-Merlin is one of the three largest chains of do-it-yourself stores in France.)

21. C. Orléach, *La rationalisation du service caisse*, Université d'Evry, Centre Pierre Naville, 1999.

22. The keen observer will remark that the central checkout is always placed at a height. The disgruntled client thus has to 'look up' to the central cashier, who outranks colleagues and is closer to store management.

23. Quoted by C. Orléach, as Nt. 21, pp. 30–1.

24. Ibid.

25. P. Alonzo, 'Les rapports au travail et à l'emploi des caissières de la grande distribution. Des petites stratégies pour une grande vertu', *Travail et Emploi*, no. 76.

26. See P. Taylor, G. Mulvey, J. Hyman and P. Bain, 'Work Organisation, Control and the Experience of Work in Call Centres', *Work, Employment and Society*, vol. 16, no. 1, 2002.

27. See M. Glucksmann, 'Call Configurations: Varieties of Call Centre and Divisions of Labour', *Work, Employment and Society*, vol.18 no. 4, 2004.

28. When tele-operators at a Level 1 call centre cannot solve a problem, it is pushed up to a Level 2 call centre. The technological qualifications of Level 1 tele-operators is so low that the work there is often called 'killing it' – and the number of calls is in keeping with that.

29. J.-P. Durand and N. Hatzfeld, *Living Labour* ...

30. Excepting large Japanese corporations which could handle the increasing mobility of the semi-skilled automobile workers – at least during the expansion period (1960–1990). See J.-P. Durand and J. Sebag, *op. cit.*

5 The Fragmentaion of the Labour Market

1. In the motor vehicle industry, the value addition achieved in the large enterprises dropped from 70 per cent in the 1970s to only 30–35 per cent in the 2000s.

2. John Allen, 'Fragmented firms, disorganized labour?' in J. Allen and D. Mossey (eds), *Restructuring Britain. The Economy in Question*, sage, 1988.

3. We can cite other examples also, such as in the field of engineering. At the time of writing, engineers and technicians from sub-contracted engineering enterprises – not only the sub-contracted parts manufacturers – have to rub shoulders and co-operate with the in-house engineers of the large enterprise.

Similarly, in the logistics sector, employees from different companies have to come together and co-operate in the order preparation stores or the package sorting platforms.

4. This model of centrifugation should be challenged with questions regarding the type, ethnicity and age in some jobs and in some sectors: the inequalities regarding the opportunities available to enter the heart of the production process (of goods or services) are central to the whole issue.

5. Presented in *Flexibility, Uncertainty and Manpower Management*, Institute of Manpower Studies, University of Sussex, 1984, and taken up by John Allen in 'Fragmented firms, disorganised labour?' in John Allen and Doreen B. Massey (eds), *Restructuring Britain. The Economy in Question*, Sage, 1988.

6. A large part of which is supported by the government, such as the 'qualification contracts', 'youth employment' or 'employment solidarity contracts' which encourage the elderly to retire so that young people can be recruited. These are some of the ways used by government in its perennial fight against unemployment.

7. Y. Lhorty *et al.*, *Flexibilité de l'emploi, rigidité des salaires*, EPEE and Centre Pierre Naville, Université d'Evry, 2002.

8. It was decided to give some €380 per month to people who had no other source of income. The initial plan called for the beneficiaries to apply compulsorily for vocational training and to look for employment. In fact, this search for employment was never insisted upon, and the RMI has become a kind of minimum guaranteed income (though truly very minimal).

9. With regard to the insecurity of fixed-term contracts, we must make a small comment. In France, if a contract specifies a clearly determined time period, it also guarantees the employee very clear rights, especially regarding job security for the duration of the contract. In contrast, holders of open-ended contracts are relatively easy to get rid of, under any economic pretext. It is thus understandable why in the retail business, and especially in the fast food sector, the general practice is to resort to these open-ended contracts as far as possible.

10. R. Castel, *Les métamorphoses de la question sociale. Une chronique du salariat*, Fayard, 1995.

11. K. Marx, *Un chapitre inédit du Capital*, UGE 10/18, 1971.

12. A. Supiot (ed.), *Au-delà de l'emploi. Transformations du travail et devenir du droit du travail en Europe*, Flammarion, 1999.

13. While A. Supiot finds some common ground between his proposition and that of Jean Boissonnat (*Le travail dans vingt ans*, Editions Odile Jacob, 1995) around the notion of *activity contract*, he makes it clear that he would rather talk of *status* instead of *contract* (in order to cover the periods that lie outside any contractual exchange on the labour market). Also, the term 'activity' is too vague to be of any legal consequence.

14. P. Stéphanon, *Les intérimaires: identités professionnelles et enjeux de pouvoir*, Université d'Evry, Centre Pierre Naville, 2000. Starting from another direction, C. Faure-Guichard distinguishes between three types of temporary work relations: the *probationary temporary*, particularly the young who can thus have an identity of their own after having meandered along different paths; the *transitional temporary workers*, who often have to face a breaking-off and loss of their professional bearings; and the *professional temporary workers*, who remain temporary by choice, their identity being established through a

mobility between employers (see. *L'emploi intérimaire. Trajectoires et identités*, Presses Universitaires de Rennes, 2000). Also, D. Glaymann, *La vie en interim*, Fayard, 2005.

15. In France, every nationalized trade union has local (in the larger towns) or federal (in every administrative division, equivalent to the British county) branches to help employees who are isolated or who work in SMEs.

16. J.-P. Durand, 'Le travail à domicile en France aujourd'hui', *Travail et Emploi*, no. 23, March 1985.

17. S. Paugam, *Le salarié de la précarité*, PUF, 2000, p. 96 *et seq.*

6 Information Technology and the Service Industry

1. Moreover, while the number of workers in the industrial sector is declining steadily, the service industries have seen a phenomenal growth. According to J. Gadrey, in France, the number of industrial workers went down from 5.1 to 2.2 million between 1962 and 1995, while in the tertiary sector it went up from 1.4 to 2.6 million during the same period (*L'économie des services*, La Découverte, 1992, pp. 13–14).

2. Including in the USA where, according to J. Téboul, the latter rose from 21 per cent of the active population in 1970 to 28.50 per cent at the time of writing. See J. Téboul, *Le temps des services*, Editions d'Organisation, 1999, p. 17.

3. J. Gadrey, as Nt. 1, p. 17

4. J. Singelmann: *From Agriculture to Services: The Transformation of Industrial Employment*, Sage, 1978.

5. J. Rifkin, *The Age of Access: The New Culture of Hypercapitalism Where All of Life Is a Paid-for Experience*, Jeremy P. Tacher/G. P. Putnam's Sons, 2000.

6. In fact, this circle is only partly virtuous and quite different from the Fordian virtuous circle. In the latter, the reduction in costs and the rise in income led to ever-increasing demand. In the present case, the reduction in production costs, particularly in the personal services (including tourism, leisure restaurants and so on), was slow in coming (the spread of the 'information services' or their public broadcasting should not hide their high production costs). On the other hand, the need to finance them also contributed to the stagnation, or at most, the meagre increase, in income of most sections of the population.

7. E. Goffman, *Asiles. Etudes sur la condition sociale des malades mentaux*, Editions de Minuit, 1968, pp. 377–92.

8. I. Joseph, *La ville sans qualité*, Editions de l'Aube, 1998, chapter entitled 'Les protocoles de la relation de service'; J. Gadrey, *Services: la productivité en question*, Desclée de Brouwer, 1996.

9. This concept is based partly on J. Habermas's ideas regarding the act of communication (*L'agir communicationnel*, Fayard, 1987). According to Habermas, communication needs a 'common world' to exist. A part of communication consists of a mutual recognition of values and of some shared knowledge, which are indispensable to communication itself. Moreover, the substance of this communication would be difficult to streamline and 'instrumentalize'. This is why we too agree with J. Habermas when he talks of the impossibility of having this sort of communication in an enterprise in order to increase efficiency and profitability. At the same time, the attempt to motivate employees and to

bring into the enterprise a service relationship by generalizing the concept of client–supplier is an attempt to 'instrumentalize' communication. This inevitably led to the contradictions that manifested themselves in protests by employees, and in the diverging interpretations given by researchers regarding ongoing changes and transformations.

10. Not only are all the sales reps' moves monitored, but their results are also checked on a daily basis. Moreover, they can be contacted at any time by mobile phone. The laptop computer is used to dispatch orders, prepare future meetings, keep track of the changing situation and attend to emails.

11. C. Magnier, *Magasin Leny-Merlin. De nouveaux services donc de nouveaux métiers*, Université d'Evry, 1997.

12. This is not the case in the USA, where this job is assigned to a specific employee; also in certain hardware stores in France, where this is done by the cashier herself.

13. For more details, see our chapter 'Travail informationnel et flux tendu' in C. Durand and A. Pichon, *Temps de travail et temps libre*, De Boeck, 2001.

14. J. Gadrey and P. Zarifian, *L'émergence d'un modèle du service: enjeux et réalités*, Editions Liaisons, 2002.

15. They were more or less sophisticated devices (with or without microelectronics) which would sound an audio or visual alarm if an operator tried to assemble something in a manner that was physically possible, but not correct.

16. Which confirms the statistics on illiteracy regarding the *comprehension* of what is read.

17. In this context one could refer to the limits of artificial intelligence as set out in *Intelligence artificielle. Mythes et réalités*, by Hubert Dreyfus, (Flammarion, 1984).

18. That is the very idea behind the so-called 'expert systems' which seek to replace experts with less qualified personnel. But the results have been rather disappointing.

19. J. Gadrey, *Services: la productivité en question*. It is only by giving undue importance to situations that exhibit a large intellectual and creative dimension at the cost of all the others, characterized by repetition, that some authors, such as P. Veltz and P. Zarifian, have concluded that there has been a positive transformation of the work. Refer to P. Veltz and P. Zarifian, 'Vers de nouveaux modèles d'organisation?', *Sociologie du travail*, 1/1993; P. Zarifian, *Communication et travail*, PUF, 1996; P. Veltz, *Le nouveau monde industriel*, Gallimard, 2000; J. Gadrey and P. Zarifian, *L'emergence d'un modèle du service*.

7   Intensification and Autonomy

1. See J.-P. Durand, *La sociologie de Marx*, La Découverte, 1995.

2. See the work of Gerpisa and in particular Y. Lung, J.-J. Chanaron, T. Fujimoto and D. Raff, *Coping with Variety. Flexible Productive Systems for Variety in the Auto Industry*, Avebury, 1999; B. Jetin and Y. Lung, 'Un ré-examen de la relation entre variété et échelle de production à partir de l'industrie automobile', *Economie et prévision*, no. 145, 4/2000.

3. R. Boyer and J.-P. Durand, *After Fordism*, Macmillan, 1997.

4. See, in particular, A. Gorgeu and R. Mathieu, *Les pratiques de livraison en juste-à-temps en France entre fournisseurs et constructeurs automobiles*, CEE, Noisy le

Grand, 1991; M. Gollac and S. Volkoff, '*Citius, altius, fortius*: l'intensification du travail', *Actes de la Recherche en Sciences Sociales*, no. 114, September 1996; G. Barisi, *Intensité et intensification du travail. Comment les mesurer? Comment mesurer les causes?*, documents from the ISERES, 2000/05.

5. See, in particular, P. Bouffartigue and C. Gadéa, *Sociologie des cadres*, La Découverte, 2000; P. Bouffartigue, *Les cadres*, La Dispute, 2001, A. Pichon, *Les chemins de la précarité. Cadres, techniciens et ingénieurs entre résignation et anticipation*, Cahiers d'Evry, 1998.

6. According to *Premières Informations* (DARES, Department of Labour and Manpower, April 2001, no. 17.2), both 23 per cent of contracts signed in 2000 change the methods of accounting for working time by excluding one or both of these elements: breaks and official holidays.

7. See *Premières Synthèses*, DARES, Department of Labour and Manpower, May 2001, no. 21.1, pp. 6 and 7.

8. A quarter of the employees said that they had not been consulted (ibid., p. 3).

9. Ibid., p. 3.

10. Ibid., p. 2.

11. C. Dejours, *Souffrance en France. La banalisation de l'injustice sociale*, Le Seuil, 1998, p. 39.

12. See G. de Terssac, *Autonomie dans le travail*, PUF, 1992.

13. See J.-D. Reynaud, 'Conflit et régulation sociale. Esquisse d'une théorie de la régulation conjointe', *Revue française de sociologie*, xx, 1979; 'Les régulations dans les organisations: régulation de contrôle et régulation autonome', *Revue française de sociologie*, xxix, 1988; *Les règles du jeu. L'action collective et la régulation sociale*, A. Colin, 1993.

14. To avoid falling into the trap of laying all suffering on the doorstep of the workplace, let us remind ourselves that all social interactions have their lot of suffering, just as they have their joys and satisfactions – be it within the family, between a couple, at a club, in the neighborhood, and so on. It is unavoidable because none of them are or can be (completely) chosen. Of course, there is no doubt that employment, being the relationship between capital and labour, carries an additional burden of constraints crystallized in the form of the alienation between labourers and their product (Marx, *Early Writings* ...).

15. We have already shown in the previous chapter how the management in the big companies fought against cashier automatism that so reduced the quality of the service.

16. B. Appay, *Individuel et collectif: questions posées à la sociologie des professions. L'autonomie contrôlée*, GEDISST, 1993, p. 63. At the same time, we are in complete agreement with critique regarding game theory. Morever, it deals with rational and calculating beings – which, by the way, we humans are not, except in very specific cases and for short periods – caught in the net of interdependence or interaction that does not allow any initiative or room for creativity. Also, game theory does not consider the possibility for rule modification which it regards as external to the game itself, while in our case, rules are at the centre and constitute the primary challenge.

17. Donald F. Roy was one of the first sociologists to point out the importance of the social game (social interaction) in making labour acceptable – his article '"Banana Time": Job Satisfaction and Informal Interaction' *Human Organization*, Winter 1959/60, vol. 18, no. 4.

18. From a completely different point of view, the process of arrangement as pointed out by C. Morel in the conquest of the 'indulgent system' (that is, a production system which was somewhat favourable to workers during the 1970s) functioned as a form of social adjustment. Morel defined arrangement as 'a more or less explicit agreement drawn up between a manager and one or more of his subordinates which tended to be favorable for the latter, an agreement which went against the official principles and set practices of the enterprise.' (*La grève froide. Stratégies syndicales et pouvoir patronal*, Les Editions d'Organisation, 1981 and Octares, 1994, p. 131). Social adjustment is a process without any end or victor, and which plays itself out in the unequal relationship of the employee.

19. See, for example, J.-P. Durand and P. Stewart, 'Manufacturing Dissent? Burawoy in a Franco-Japanese Workshop', *Work, Employment and Society*, vol. 12, no. 1 March 1998.

20. See J.-P. Durand and N. Hatzfeld, *Living Labour. Life on the Line at Peugeot France*, Palgrave Macmillan, 2003.

21. see N. Dodier discusses an 'arena of virtuosity' regarding these shows of control over work or working conditions in *Les hommes et les machines. La conscience collective dans les sociétés technicisées*, Métailié, 1995 (ch. 6).

22. See Durand and Hatzfeld, *Living Labour...*, ch. 3.

23. J.-D. Reynaud, as Nt. 13 p. 32.

24. C. Teiger and A. Laville, 'Nature et variation de l'activité mentale dans les tâches répétitives: essai d'évaluation de la charge de travail', *Le travail humain*, no. 1/1972; or A. Wisner, 'Contenu des tâches et charge de travail', *Sociologie du travail*, no. 4/1974.

25. G. de Terssac, as Nt. 12 ch. 6.

26. It is here that we must make a distinction with the interpretations of P. Veltz (*Le nouveau monde industriel*, Gallimard, 2000); or P. Zarifian (*La nouvelle productivité*, L'Harmattan, 1990; *Le travail et l'événement*, L'Harmattan, 1995; *Travail et communication*, PUF, 1996). They give so much importance to 'relational work' in a post-Taylorian world that they underestimate the role of social control in work – and of its necessity – especially work carried out under time constraints, to which they only make an allusion.

27. See Y. Clot, *Le travail sans l'homme*.

28. J. Sebag, *Un siècle de rationalisation taylorienne: sociologie du travail, représentations et subjectivité*, Université de Paris VIII, 1992.

29. M. Burawoy, Manufacturing Consent ... p. 82.

8 Unionism and Globalization

1. For France, one could consult R. Mouriaux, *La CGT*, Points-Seuil, 1982; *Le syndicalisme en France depuis 1945*, La Découverte, 1994; G. Groux and R. Mouriaux, *La CFDT*, Economica, 1992; and *La CGT. Crises et alternatives*, Economica, 1992; V. Aubert *et al.*, *La forteresse enseignante. La Fédération de l'Education Nationale*, Fayard, 1985; D. Labbé and M. Croisat, *La fin des syndicats?*, L'Harmattan, 1992; P. Rosanvallon, *La question syndicale*, Calmann-Lévy, 1988; J.-D. Reynaud, *Les syndicats en France*, Seuil, 1975, 2 vols; D. Labbé and S. Courtois, *Regards sur la crise du syndicalisme*, L'Harmattan, 2001; G. Nicolas,

Une nouvelle énergie sociale, Editions sociales, 1999; R. Guillon, *Syndicalisme et mondialisation. Une stratification de l'action syndicale*, L'Harmattan, 2000. Also ch. 4, 'Travail et organisation collective' in A. Supiot (ed.), *Au-delà de l'emploi*.

2. This process of elimination has accelerated greatly with the implementation of the 35-hour week, which made management take notice and actively hunt out the downtime.

3. There are, of course, differences in the success of the demand depending on the action of the union (CISL, CFTC, FO) or the CGT (and sometimes the CFDT).

4. It is another matter that, today, employees, especially white-collar workers, want the implementation of badges to show to the management when they have completed the legal number of working hours. But that too can cut both ways, as a precise knowledge of the hours worked could also lead to a better management of human resources: differentiation and competition between employees, the possibility of distributing the work over the year and consequently the disappearance of overtime income, and so on.

5. The general rise in the standard of living of the lowest-paid employees and their identification with other, higher categories – even though that brought its own frustrations – greatly reduced union participation.

6. The same reasoning is as valid for Latin-American countries with their weak unions as it is for Germany or the Scandinavian countries. Although the latter had strong labour unions with considerable amounts of finance at their disposal, the infrequent meetings and the disavowal of the agreement signed by the elected members seems to my mind to exhibit the same crisis of representativeness.

7. See J. P. Durand (ed.), *Le syndicalisme au futur*, Syros, 1995.

8. For details of the legal procedures and results, see J. P. Durand and N. Hatzfeld, *Living Labour ...*

9. Who would dare blame a unionist who applied him/herself a little more to writing pamphlets and organizing meetings than to his/her job – a job that had little autonomy and evoked no interest (and that was assigned in the first place because these personal absences prevented the worker from getting a more enriching job)?

10. 'Etats-Unis: crise et incertitude des relations industrielles', in H. Nadel and R. Lindley, *Les relations sociales en Europe. Economie et institutions*, Paris, L'Harmattan, 1998.

11. By saying that Fordian consumption norms have diminished in the industrialized countries, we are in fact saying that households in these countries now have most of the appliances they need, and that the market is now more of a replacement market rather than one of new acquisitions. Although we are talking of a general trend, it is painfully clear that developed countries do still have poorer sections, and that the major part of the world's population does not even have access to such industrialized goods.

12. This brings to our mind the situation in the USA and the UK. Although the official rate of unemployment in the UK is lower than in other European countries, we need to look at it a little more closely: on the one side, it must be kept in mind that British demographical structure is quite different from that of Southern European countries (the number of young entrants into the labour market is much lower, for example) and on the other, more than half of the newly-created jobs are low-paying, flexible ones. The inequalities keep

growing – faster than elsewhere in Europe – not only between employees, but also between the types of income (labour or ownership). Through to an uninterrupted growth of its economy over many years, the USA remains an exception on several counts. One of the main reasons (which is only rarely admitted) is the clear under-valuation of the dollar, the dominant currency of the world. By regulating its appreciation, the US captains of industry can help exports and at the same time maintain a passive trade balance. The recent weakening of the euro and the yen is nothing but a belated acknowledgment of the real value of the dollar. The dominant position enjoyed by the USA allowed it the luxury of long-term full employment, but the mid-term effects of their budget deficit could spring some surprises, including in terms of employment.

13. See. B. Brunhes, D. Clerk, D. Méda, B. Perret, *35 heures: le temps du bilan*, Paris, Desclée de Brouwer, 2001.
14. See D. Linhart (ed.), *Perte d'emploi, perte de soi*, Erès, 2002.
15. To show its feasibility, it might be necessary to give a more detailed account of the manner in which the jobs could be shared:

    • Today, the 27 million active members of society can be divided into two groups: Group A consists of the 22 million who have a job (taken as more-or-less full-time, in order to avoid complicating matters too much), and Group B made up of the remaining 5 million.
    • If we shift 5 million from Group A to Group B, we would have 17 million in Group A with full-time and full-salaried jobs, and 10 million in Group B with only 5 million full-time jobs and full salaries. The 5 million full-time jobs could be turned into 10 million part-time jobs, and at the same time, the half salaries could be turned into full salaries by the addition of the €60 billion, which, as we have seen, is the cost of unemployment.
    • Obviously, that would elicit howls of protest from the employees who are working full-time. To avoid this, we could shift 10 million more from Group A to Group B, and would thus have 20 million people working for 75 per cent to 80 per cent of the legal working hours while enjoying the benefit of full wages. Similarly, there could be any kind of mix, 50%, 60%, 70%, 80%, and so on depending on local or national accords, or a law that would draw up a list of difficult and strenuous jobs. Groups A and B used for this demonstration are actually only one group, as all jobs would have a tendency to be paid on a full-time basis.

16. Here we have in another form the principle of 'deuxième chèque', which for a long time has been championed by G. Aznar – for example, in *Travailler moins pour travailler tous*, Syros, 1993.
17. See Durand, *Le syndicalisme au futur*.
18. Who would have thought in the post-war period that social work would generate hundreds of thousands of jobs in Europe to de-politicize the effects of the employment crisis? Questions of finance were resolved as soon as they were raised!
19. P.-L. Brodier, 'Les comptes de l'entreprise ne sont pas faits pour elle', *L'Expansion Management Review*, 1996.
20. Especially the works of D. Bachet, 'Le travail, le capital … et l'entreprise', *Issues*, no. 55–6, 2000; P.-L. Brodier, as Nt. 19; J. Lojkine, *Les tabous de la gestion*,

L'Atelier, 1996; T. Rochefort, 'Invention du travail et nouvelles combinaisons productives efficaces', *Issues*, no. 55–6, 2000.

21. See, in particular, J.-P. Le Goff and A. Caillé, *Le tournant de décembre*, La Découverte, 1996; C. Leneveu and M. Vakaloulis, *Faire mouvement. Novembre–décembre 1995*, PUF, 1998.

22. The French acronym for the *Association pour la Taxation des Transactions Financières Au bénéfice des Citoyens* (Association for the Taxation of Financial Transactions for the Benefit of Citizens).

23. See A. Fouquet, U. Rehfeldt, S. Le Roux, *Le syndicalisme dans la mondialisation*, L'Atelier, 2000; C. Aguiton, *Le monde nous appartient*, Plon, 2001. In ch. 2 of Aguiton (2001), the author gives his no-holds-barred diagnosis of the difficulties faced by unions because of globalization, while emphasizing the competitive role of the NGOs (non-governmental organizations), the impossibility of forming labour unions in the newer sectors or within the new professional categories; at the same time, the author asks us not to make too much of the creation of new unions.

24. The three biggest Motor vehicle manufacturers in the USA have made extensive use of this internal competition since the 1980s and continue to do so to the present day. They threaten the Michigan workers with moving the whole installation to Mexico or to the south of the USA, where there are no unions. They even encouraged their suppliers, who were often their own subsidiaries, to do the same.

25. See J.-C. Delaunay, *La mondialisation en question*, L'Harmattan, 1999.

26. G. Barisi, *Les comités d'entreprise européens*, La Documentation française, 2001, p. 168.

27. R. Guillon, *Syndicalisme et Mondialisation*, p. 54. Also see G. Caire, 'Mondialisation et relations professionnelles', *Syndicalisme et société*, no. 1/1998; A. Fouquet, U. Rehfeldt, S. Le Roux, *Le syndicalisme dans la mondialisation*.

28. The André Renard Foundation, *Le syndicalisme à l'ère de la mondialisation*, Liège, no. 221/222, 2000, p. 43.

29. R. Guillon, *syndicalisme et mondialisation*, p. 61.

30. The André Renard Foundation, as Nt. 28 p. 46.

31. See G. Barisi, *Les Comités d'entreprise européens*, pp. 155–64.

32. Ibid., p. 16.

33. See R. Guillon, *Syndicalisme et mondialisation*, ... p. 30 *et seq.*

34. The internationalization of trade and manufacturing process characterizes the period when capitalism came of age with the development of multinational companies that still retained a sense of nationality at the heart of their capital. Globalization, however, designates that post-Fordian period that saw a rapid increase in the number of commercial, and especially financial, deregulations that allowed capital to cross the boundaries of the nation-state in order to try to solve the contradictions that it could not reconcile within the country – hence the idea that these nation-states had lost their grip on economic, and especially financial, spheres. In the original French, the term 'mondialisation' has been used to denote this phase of capitalism, and the concept of 'globalization' has been imported to define the ongoing process that, according to the authors, is characterized by the financialization of the economy and the advent of a new phase of capitalism. In fact however, it proves inadequate because, from the point of view of the enterprise, or to be more

precise, the group, to say that its strategy has turned 'global' is to give it a more definite meaning: the consortium conceives first its financial strategy and then economies on the scale of the entire planet. It sets up its research and engineering centres, its production units and later its distribution network according to the advantages it perceives in each region – the consortium has turned into a vast Lego construction whose overall structure is managed by a core of directors who assemble and disassemble networks at their discretion. This adds to the vulnerability of these consortiums as well as to the 'financialized economy'. For a more detailed study, see F. Chesnais, *La mondialisation du capital*, Syros, 1997.

35. We can establish a direct link between the position occupied by the USA within the WTO and the power that it wields in the political field. See Rémy Herrera, *L'empire en guerre. Le monde après le 11 septembre...*, Le temps des cerises/EPO, 2001.

36. Named after an American liberal economist and Nobel Laureate who had proposed in 1972 to tax all short-term financial transactions in order to reduce financial confusion prevalent all over the world.

37. See J. Bové and F. Dufour, *Le monde n'est pas une marchandise*, La Découverte, Paris, 2000.

38. See C. Aguiton, *Le monde nous appartient*.

39. A. Bihr, *La reproduction du capital*, Lausanne, 2001, p. 2.

40. See D. Plihon, *Le nouveau capitalisme*, Flammarion, 2001; R. Passet, *Éloge du mondialisme par un 'anti' présumé*, Fayard, 2001; P. de Senarclens (ed.), *Maîtriser la mondialisation, la régulation sociale internationale*, PFNSP, 2000.

41. In this regard, see Kostas Vergopoulos, *Mondialisation, la fin d'un cycle*, Séguier, 2002.

Conclusion

1. The fact that evaluators at IBM and later at Hewlett Packard were asked to be overstrict in judging the employees just before a new social plan shows what it means to go from the core to the periphery.

2. In an interview with *France Inter* (November 2002), Dr P. Davezie defined stress as 'the inability to act in the face of a constraint'. This definition corresponds quite accurately to the situation faced by many employees who do not have the necessary means to meet the objectives fixed by others.

3. É. de La Boétie, *La Servitude volontaire*, Paris Arléa, 2003, p. 42.

4. Ibid. pp. 42–3.

Bibliography

Aguiton, Christophe, *Le monde nous appartient*, Plon, 2001.

Allen, John, 'Fragmented firms, disorganized labour?' in John Allen and D. Mossey (eds), *Restructuring Britain. The Economy in Question*, London, Sage, 1988.

Althusser, Louis, *Positions*, Editions sociales 1976.

Amadieu, Jean-François, *Le poids des apparences,. Beauté, amour et gloire*, Odile Jacob, 2002.

Anger, Michel and Bénédicte Roy, *Développement des compétences. La position des partenaires sociaux*, Anact, June–July 1999.

Appay, Béatrice, *Individuel et collectif: questions posées à la sociologie des professions. L'autonomie contrôlée*, Mimeo, Gedisst, 1993.

Appay, Béatrice, 'Vers une nouvelle rationalisation du travail? Le cas de la grande distribution', *viiièmes Journées de Sociologie du Travail*, 'Marchés du travail et différenciations sociales', Aix en Provence, 21–23 June 2001.

Ariès, Paul, *Les fils de McDFo. La McDonalisation du Monde*, L'Harmattan, 1997.

Ascher, François, *Ces évènements nous dépassent, feignons d'en être les organisateurs. Essai sur la société contemporaine*, Editions de l'Aube, 2001.

Aznar, Guy, *Travailler moins pour travailler tous*, Syros, 1993.

Aznar, Guy, *Emploi: la grande mutation*, Hachette, 1998.

Bachet, Daniel (ed.), *Décider et agir dans le travail*, Ed. du Cesta, 1986.

Bachet, Daniel, 'Le travail, le capital … et l'entreprise', *Issues*, no. 55–6, 2000.

Bandt, Jacques de (ed.), *Les services dans les sociétés industrielles*, Economica, 1985.

Bandt, Jacques de, *Les services: productivité et prix*, Economica, 1991.

Baret, Jean, Jean Gadrey and Carmal Gallouj, 'Le temps de travail dans la grande distribution alimentaire en France, Allemagne, Grande Bretagne', *Travail et emploi*, no. 74.

Barisi, Giusto, 'Intensité et intensification du travail. Comment les mesurer? Comment mesurer les causes?', Les documents de l'ISERES, 2000/05.

Barisi, Giusto, *Les Comités d'Entreprise européens*, La Documentation française, 2001.

Barlow, Maude and Tony Clarke, *La bataille de Seattle. Sociétés civiles contre mondialisation marchande*, Fayard, 2002.

Beaud, Stéphane and Michel Pialoux, *Retour sur la condition ouvrière, Enquête aux usines Peugeot de Sochaux-Montbéliard*, Fayard, 1999.

Berggren, Christian and Masami Nomura, *The Resilience of Corporate Japan: New Competitive Strategies and Personal Practices*, Paul Chapman Publishing, 1997.

Bertrand, Agnès and Laurence Kalafatides, *OMC, Le pouvoir invisible*, Fayard, 2002.

Bihr, Alain, *La reproduction du capital*, Page 2, Geneva, 2001.

Boisseau, Christian, *Les pratiques du juste-à-temps: enjeux et conditions favorables*, doctoral thesis, Université de Paris X-Nanterre, 1994.

Boissonnat, Jean, *Le travail dans vingt ans. Rapport de la Commission Boissonnat*, Editions Odile Jacob, 1995.

Boltanski, Luc and Ève Chiapello, *Le nouvel esprit du capitalisme*, Gallimard, 1999.

Bouffartigue, Paul, *Les cadres*, La Dispute, 2001.

Bouffartigue, Paul and Charles Gadéa, *Sociologie des cadres*, La Découverte, coll. 'Repères', 2000.

Bové, José and François Dufour, *Le monde n'est pas une marchandise*, La Découverte, Paris, 2000.

Boyer, Robert, *La théorie de la régulation: une analyse critique*, La Découverte, 1986.

Boyer, Robert and Durand Jean-Pierre, *After Fordism*, Macmillan, 1996.

Boyer, Robert and Michel Freyssenet, *The Productive Models*, Palgrave Macmillan, 2002.

Briole, Alain, Sylvie Craipeau and Béatrice Faguet-Picq, *Groupware, contrôle et gestion des activités: le sens des convergences*, Mimeo, Int-Evry, n. d.

Brunhes, Bernard, Denis Clerc, Dominique Méda and Bernard Perret, 35 *heures: le temps du bilan*, Desclée de Brouwer, 2001.

Burawoy, Michael, *Manufacturing Consent. Changes in the Labor Process under Monopoly Capitalism*, University of Chicago Press, 1979.

Caire, Guy, 'Mondialisation et relations professionnelles', *Syndicalisme et société*, no. 1/1998.

Castel, Robert, *Les métamorphoses de la question sociale*, Fayard, 1995.

Castells, Robert, *The Rise of the Network Society*, Blackwell, 1996.

Cézard, Michel and Lydia Vinck, *Les rythmes du travail*, Dares, ministère du Travail, Documents d'Etude, no. 10, 1996.

Cfdt, *Le travail en questions. Enquêtes sur les mutations du travail*, Syros, 2001.

Charlot, Bernard, *Du rapport au savoir*, Anthropos, 1997.

Chatzis, Kostas, Céline Mounier, Pierre Veltz and Philippe Zarifian, *L'autonomie dans les organisations. Quoi de neuf?*, L'Harmattan, 1999.

Chenu, Alain, *L'archipel des employés*, INSEE Etudes, 1990.

Chenu, Alain, *Les employés*, La Découverte, coll. 'Repères', 1994.

Chesnais, François, *La mondialisation du capital*, Syros, 1995.

Clark, Kim B. and Takahiro Fujimoto, *Product Development Performance. Strategy, Organization and Management in the World Auto Industry*, Harvard Business School Press, 1991.

Clot, Yves, *Le travail sans l'homme*, La Découverte, 1995.

Clot, Yves, Jean-Yves Rochex and Yves Schwartz, *Les caprices du flux. Les mutations technologiques du point de vue de ceux qui les vivent*, Editions Matrice, 1990.

Cnpf, *Journées internationales de la Formation. Objectif compétences*, 1998, 12 vols.

Coase, Ronald, 'La nature de la firme', *Revue française d'économie*, Winter 1987.

Cohendet, Patrick and Patrick Llerena (eds), *Flexibilité, information et décision*, Economica, 1989.

Commissariat, Général au Plan, *Réduction du temps de travail: les enseignements de l'observation*, La Documentation française, 2001.

Coninck, Frédéric de, *Travail intégré, société éclatée*, PUF, 1995.

Copernic (Fondation), *Retraites: l'autre diagnostic*, Notes de la Fondation Copernic, June 1999.

Copernic (Fondation), *Retraites: d'autres propositions*, Notes de la Fondation Copernic, February 2000.

Copernic (Fondation), *Un social libéralisme à la française? Regards critiques sur la politique économique et sociale de Lionel Jospin*, La Découverte, 2001.

Coriat, Benjamin, *'Penser à l'envers'. Travail et Organisation dans l'Entreprise japonaise*, Christian Bourgois, 1991.

Coriat, Benjamin and Olivier Weinstein, *Les nouvelles théories de l'entreprise*, Le Livre de Poche, 1995.

Courpasson, David, 'Eléments pour une sociologie de la relation commerciale. Les paradoxes de la modernisation dans la banque', *Sociologie du travail*, 2/1995.

Courpasson, David, *L'action contrainte. Organisations libérales et domination*, PUF, 2000.

Coutrot, Thomas, *L'entreprise néo-libérale, nouvelle utopie capitaliste?* La Découverte, 1998.

Craipeau, Sylvie, *L'entreprise commutante. Travailler ensemble séparément*, Hermès, 2001.

Degenne, Alain and Michel Forsé, *Les réseaux sociaux*, Armand Colin, 1994.

Dejours, Christophe, *Souffrance en France. La banalisation de l'injustice sociale*, Le Seuil, 1998.

Delaunay, Jean-Claude, *La mondialisation en question*, L'Harmattan, 1999.

Delaunay, Jean-Claude, *Le capitalisme contemporain. Questions de fond*, L'Harmattan, 2001.

Delaunay, Jean-Claude and Jean Gadrey, *Les enjeux de la société de service*, PFNSP, 1987.

Dodier, Nicolas, *Les hommes et les machines. La conscience collective dans les sociétés technicisées*, Métailié, 1995.

Dreyfus, Hubert, *Intelligence artificielle. Mythes et réalités*, Flammarion, 1984.

Dubar, Claude, *La formation professionnelle continue*, La Découverte, coll. 'Repères', 4th edn, 2000.

Dubuisson-Quellier, Sophie, 'Le prestataire, le client et le consommateur. Sociologie d'une relation marchande', *Revue française de Sociologie*, 4/1999.

Dupuy, Yves and Françoise Larré, 'Entre salariat et travail indépendant: les formes hybrides de mobilisation du travail', *Travail et emploi*, 4/1998.

Durand, Jean-Pierre, 'Le travail à domicile en France aujourd'hui', *Travail et emploi*, no. 23, March 1985.

Durand, Jean-Pierre (ed.), *Le syndicalisme au futur*, Syros, 1995.

Durand, Jean-Pierre, 'Is the "Better Job" Still Possible Today?', *Economic and Industrial Democracy*, 1998.

Durand, Jean-Pierre, 'Le nouveau modèle productif', in G. Bollier and C. Durand (eds), *La nouvelle division du travail*, L'Atelier, 1999.

Durand, Jean-Pierre and Paul Stewart, 'La transparence sociale dans une usine française à capitaux japonais', *Sociologie du travail*, 4/1998.

Durand, Claude and Alain Pichon, *Temps de travail et temps libre*, De Boeck, 2001.

Durand, Jean-Pierre and Nicolas Hatzfeld, *Living Labour. Life on the Line at Peugeot France*, Palgrave Macmillan, 2003.

Durand, Jean-Pierre, Paul Stewart and Juan-José Castillo (eds), *Teamwork in the Automobile Industry: Radical Change or Passing Fashion?*, Macmillan, 1998.

Duval, Guillaume, *L'entreprise efficace à l'heure de Swatch et McDonald's. La seconde vie du taylorisme*, Syros, 1998.

Eymard-Duvernay, François and Emmanuelle Marchal, 'Les règles en action', *Revue française de sociologie*, xxxv, 1994.

Faure-Guichard, Catherine, *L'emploi intérimaire. Trajectoires et identités*, Presses Universitaires de Rennes, 2000.

Fondation, André Renard, *Le syndicalisme à l'ère de la mondialisation*, Liège, no. 221/222, 2000.

Fouquet, Annie, Udho Rehfeldt and Serge Le Roux, *Le syndicalisme dans la mondialisation*, L'Atelier, 2000.

Fourmont, Nicolas, *Quel modèle de relation salariale pour le transport aérien?*, Centre Pierre Naville, Université d'Evry, 1998.

Freyssenet, Michel and Jean-Claude Thénard, 'Choix d'automatisation, efficacité productive et contenu du travail', *Cahiers du GIP Mutations Industrielles*, 1988.

Gadrey, Jean, *L'économie des services*, La Découverte, coll. 'Repères', (1992) 1996.

Gadrey, Jean, *La productivité en question*, Desclée de Brouwer, 1996.

Gadrey, Jean and Philippe Zarifian, *L'émergence d'un modèle du service: enjeux et réalités*, Editions Liaisons, 2002.

Gaulejac, Vincent (de) and Nicole Aubert, *Le coût de l'excellence*, Le Seuil, 1992.

George, Susan and Martin Wolf, *La mondialisation libérale*, Grasset, 2002.

Gerritsens, Danielle and Dominique Martin, *Effets et méfaits de la modernisation dans la crise*, Desclée de Brouwer, 1998.

Goffman, Erwing, *Asiles. Etudes sur la condition sociale des malades mentaux*, Editions de Minuit, 1968.

Gollac, Michel and Serge Volkoff, '*Citius, altius, fortius*: l'intensification du travail' *Actes de la Recherche en Sciences Sociales*, no. 114, September 1996.

Gollac, Michel and Serge Volkoff, *Les conditions de travail*, coll. 'Repères', La Découverte, 2000.

Gorgeu, Armelle and René Mathieu, *Les pratiques de livraison en juste-à-temps en France entre fournisseurs et constructeurs automobiles*, CEE, Noisy le Grand, 1991.

Gorgeu, Armelle and René Mathieu, *Recrutement et production au plus juste*, Centre d'Etudes de l'Emploi, 1995.

Gorgeu, Armelle, René Mathieu and Michel Pialoux, *Organisation du travail et gestion de la main-d'œuvre dans la filière automobile*, Centre d'Etudes et de l'Emploi, 1998.

Groux, Guy and René Mouriaux, *La CFDT*, Economica, 1992.

Groux, Guy and René Mouriaux, *La CGT. Crises et alternatives*, Economica, 1992.

Guillon, Roland, *Syndicalisme et mondialisation. Une stratification de l'action syndicale*, L'Harmattan, 2000.

Habermas, Jürgen, *L'agir communicationnel*, Fayard, 1987, 2 vols.

Herrera, Rémy, *L'empire en guerre. Le monde après le 11 septembre ...* , Le temps des cerises/EPO, 2001.

Hirigoyen, Marie-France, *Le harcèlement moral. La violence perverse au quotidien*, Syros, 1998.

Hubault, François (coord.), *La relation de service, opportunités et questions nouvelles pour l'ergonomie*, Octavès Editions, 2002.

Imai, Masaaki, *Kaizen: la clé de la compétitivité japonaise*, Eyrolles, 1989.

Isaac, Joseph, *La ville sans qualité*, Editions de l'Aube, 1998.

Jacot, Jacques-Henri (ed.), *Du fordisme au tokyoïte. Les voies de la modernisation du système automobile en France et au Japon*, La Documentation française, 1990.

Jacot, Jacques-Henri, Damien Brochier and Myriam Campinos-Dubernet (eds), *La formation professionnelle en mutation*, Editions Liaisons, 2001.

Jacquiau, Christian, *Les coulisses de la grande distribution*, Albin Michel, 2000.

Jetin, Bruno and Yannick Lung, 'Un ré-examen de la relation entre variété et échelle de production à partir de l'industrie automobile', *Economie et prévision*, no. 145, 4/2000.

La Boétie, Etienne (de), *La servitude volontaire*, Arléa, 2003.

Labbé, Dominique and Stéphane Courtois, *Regards sur la crise du syndicalisme*, L'Harmattan, 2001.

Labbé, Dominique and M. Croisat, *La fin des syndicats?*, L'Harmattan, 1992.

Lamy, Pascal, *L'Europe en première ligne*, Le Seuil, 2002.

Larson, E. and F. M. J. Lafasto, *Teamwork. What Must Go Right/What Can Go Wrong*, Sage, 1989.

Le Goff, Jean-Pierre and Alain Caillé, *Le tournant de décembre*, La Découverte, 1996.

Leclercq, Emmanuelle, 'Gestion des compétences en réseaux et différenciations biographiques', *viiièmes Journées de Sociologie du Travail 'Marchés du travail et différenciations sociales'*, Aix en Provence, 21-23 June 2001.

Lehndorff, Steffen, *Human Beings as Buffers. Time Constraints and Autonomous Time Management under the Just-in-time Regime*, Mimeo, Gerpisa, Université d'Evry, 1997.

Leneveu, Claude and Michel Vakaloulis, *Faire mouvement. Novembre-décembre 1995*, PUF, 1998.

Linhart, Danièle, *Le torticolis de l'autruche. L'éternelle modernisation des entreprises*, Seuil, 1991.

Linhart, Danièle, *La modernisation des entreprises*, La Découverte, coll. 'Repères', 1994.

Linhart, Danièle (ed.), *Perte d'emploi, perte de soi*, Erès, 2002.

Linhart, Robert, *L'établi*, Les Editions de Minuit, 1978.

Lojkine, Jean, *La révolution informationnelle*, PUF, 1992.

Lojkine, Jean, *Les tabous de la gestion*, L'Atelier, 1996.

Lojkine, Jean and Jean-Luc Malétras, *La guerre du temps. Le travail en quête de mesure*, L'Harmattan, 2002.

Lordon, Frédéric, *Fonds de pension, piège à cons? Mirage de la démocratie actionnariale*, Ed. Raisons d'agir, 2000.

Lung, Yannick, Jean-Jacques Chanaron, Takahiro Fujimoto and Daniel Raff, *Coping with Variety. Flexible Productive Systems for Variety in the Auto Industry*, Avebury, 1999.

Martinet, Bruno and Yves-Michel Marti, *L'intelligence économique. Les yeux et les oreilles de l'entreprise*, Editions d'Organisation, 1995.

Marx, Karl, *Capital*, Pelican Marx Library, Penguin, London, 1973 (1867-94)

Marx, Karl, *Un chapitre inédit du Capital*, UGE 10/18, 1971.

Math, Antoine, *Quel avenir pour les retraites par répartition?*, IRES, May 2001.

Méhaut, Philippe, *Vers une nouveau rapport de l'entreprise à la formation*, GREE, 1999.

Midler, Christophe, *L'auto qui n'existait pas*, Interéditions, 1994.

Mispelblom, Frederik, *Au-delà de la qualité*, Syros, 1999.

Moati, Philippe, *L'avenir de la grande distribution*, Editions Odile Jacob, 2001.

Monami, Eric and Agnès Lejeune, *La chaîne du silence*, RTBF Liège, 2001.

Monden, Yves, *Toyota Production System*, Institute of Industrial Engineering and Management Press' Atlanta, 1983.

Morel, Christian, *La grève froide. Stratégies syndicales et pouvoir patronal*, Les Editions d'Organisation, 1981; and Octares, 1994.

Mouriaux, René, *La CGT*, Points-Seuil, 1982.

Mouriaux, René, *Le syndicalisme en France depuis 1945*, La Découverte, coll. 'Repères', 1994.

Munck, Jean de and Maris Verhoeven, *Les mutations du rapport à la norme. Un changement dans la modernité*, De Boeck, 1997.

Nadel, Henri and Robert Lindley, *Les relations sociales en Europe. Economie et institutions*, L'Harmattan, 1998.

Naville, Pierre, *L'automation et le travail humain*, CNRS, 1961.

Naville, Pierre, *Vers l'automatisme social? Problèmes du travail et de l'automation*, Gallimard, 1963.

Neuville, Jean-Pierre, *Le modèle japonais à l'épreuve des faits*, Economica, 1997.

Nicolas, Grégoire, *Une nouvelle énergie sociale*, Editions sociales, 1999.

Nkuitchou, Raoul, *Les enjeux sociaux du Juste-à-Temps dans la restauration rapide*, Centre Pierre Naville, Evry, 2000.

Ohno, Taiichi, *Toyota Production System: Beyond Large-scale Production*, Productivity Press, 1988.

Osada, Takashi, *Les 5 S. Première pratique de la qualité totale*, Dunod, 1993.

Paradeise, Catherine and Yves Lichtenberger, 'Compétence, compétences', *Sociologie du travail*, no. 43, 1/2001.

Paugam, Serge, *Le salarié de la précarité*, PUF, 2000.

Pécout, Marie-Noëlle, 'La maintenance productive', in G. Bollier and C. Durand, *La nouvelle division du travail*, L'Atelier, 1999.

Petit, Pascal, *L'économie de l'information. Les enseignements des théories économiques*, La Découverte, 1998.

Philonenko, Grégoire and Véronique Guienne, *Au carrefour de l'exploitation*, Desclée de Brouwer, 1997.

Pichon, Alain, *Les chemins de la précarité. Cadres, techniciens et ingénieurs entre résignation et anticipation*, Cahiers d'Evry, 1998.

Pillon, Thierry and François Vatin, *Traité de Sociologie du Travail*, Octarès, 2002.

Piore, Michael J. and Charles F. Sabel, *Les chemins de la prospérité. De la production de masse à la spécialisation flexible*, Hachette, 1989.

Polanyi, Karl, *La grande transformation. Aux origines économiques et politiques de notre temps*, Gallimard, 1983.

Reynaud, Jean-Daniel, *Les syndicats en France*, Seuil, 1975, 2 vols.

Reynaud, Jean-Daniel, 'Conflit et régulation sociale. Esquisse d'une théorie de la régulation conjointe', *Revue française de sociologie*, xx, 1979.

Reynaud, Jean-Daniel, 'Les régulations dans les organisations: régulation de contrôle et régulation autonome', *Revue française de sociologie*, xxix, 1988.

Reynaud, Jean-Daniel, *Les règles du jeu. L'action collective et la régulation sociale*, A. Colin, 1993.

Rifkin, Jeremy, *L'âge de l'accès. La révolution de la nouvelle économie*, La Découverte, 2000.

Ritzer, George, *The McDonaldization of Society*, Pine Forge Press/Sage, 1993.

Rochefort, Thierry, 'Invention du travail et nouvelles combinaisons productives efficaces', *Issues*, no. 55–6, 2000.

Rosanvallon, Pierre, *La question syndicale*, Calmann-Lévy, 1988.

Rozet, Pierre-Jean, 'Des négociations (provisoirement?) interrompues', *Nouveaux Regards*, revue de l'Institut de recherche de la FSU, no. 15, Autumn 2001.

Schor, Juliet, *The Overworked American*, Basic Books, 1991.

Sebag, Joyce, *Un siècle de rationalisation taylorienne: sociologie du travail, représentations et subjectivité*, Université de Paris viii, 1992.

Sebag, Joyce and Jean-Pierre Durand, *Rêves de chaîne*, Production Centre Pierre Naville, Université d'Evry, 2001.

Sennett, Richard, *Le travail sans qualité. Les conséquences humaines de la flexibilité*, Albin Michel, 2000.

Shimizu, Koïchi, *Le toyotisme*, La Découverte, coll. 'Repères', 1999.

Singlemann, Joachim, *From Agriculture to Services: The Transformation of Industrial Employment*, Sage, 1978.

Stéphanon, Pierre, *Les intérimaires: identités professionnelles et enjeux de pouvoir*, Université d'Evry, Centre Pierre Naville, 2000.

Stroobants, Marcelle, *Savoir-faire et compétences au travail. Une sociologie de la fabrication des aptitudes*, Editions de l'Université de Bruxelles, 1993.

Supiot, Alain (ed.), *Au-delà de l'emploi. Transformations du travail et devenir du droit du travail en Europe*, Flammarion, 1999.

Téboul, James, *Le temps des services. Une nouvelle approche de management*, Editions d'Organisation, 1999.

Teiger, Catherine and Alain Laville, 'Nature et variation de l'activité mentale dans les tâches répétitives: essai d'évaluation de la charge de travail', *Le travail humain*, no. 1/1972.

Terssac, Gilbert de, *L'autonomie dans le travail*, PUF, 1992.

Terssac, Gilbert de and Jean-Luc Soubie, 'Systèmes à base de connaissances et organisations', *Sociologie du travail*, 1/1995.

Vatin, François, *La fluidité industrielle*, Les Méridiens-Klincksieck, 1987.

Vatin, François, *Le travail, économie et physique (1780-1830)*, PUF, 1993.

Veltz, Pierre, *Le nouveau monde industriel*, Gallimard, 2000.

Veltz, Pierre and Philippe Zarifian, 'Vers de nouveaux modèles d'organisation?', *Sociologie du travail*, 1/1993.

Williamson, Oliver E., *The Economic Institutions of Capitalism*, The Free Press, 1985.

Wisner, Alain, 'Contenu des tâches et charge de travail', *Sociologie du travail*, no. 4/1974.

Womack, James P., Daniel T. Jones and Daniel Roos, *The Machine that Changed the World*, Rawson, 1990.

Wood, Stephen, *The Transformation of Work?* Unwin Hyman, 1989.

Wood, Stephen, 'Le modèle japonais: postfordisme ou japonisation du fordisme?' in J.-P. Durand, *Vers un nouveau modèle productif?*, Syros, 1993.

Zarifian, Philippe, *La nouvelle productivité*, L'Harmattan, 1990.

Zarifian, Philippe, *Le travail et l'événement*, L'Harmattan, 1995.

Zarifian, Philippe, *Travail et communication*, PUF, 1996.

Zarifian, Philippe, 'L'agir communicationnel face au travail', *Sociologie du travail*, 2/1999a.

Zarifian, Philippe, *Objectif compétence. Pour une nouvelle logique*, Editions Liaisons, 1999b.

Index